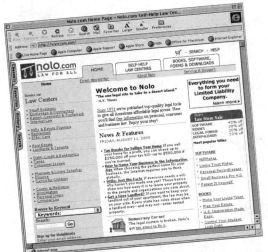

Read This First

The information in this book is as up to date and accurate as we can make it. But it's important to realize that the law changes frequently, as do fees, forms and procedures. If you handle your own legal matters, it's up to you to be sure that all information you use—including the information in this book—is accurate. Here are some suggestions to help you:

First, make sure you've got the most recent edition of this book. To learn whether a later edition is available, check the edition number on the book's spine and then go to Nolo's online Law Store at www.nolo.com or call Nolo's Customer Service Department at 800-728-3555.

Next, even if you have a current edition, you need to be sure it's fully up to date. The law can change overnight. At www.nolo.com, we post notices of major legal and practical changes that affect the latest edition of a book. To check for updates, find your book in the Law Store on Nolo's website (you can use the "A to Z Product List" and click the book's title). If you see an "Updates" link on the left side of the page, click it. If you don't see a link, that means we haven't posted any updates. (But check back regularly.)

Finally, we believe accurate and current legal information should help you solve many of your own legal problems on a cost-efficient basis. But this text is not a substitute for personalized advice from a knowledgeable lawyer. If you want the help of a trained professional, consult an attorney licensed to practice in your state.

5th California edition

How to Collect When You Win a Lawsuit

by Attorney Robin Leonard

Fifth Edition	FEBRUARY 2003
Editor	LISA GUERIN
Illustrations	MARI STEIN
Cover Design	KEN ARMISTEAD
Book Design	TERRI HEARSH
Proofreading	SUSAN CARLSON GREENE
Index	NANCY BALL
Printing	CONSOLIDATED PRINTERS, INC.

Leonard, Robin
   How to collect when you win a lawsuit/by Robin Leonard.--5th Calif. ed.
     p. cm.
   Includes index.
   ISBN 0-87337-840-7
    1. Executions (Law)--California--Popular works. 2. Judgments--California--Popular works. 3. Collection laws--California--Popular works. I. Title.

KFC1065.Z9 S25 2002
347.794'077-dc21   2002029521

For information on bulk purchases or corporate premium sales, please contact the Special Sales Department. For academic sales or textbook adoptions, ask for Academic Sales. Call 800-955-4775 or write to Nolo, 950 Parker Street, Berkeley, CA 94710.

Acknowledgments

For the first edition, thanks to:

Attorney Michael Perna (of Marsh and Perna, Oakland, California) for his valuable suggestions and guidance in assembling the manuscript.

Attorney Sheldon Greene and the law firm of Greene, Kelley, Tobriner and Farren (San Francisco, California) for their generosity in allowing us to use forms and procedures that were developed for the law firm.

Attorney Irwin Eskanos (of Eskanos and Adler, Oakland, California) and Judge Allen Norris (Richmond, California) for their experienced and insightful overviews of the judgment collection process.

For the fifth edition, thanks to:

Crystal Bergstrom (of Judicial Judgment Enforcement Services, in Laguna Niguel, California) for all of her generous help in bringing this material up-to-date.

Table of Contents

Appendix

Tear-Out Forms

Index

Chapter 1

How to Use This Book

Congratulations! You have a court judgment ordering someone to pay you money. You won your small claims court case or your case in regular civil court—a California state court, or maybe even a federal court. You've spent some time celebrating—after all, you were wronged and deserve to be compensated, and a judge, even perhaps a jury, agreed.

But your celebration is not yet complete. While the court decided in your favor, the court did not pay you or force the defendant to write you a check on the spot. Collecting the judgment is your job. You may have no idea where or how to begin. If you've already made some attempts at collecting, you may be frustrated and feel like you keep hitting a dead end.

It's true that some judgments are uncollectible, but those judgments are the minority. With information and perseverance, most people can collect what they are owed—without having to hire an attorney and often without much additional expense.

If you don't yet have a court judgment. This book is for people who already have been to court and been awarded a court judgment. If you have not yet filed your case or your case is still pending and you don't yet have a judgment, you'll need to wait until you get your judgment before using this book. If you haven't yet filed a lawsuit, take a look at *Everybody's Guide to Small Claims Court*, by Ralph Warner (Nolo) or *Represent Yourself in Court*, by Paul Bergman & Sara Berman-Barrett (Nolo). If you're represented by an attorney, check out *The Lawsuit Survival Guide*, by Joseph Matthews (Nolo). Of course, you can read this book while awaiting your day in court just to prepare for your victory!

A. Nineteen Ways to Collect a Court Judgment

This book covers 19 different ways to collect a court judgment. The methods are introduced in this chapter and explained in detail in other chapters. After you read this chapter, you'll need to read only those portions of the book that apply to your situation—and will help you collect.

Bankruptcy or death of debtor. If the debtor has either filed for bankruptcy or died, your collections options are greatly limited. Instead of reading the rest of this chapter, go directly to Chapter 17 (bankruptcy of the debtor) or Chapter 18 (death of the debtor) to find out more.

B. Laying the Groundwork

No matter what type of judgment you have (small claims court or regular civil court) and what kind of debtor owes you money (individual or business), you should take several steps right away to put yourself in the best possible position to collect your judgment.

1. Set Up a Case File

You may have already organized all of your documents relating to the debtor when you prepared your case for court. Using those organizational skills—or using new ones if you didn't arrange anything before going to court—set up a system for all documents related to your collection efforts. One possible method is to use an accordion folder for your papers, creating separate sections for court papers (such as the judgment), letters you write and receipts for costs you incur in trying to collect. If your collection efforts are extensive, you can set up files by the type of assets the debtor owns—such as vehicles, bank accounts, real estate and wages.

Keeping complete records of your collection efforts is well worth the trouble and will pay off in the end. You are entitled to collect not only your judgment, but also all of your collection costs and accrued interest from the date of the judgment. Chapter 16 includes instructions and

Nineteen Ways to Collect a Court Judgment

Basic Collection Techniques
(Least Costly, Generally Most Effective)

1. Place lien (legal claim) on real estate	Chapter 4
2. Place lien on business property	Chapter 4
3. Negotiate voluntary payments	Chapter 5
4. Conduct a debtor's examination; have debtor turn over property at exam	Chapter 6
5. Seize wages	Chapter 9
6. Seize bank accounts and contents of safe-deposit boxes	Chapter 8
7. Collect from business debtor's cash register (till tap)	Chapter 11
8. Collect money from business as it comes in, for specified time (keeper)	Chapter 11
9. File proof of claim, if debtor files for bankruptcy	Chapter 17
10. File creditor's claim, if debtor has died	Chapter 18
11. Seize debts owed to debtor by third parties	Chapter 10
12. Have debtor's driver's license suspended	Chapter 1, Section D3

Advanced Collection Techniques
(Often Expensive, Usually Least Effective)

13. Seize and sell business assets	Chapter 11
14. Seize and sell vehicle	Chapter 12
15. Seize and sell personal assets	Chapter 13
16. Obtain court order to seize property located in private home	Chapter 19
17. Obtain court order requiring debtor to hand over specific property	Chapter 19
18. Obtain court order requiring debtor to assign (transfer) to you right to receive certain payments	Chapter 19
19. Force sale of real estate	Chapter 14

worksheets for keeping track of payments received, costs incurred and interest due.

2. Establish Liens

A lien is a legal assertion that you have a claim of a specific value against certain property, such as a house or car. In another words, a lien changes your general judgment against the debtor into a specific claim against whatever property is subject to the lien. Anytime you win a court judgment, you can use that judgment to create liens. When a debtor sells, refinances or transfers the property, all liens against the property must be paid or otherwise dealt with beforehand. In theory, you can also collect on your lien by forcing the sale of the debtor's house, but this is very costly and time consuming—and not covered in this book.

Liens are paid in the order that they were placed against the property. For example, if the debtor still owes money to the lender, like a mortgage lender, the lender will be paid ahead of you and any other creditors who filed liens—because the lender's lien was established at the time of the original purchase. You and the other creditors, such as the taxing authority, will be paid out of the balance of the proceeds, if any, when the property is sold or refinanced. If there aren't any proceeds left to pay the creditors, the debtor will have to get the money elsewhere.

Chapter 4 discusses liens in detail and tells you how to create real estate liens and personal property liens, if the debtor is a business.

3. Know What You Can and Can't Do

Debtors have certain legal rights and protections, such as the right to appeal their case in most instances, the right to a certain grace period before you begin collection efforts and protections against collection harassment. Read Chapter 2 to figure out when to start collecting and Chapter 3 for an

overview of actions you must avoid when collecting your judgment.

4. Attempt Voluntary Collection

A debtor who has lost in court may finally be willing to pay you. If you get the debtor to make voluntary payments, you won't need to engage in active collection measures. But you won't know if the debtor will voluntarily pay unless you ask. Chapter 5 gives suggestions for negotiating voluntary payments.

⚠ **Establish liens regardless.** Even if your debtor agrees to pay voluntarily, you will want to create liens. If the debtor stops paying or declares bankruptcy, you want to be on record as a lienholder—and because earlier liens are paid first, you should get your liens on file as soon as possible.

5. Find Out About the Debtor's Job and Assets

If the debtor won't make voluntary payments, you'll have to force collections—often by garnishing the debtor's wages (where a portion of debtor's wages are diverted to you) or seizing—called levying on—certain assets owned by the

debtor. If you don't know where the debtor works or what property the debtor owns, you can use routine information discovery procedures, such as debtor's examinations, subpenas and investigation of court files. We discuss these information-gathering tools in Chapter 6. You need to know where the debtor works and what kinds of assets the debtor has before you can decide on the best methods of collecting.

6. Obtain a Writ of Execution

If you will have to force collections because the debtor doesn't voluntarily pay, you will need a Writ of Execution—a sort of legal permission slip from a court in the county where the debtor has assets. This may be the county where the debtor lives or works, or anywhere the debtor owns property—for example, a debtor who lives in El Sobrante may also own a vacation house on Lake Tahoe. Chapter 7 tells you how to obtain a Writ of Execution.

C. Create a Collections Plan

Coming up with a collection strategy isn't that difficult. Nevertheless, there's no set formula that will work for every judgment and every debtor. Other than the steps described in Section B, the collections process you use depends almost entirely on you and the debtor. No one procedure is right for collecting every judgment—even the order in which the various procedures might be used will vary depending on the circumstances.

For example, in some cases, the best approach will be to go after the debtor's wages—you'll be paid a set amount each month until the debt is paid off, unless the debtor quits her job. But some debtors are self-employed or earn income that's hard to track and garnish, such as tips earned waiting tables. In those situations, a wage garnishment is likely to come up empty—either because the self-employed person will ignore your attempts to collect or because the person doesn't earn enough to have his or her wages garnished.

Similarly, forcing the sale of a debtor's real estate after you have created a lien is extremely costly and complex—and usually requires a lawyer's help. Most people wait until the debtor sells or refinances to be paid, rather than forcing a sale. But if you have a very large judgment and the debtor has a lot of equity in his house, forcing the sale may be the best way to collect.

Collecting From Multiple Debtors

If the court awarded you a judgment against two or more defendants, the defendants are usually considered jointly and separately liable for the full amount of the judgment, unless the judgment says otherwise. Joint and separate liability means that you are entitled to collect the entire judgment from a single defendant (separate liability), or portions of it from each defendant (joint liability).

If multiple defendants are liable on your judgment, a good strategy is to seek to collect from them simultaneously, unless you know one will be especially easy to collect from. If you collect more than "his share" from a particular defendant, that's his problem—it is up to him to get the other defendants to chip in their fair share.

1. Make a Cost-Benefit Analysis

How do you assess how much time, money and energy you'll have to spend to collect your judgment? The answer, of course, depends on your situation and personality. It also depends on luck. Debt collection can be unpredictable. You may think you can easily garnish the debtor's wages—until the debtor quits her job. Or you may believe you'll never see your money—until a single letter convinces the debtor to pay up.

Consider the following factors in evaluating the costs and benefits of using specific collection techniques:

- size of your judgment
- current value of the debtor's assets
- whether the debtor is likely to come into assets in the future
- whether the debtor's assets are protected against forced collections ("exempt," in legalese)
- cost of undertaking a particular collection method
- competition from other creditors seeking to collect
- time and energy you're willing to put into your collection efforts, and
- any special circumstances affecting your likelihood of collecting.

2. Use Rating Charts

To help you choose among the collection procedures, each chapter describing a collection method opens with the following rating chart, with checkmarks in the appropriate columns.

Collection Factor			
	High	**Moderate**	**Low**
Potential cost to you			
Potential for producing cash			
Potential for settlement			
Potential time and trouble			
Potential for debtor bankruptcy			

The charts will quickly tell you if the method will be costly or time-consuming, and whether it has a high potential for producing cash—meaning that you'll be able to grab actual cash or an item that can easily be sold. The charts also assess how likely the method is to convince the debtor to enter into a payment schedule (a settlement). The more coercive the collection method, the more likely the debtor will want to settle the matter rather than lose property.

Finally, the charts tell you if the method is likely to send the debtor to bankruptcy court. There are two kinds of bankruptcy—liquidation (Chapter 7 bankruptcy) and reorganization (Chapter 13 bankruptcy for individuals or Chapter 11 bankruptcy for corporations or individuals with extremely high debt burdens). If a debtor files for bankruptcy, you must cease all collection efforts unless you file a motion with the court and are granted an order allowing you to proceed—which is highly unlikely. Most judgments are either wiped out in bankruptcy or paid off at a fraction of their worth. Even if you've created a lien against the debtor's property, there's a good chance the debtor will be able to wipe it out in bankruptcy. A few judgments do survive bankruptcy, however. We deal with bankrupt debtors in Chapter 17.

Obviously, you don't want to pursue aggressive collection techniques that will push a debtor into bankruptcy. Nor is there any need to do so. Judgments last for ten years and can be renewed for another ten years. If the debtor is having serious financial difficulties, you may want to wait for his luck to change.

If the debtor threatens to file for bankruptcy, how can you assess whether he's really in dire financial straits or is just making threats to scare you off? There's no foolproof way to tell, but the greater his total debt burden, the more likely he is to go bankrupt. If you're the only one trying to collect on the debt, he's not likely to file. But if he owes a great deal of money to several creditors, he's a good candidate for bankruptcy.

3. Select One or More Procedures

For most creditors holding a court judgment, the best collection methods are those that cost the least and get you the best results. Consider these examples:

> **EXAMPLE 1:** Sheila obtained a small claims court judgment against her former friend, Fred, for $1,000. She wrote several letters demanding payment, with no results. Sheila knew that Fred was employed and owned a late model car and his home. Sheila created a lien on Fred's home. She decided not to seize his car or force the sale of his home because the potential cost of both was likely to be greater than any money Sheila would get. Sheila also decided to garnish Fred's wages, figuring he was unlikely to quit his job or file for bankruptcy. Through the garnishment, Sheila's judgment, including collection costs, was paid in six months.

> **EXAMPLE 2:** Small Press, a book publisher, obtained a $5,000 judgment against Terry Wittgenstein and his small bookstore, Protos. Small Press knew that Protos did a brisk business and had a relatively extensive inventory. Terry owned a BMW automobile, a house and a 25-foot cabin cruiser, which he kept docked at a local marina. Small Press discovered that the BMW and boat were heavily financed, and that the cost of having them seized, stored and sold probably exceeded the amount of money Small Press would get. Small Press did create a lien on Terry's house, but decided not to force a sale because of the cost involved.
>
> Small Press decided that the best way to collect was to impose a "keeper" on the business, where a law enforcement officer stands by the cash register and collects money as it comes in. The law enforcement officer charged a fee of $150. When the sheriff phoned Terry at the bookstore and told him he was sending a deputy down to stand by his cash register, Terry quickly came to terms with Small Press, signing an agreement to pay off the judgment in installments over the next six months. Small Press knew that if Terry didn't honor the terms of the agreement, it could send the keeper and even have the sheriff seize and sell the bookstore inventory and assets to satisfy the judgment.

D. Special Situations

In several collection situations, you have remedies other than the 19 listed in Section A, or there are limitations on how you can collect. Keep reading if any of the following are true:

- you have a judgment from small claims court
- you have a judgment from a federal court
- you have a judgment stemming from a motor vehicle accident
- you have a judgment for child or spousal support
- you have a restitution order
- the debtor is married
- the debtor is a government agency
- the debtor is on active military duty
- the debtor is a licensed contractor
- the debtor is a licensed real estate agent
- the debtor is a private vocational school
- the debtor is subject to a conservatorship or guardianship, or
- the judgment doesn't reflect the debtor's correct name.

1. Judgment From Small Claims Court

Sometimes a judgment debtor is willing to pay up, but doesn't want to deal directly with you, the judgment creditor. A small claims court judgment debtor has the option of paying a judgment directly to the court. The court can charge the debtor up to $25 for this service.

If your judgment debtor opts for this, the court will notify you once it receives payment. You have three years to claim the payment. Make sure you notify the small claims court clerk if you change your address. (See Section E1, below.) If you fail to collect within three years, the state gets to keep the money.

If you receive notice from the court that the debtor is paying off the judgment through the court, it makes sense to cease all other collection efforts. Otherwise, the debtor will probably get angry and stop making the payments.

Once the debt is paid off, read Chapter 22 for information on the few additional steps you'll need to take.

2. Judgment From Federal Court

In general, federal judgments are enforced only by federal courts. But still, state law governs procedures for enforcing judgments if a specific state law applies. In California, the procedures described in this book apply if you are collecting a judgment awarded by a federal court in California.

However, even though the rules apply, the forms may not. Instead, you will have to use forms for enforcing federal court judgments. One book that might help, available at a law library, is *West's Federal Forms*. Look at forms 5501 through 5671.

If the federal court that awarded the judgment is not within California, you must register the judgment with a federal district court in California by filing a certified copy of the judgment with the court (28 U.S.C. § 1963). Once registered, the judgment may be collected as if it had been initially awarded by a federal court within California.

3. Judgment Stemming From Motor Vehicle Accident

If you get a judgment against a California licensed driver and the debtor doesn't pay, the Department of Motor Vehicles (DMV) can suspend the debtor's license in either of the following situations.

- **The accident occurred on a California road, and the judgment is for $500 or less and remains unpaid at least 90 days from the date it was entered.** DMV will notify the debtor and give her 20 days to pay or prove that insurance will cover the damage. If the debtor does neither, her license will be suspended for 90 days (Code of Civil Procedure § 116.880, Vehicle Code § 16370.5).

- **The judgment is for more than $500 or for personal injury or death, and resulted from an accident caused by an uninsured debtor's operation of a motor vehicle.** DMV will suspend the debtor's license until the judgment is paid or converted to a judgment under which payments are made in installments, for a maximum of six years. If the judgment is still not paid at the end of six years, you can't simply renew the suspension. However, you can request a new suspension (Vehicle Code § 16371).

If the debtor drives to work, license suspension may lead to job loss, leaving you with no source from which to collect. The debtor might even file for bankruptcy. Before taking the drastic step of getting the debtor's license suspended, negotiate with the debtor. You may be able to work out a payment plan.

If you decide to proceed with the suspension, gather together the following:

- a certified copy of your judgment or a docket entry showing the judgment
- the required fee, and
- Form DL-30, Certificate of Facts Re Unsatisfied Judgment.

The court may have Form DL-30 because the court must complete part of it. Otherwise you can request a copy from DMV at 800-777-0133. Ask how much the fee is when you request the form. Send the judgment, fee and form to the DMV Financial Responsibility–Civil Judgments Division, in Sacramento.

4. Judgment or Order For Child or Spousal Support

The district attorney's office, or sometimes another government agency charged with support enforcement, will provide free help collecting support orders or judgments. Unfortunately, these offices usually have more cases than they can handle, and the backlog means that it may take years before they get to your case. Still, if you want a support enforcement agency to take over collection of your support order or judgment, contact the district attorney's office in your county to make arrangements.

Can You Push the Agency?

ACES—Association for Children for Enforcement of Support—is a national nonprofit agency that works with parents entitled to receive child support. It helps custodial parents deal with their local child support enforcement agency and provides specific advice on how to be heard and get a case processed, or if necessary, how to file a complaint with the agency. You can call ACES at 800-738-ACES, or check out their website at www.childsupport-aces.org.

If you decide to collect your own support order or judgment, we'll point out where your collection efforts may be slightly different from what we explain in the book. In addition, you may have collection methods available to you that are not available to other creditors, including the following:

- automatic deduction from the debtor's paycheck—called a wage withholding order
- suspension of the debtor's professional or business licenses

- requiring the debtor to deposit one year's worth of child support payments in a special security fund or post two year's worth of child support with the court
- requiring the debtor to prove he is looking for work or undergoing job training, and
- interception of the debtor's income tax refund or lottery winnings.

You can use some of these collection methods if you simply have a court order for support; for others, you will have to turn that order into a court judgment. You may need a lawyer's help; see Chapter 23. If you want to try on your own, take a look at *California Practice Guide: Enforcing Judgments and Debts*, published by the Rutter Group and available in most law libraries.

5. You Have a Restitution Order

California law requires a judge who sentences a person convicted of a crime to also order the person to compensate the victims of the crime for any economic losses they suffered—called making restitution (Penal Code § 1202.4(f)). The judge must calculate the amount of the restitution at the time of the sentencing or later, at the judge's discretion.

You can convert a restitution order to a civil judgment and collect using the procedures outlined in this book. To do so, take the following steps:

1. Visit the clerk of the court in which the defendant was sentenced and give the clerk the defendant's name and the court docket number—this should appear on the papers sent to you by the district attorney's office.
2. Ask the clerk to provide you with a free certified copy of the sentencing order, which will include the restitution order (Penal Code § 1214(b)).
3. Use this certified copy of the restitution order as your "civil judgment" to collect.

Is Trying to Collect From a Person Convicted of a Crime Worth the Effort?

You have the best chance of collecting from a defendant who is not sentenced to jail, but is fined or placed on probation and required to make restitution payments as a condition of staying out of jail.

But what if the defendant is sentenced to prison? For starters, you aren't likely to collect while he's in jail. Defendants rarely have assets that can be seized to satisfy a judgment, at least at the time of their sentencing, and may well shield what assets they do have. Defendants can take advantage of the California exemption laws (see Chapters 9-14), which protect basic necessities from being grabbed to satisfy a judgment. And even if the defendant has assets, it may cost you more to try to collect them than you are willing to risk.

Once the defendant is released and on parole, however, you might be able to collect if he finds a job. In addition, the parole board may order him to make restitution payments as a condition of remaining free.

As a victim due restitution, you can act as a squeaky wheel to make sure the appropriate agency (probation or parole) knows you expect to be paid and are watching to make sure that a restitution order is not ignored. But even they can't squeeze blood out of a turnip—if the person on probation or parole truly can't pay, he won't be forced to do so.

If the defendant files for bankruptcy, your restitution order cannot be discharged (wiped out). Stop your collection efforts while the bankruptcy is pending, but feel free to resume them when the case ends. (See Chapter 17.)

In addition to ordering the defendant to make restitution for your economic losses, the court usually will impose what's called a "restitution fine," which the defendant must pay to the state Restitution Fund. This Fund is responsible for paying restitution to victims for their noneconomic injuries—such as emotional distress caused by the murder of a loved one. You can get information on how to apply for recovery from this fund through the victims' assistance division of your local district attorney's office or by calling 800-777-9229. If you collect money from the fund for any losses covered by your restitution order, do not attempt to recover that money directly from the defendant.

If you collect your restitution order in full, plus interest and the costs of collection, inform the court clerk for the court in which the defendant was convicted.

6. Debtor Is Married

If your judgment debtor is married, you may have more assets available to you for collection. This is because California follows what are known as "community property" laws for married couples. Under community property laws, income earned by either spouse and most property accumulated during the marriage is considered jointly owned—which means you can collect it to satisfy your judgment against either spouse. The only property considered the separate property of one spouse is property she brought into the marriage or acquired after permanent separation, property purchased during the marriage with separate funds, received as a gift or inherited or property made separate under a written agreement.

Of course, if your judgment is against both spouses, you can go after their community property and each spouse's separate property. If your judgment is against only one spouse, you can collect from that person's wages and separate property.

Furthermore, you can usually go after community property, even if the judgment is for a debt incurred before marriage. For example, if a debtor and his wife own a grand piano, you can go after the whole piano even though the wife owns half as her community property share.

Going after the wages or separate property of the non-debtor spouse is tricky, but not impossible. You can garnish the non-debtor spouse's wages if you obtain a court order (Code of Civil Procedure § 706.109). If the debt was incurred before marriage, you cannot collect from the non-debtor spouse's wages if they are deposited in a separate bank account to which the debtor has no access. You can collect from the non-debtor spouse's separate property—such as the property she owned before marriage—only if your judgment is for a debt incurred during marriage for food, clothing, shelter or other necessaries of life.

If the couple divorces after you created liens on community property, the liens will remain. For example, if a non-debtor spouse is awarded the family home as part of a divorce settlement, any real estate lien you have created will remain intact. Of course, if the non-debtor spouse tries to refinance the mortgage during the divorce, you're likely to get paid. (See Section B2, above.)

And if the non-debtor spouse has taken responsibility for a debt in the divorce decree, you have the right to collect from that spouse, even if the other spouse incurred the debt.

7. Debtor Is Government Agency

If you have a money judgment against a California government agency—including the State; a county, city or district; a public authority or agency; or any other political subdivision—you must follow special procedures to collect (Code of Civil Procedure § 708.710).

As soon as you receive notice that the judgment has been entered, do the following:

1. Prepare a written declaration under penalty of perjury specifying that you have a judgment, identifying the agency, stating that you want to be paid and indicating the amount. A sample is below.

2. Obtain a certified copy of the judgment or an abstract of judgment from the court clerk. You will have to pay a small fee.

3. Contact the agency you have the judgment against and find out its fee for registering a court judgment and getting paid. It will be small, around $6 (Code of Civil Procedure § 708.785(a)).

Your next step is to deliver these documents to the agency. Legally, you must let the agency and the court know that you've delivered the documents to the agency. So first you should take or send the documents to the agency. Then, have a friend mail photocopies of the declaration and judgment to the agency and sign and file a proof of service. (See Chapter 21, Section E, for information on signing and filing proofs of service.) Be sure to keep copies of the documents for yourself.

The agency must notify its controller, who is required to deposit the money owed to you with the court. Make sure you have your current address on file with the court. (See Section E1, below.)

Sample Declaration

I, Horace Honeycutt, declare as follows:

1. I have a judgment against the City of Los Angeles (Los Angeles Municipal Court case #11212).

2. I desire the relief provided by Code of Civil Procedure Sections 708.710–708.795.

3. The exact amount required to satisfy the judgment is $3,566.90, plus interest at the rate allowable by law from February 16, 20___, until the judgment is paid in full.

I declare under penalty of perjury under the laws of the State of California that the foregoing is true and correct.

2/16/20xx   _Horace Honeycutt_
Date   Horace Honeycutt

8. Debtor Is Federal Employee or on Active Military Duty

If the debtor is an employee of a federal government agency or is on active military duty, you will need to follow rules established by the federal government if you want to use a wage garnishment as part of your collection activities. These special rules are explained in Chapter 9. You may be restricted in trying to collect your judgment in any way against a person on active military duty. Practically, the person may have no property in California. Furthermore, laws may restrict your collection efforts. If a wage garnishment doesn't work for a member of the military, try contacting the person's commander.

9. Debtor Is Licensed Contractor

If your judgment is against a California licensed contractor for a matter arising out of his contracting business, you can ask the Contractor's State License Board (www.cslb.ca.gov) for help in collecting. Submit a legible copy of the judgment and the complaint you filed in the case or a statement briefly describing the reasons for the lawsuit to: Registrar of the Contractor's State License Board, Judgment Unit, P.O. Box 26000, Sacramento, CA 95826, 916-255-3900.

The Board will send a notice to the contractor, usually within a month. The contractor has 90 days to pay the judgment in full, sign a written agreement before a notary public to pay in installments or post bond. If the contractor doesn't pay the judgment or post bond, the Board will suspend his license.

10. Debtor Is Licensed Real Estate Agent

If your judgment is against a California licensed real estate agent or broker, you can ask the California Department of Real Estate for help in collecting, or at least in disciplining the agent or broker. The Department may suspend or revoke an agent's license for fraudulent or dishonest acts. If the court not only awarded you money but also found that the agent or broker engaged in any of these types of misconduct, you'll want to contact the Department:

- made a substantial misrepresentation
- made a false promise
- acted for more than one party to a transaction without the consent of all
- commingled money entrusted to him with his own money
- made a secret profit
- demonstrated negligence or incompetence in performing an act that requires a real estate license, or
- failed to reasonably supervise an agent.

You can contact the Department of Real Estate at:

Fresno	559-445-5009
Los Angeles	213-620-2072
Oakland	510-622-2552
Sacramento	916-227-0931
San Diego	619-525-4192

In addition, you can try to collect your judgment out of the California Real Estate Recovery Fund (Business and Professions Code § 10471). You must complete and return a form available from the Department of Real Estate; call 916-227-0931 or visit www.dre.cahwnet.gov for more information.

11. Debtor Is Private Vocational School

If your judgment is against a private vocational school—perhaps for failing to refund your money after you dropped out—a couple of places may be able to help you get your money.

Vocational schools must post a bond before opening their doors. Contact the Bureau for Private Postsecondary and Vocational Education, at 400 R Street, Suite 5000, Sacramento, CA 95814, (916) 445-3427, for more information—or visit the Bureau's website at www.bppve.ca.gov. If the bond money is all used up, you may be eligible to collect from the California Student Tuition Recovery Fund. The Bureau can give you more information.

Other Recovery Funds

Recovery funds that will pay you money you are owed by a licensed contractor, a licensed real estate broker or agent or a private vocational school have been around a while. Every so often, other recovery funds are established—sometimes for the long haul and sometimes temporarily.

If you have a judgment against any licensed professional, check to find out whether there's a recovery fund where you can submit a claim. The California Department of Consumer Affairs licenses more than 2.1 million Californians in more than 180 different professions, ranging from doctors to accountants to mechanics to security guards. Call 800-952-5210 or visit www.dca.ca.gov.

---

12. Debtor Is Subject to Conservatorship or Guardianship

The property of a person subject to a conservatorship or guardianship is under the jurisdiction of a probate court. This means that the property isn't accessible to creditors through traditional channels, and therefore you cannot use the collection methods described in this book. But the property may not be completely beyond your reach. You can file a motion in the probate court asking that your judgment be paid out of the property under the court's jurisdiction (Code of Civil Procedure § 709.030). How to pursue collections in this situation is beyond the scope of this book.

13. Judgment Does Not Reflect Debtor's Correct Name

If the judgment incorrectly lists the judgment debtor's name or neglects to list all names by which the debtor is known, you will have to file a form called an Affidavit of Identity. You must file this form when you file for a writ of execution (see Chapter 7) or an abstract of judgment (see Chapter 4).

In the Affidavit of Identity, you must list the case name and number, the name of the debtor as stated in the judgment, the additional name or names the debtor uses and the facts on which you base your assertions. Some counties have created their own forms for the Affidavit of Identity—check with the court that issued your judgment to see whether it has a form you can use. If your county does not have a form, you can adapt the sample, below, to meet your needs. Make sure to put the affidavit on numbered pleading paper (you'll find a blank sheet in the Appendix) and sign your name.

You can only use the Affidavit of Identity to include additional names for the debtor, not to add a new debtor. For example, you can state, in the Affidavit, that Harry Smith also goes by the name Harvey Smithers. However, if Harry Smith and Harvey Smithers are two different people, you cannot use an Affidavit to add one of them to your judgment.

And the Affidavit can be used only for a writ of execution or an abstract of judgment. If you want to use one of the more complicated collection procedures (for example, getting an assignment order—see Chapter 19), you will have to file a motion to amend the judgment to reflect the debtor's additional names.

Sample Affidavit of Identity

I, Frank Harrison, declare as follows:

1. I obtained a judgment against Michael Moorhouse from the Stanislaus County Superior Court on June 26, 20XX (*Harrison v. Moorhouse*, Case No. 0010-0020).

2. At the time of the judgment, I knew the judgment debtor only as Michael Moorhouse. He used this name in our correspondence and on his business card. Therefore, I sued him and obtained a judgment against him under that name.

3. Since I obtained this judgment, I have learned that Michael Moorhouse has also used the name Michael Raphael and owns property under this name. I questioned Mr. Moorhouse during a debtor's examination on August 22, 20XX. Mr. Moorhouse said that he owned a home at 346 Magnolia Lane in Modesto, California. Mr. Moorhouse also stated that he used to use the name Michael Raphael, and that he might have purchased this property under that name. I checked at the Stanislaus County Recorder's Office, and found that this property is owned by Michael Raphael.

I declare under penalty of perjury under the laws of the State of California that the foregoing is true and correct.

3/24/20xx   *Frank Harrison*
Date   Frank Harrison

AFFIDAVIT OF IDENTITY

E. Miscellaneous Information About Collections

There are a few things you can do to make collection of your court judgment go as smoothly as possible.

1. Notify Court of Change of Address

Promptly report any change of your address to the court—and to the defendant. Even years after you get your judgment, the court might need to notify you, especially if the debtor wants to pay off the judgment or wants to have a lien removed after paying the judgment. Similarly, if the debtor files for bankruptcy, she'll need to notify you of the new proceeding. And if the debtor dies, the executor of the estate should notify you.

The notice of change of address need not be elaborate; a sample is below. You can notify the court by simply sending a copy. Be more formal with the debtor—have the debtor served either by mail or in person, and file a Proof of Service with the court. How to serve documents is covered in Chapter 21.

Sample Notice of Change of Address

Your name
Your address
Your phone number

SUPERIOR COURT OF CALIFORNIA

COUNTY OF _____

[plaintiff's name],)	Case No. _____
PLAINTIFF)	
)	
v.)	NOTICE OF CHANGE OF
)	ADDRESS
[defendant's name],)	
DEFENDANT)	

To all parties and their counsel of record:

PLEASE TAKE NOTICE THAT _____ *[your name]* _____,
plaintiff in pro per in this case, has moved to:

[indicate your new address and new phone number].

All communications to plaintiff in this case should be directed to the new address.

_____   _____
Date   Plaintiff's Signature

NOTICE OF CHANGE OF ADDRESS

2. Find Out About Fees and Deposits

Most collection procedures require you to lay out money up front to cover costs, such as court fees, fees for serving papers and fees for levying on (seizing) property. We try to estimate the fees for particular collection methods to help you evaluate whether or not to use that remedy. You can get the exact fees from the levying officer—usually a sheriff or marshal—who has responsibility in a particular county for making levies. You should be able to add your collection costs on to the judgment. (See Chapter 16.)

If your income is low, you may qualify for a waiver of some or all court fees and levying fees. Check with the clerk of the court that issued the judgment.

3. Use the Correct Forms and Court Documents

The Appendix contains most of the forms you will need to use the procedures discussed in this book. Make photocopies of any forms before you fill them in. Otherwise, you may find yourself empty-handed if you need to use a particular form more than once. Most of the forms are issued by the California Judicial Council, and are available from the court clerk's office, a law library or on the Internet. (See Chapter 23, Section A3.)

4. Substitute Yourself for Your Attorney

If an attorney handled your case in court, you'll need to file a document called a Substitution of Attorney with the court. In this paper, your attorney agrees to withdraw from the case so you can represent yourself. A sample notice is below; use numbered pleading paper following the format outlined in Chapter 19. You will need to have the debtor served with a copy of the Substitution of Attorney. You can use service by mail or in person; see Chapter 21. Whoever serves the Substitution of Attorney must file the original and proof of service with the court.

Sample Notice of
Substitution of Attorney

Your name
Your address
Your phone number

SUPERIOR COURT OF CALIFORNIA

COUNTY OF _____

[plaintiff's name] ,) Case No. _____
     PLAINTIFF   )
)
    v.   ) NOTICE OF SUBSTITUTION
) OF ATTORNEY
[defendant's name],)
   DEFENDANT)

[Attorney's name] , having represented me in the
above-entitled action as my attorney, is hereby
discharged. I substitute myself in his/her place and
stead.

_____   _____
Date   Plaintiff's Signature

Consent is hereby given to the above discharge and
substitution.

_____   _____
Date   Attorney's Signature

NOTICE OF SUBSTITUTION OF ATTORNEY

■

Chapter 2

Getting Started

*I*n Chapter 1, we reviewed the many methods available to you to collect your judgment. You are probably anxious to get started—but don't move too fast. As odd as it may sound, just because you have a judgment in your hands doesn't mean you can—or even should—immediately start collecting. Delays are sometimes required by law. If you start in before the law says it's okay for you to proceed, your collection efforts will be invalid. In extreme cases, the debtor might even be able to sue you for damages.

Other times, waiting can be a sound collection strategy. For example, let's say you obtained a default judgment—the defendant failed to respond to your complaint in the time required. A defendant might be able to file a motion to have a default judgment set aside and be given a chance to respond if she had a good reason for failing to respond in the first place. For this reason, it makes sense to hold off your collection efforts until the time to file a motion to set aside the default judgment has expired. You don't want to remind the debtor of an opportunity to contest your original judgment.

And sometimes delay is inevitable. If you can't find the debtor, for example, you'll need to do a bit of detective work before you start collecting.

This chapter explains some legal and practical reasons why you might want to delay your collection efforts. It also covers some basic information-gathering techniques that you can use to track down the debtor.

A. How Long Must You Wait?

As mentioned, you must wait a certain number of days before you can begin collecting your judgment. The length of the waiting period depends on which court awarded the judgment.

1. California Small Claims Judgments

If you have a judgment from a small claims court, the waiting periods for collecting depend on how you won the case.

If the defendant showed up at the original small claims hearing and lost, you must wait at least 30 days from the date the verdict is issued before you can begin to collect. The debtor has 30 days to file an appeal in the superior court asking for a new trial, called a "trial de novo." You will be frustrated if you try to collect before this appeal period has passed—the court clerk will not provide you with an abstract of judgment until the 30 days have elapsed (Code of Civil Procedure § 116.810(a)).

If you obtained a default judgment because the defendant didn't show up at the hearing, you must wait at least 30 days from the date the clerk sends the defendant notice of the judgment before you can begin to collect (Code of Civil Procedure § 116.730). This is because the defendant might file a motion to set aside the judgment. If the debtor files a motion, you will be notified of the hearing date. You must hold off collections until the motion is decided.

Some judges almost always allow defendants to vacate a default judgment. If the judge does so in your case, she will either consider the merits of the dispute right then or set another date for a hearing. If you win this contested small claims hearing, you must wait at least 30 days after the decision is issued to see if the debtor appeals.

Some judges vacate default judgments only if a defendant acts very quickly and has a very good excuse. If the defendant's motion is denied, you can begin collecting. Although the debtor can theoretically appeal the denial of the motion, it is unlikely—and even less likely for an appeal to succeed. If the defendant does file an appeal, stop collecting until the appeal is resolved.

The defendant may show up six months later. If you obtained a default judgment, it is possible that the debtor will file a motion requesting a hearing, arguing that she was not served properly—that is, that she didn't attend the hearing because you didn't give her sufficient notice of the lawsuit. The debtor has six months after the judgment was entered to request this type of hearing (Code of Civil Procedure § 116.740). Debtors rarely bring these motions—they are complicated and usually aren't granted—so we don't recommend that you wait six months before starting to collect. But be warned that many courts will try to find a way to give a person her day in court if she really didn't know about a case. If the defendant requests a hearing, you may have to put your collection efforts on hold.

Small claims court help. For guidance on small claims court procedures, see *Everybody's Guide to Small Claims Court in California*, by Ralph Warner (Nolo).

2. California Superior Court Judgments

If your judgment was awarded by a California "regular" civil court—meaning a superior court— you must hold off your collection efforts until the clerk properly enters your judgment in the court records. Even after the judgment is entered, however, there are practical reasons why you might want to hold off on starting your collection efforts.

a. Defendant Might File a Motion to Set Aside the Judgment

If the defendant didn't appear at the trial, the law gives him 180 days to file a motion to set aside the judgment. A court may very well grant the motion if the defendant has a good excuse, such as an unexpected serious emergency. In some very rare situations, a court may set aside a judgment up to two years after it is entered if the debtor can show that he wasn't served with notice of the lawsuit and only recently learned of the judgment.

If you believe that the debtor disputes your version of the facts, the most prudent course of action is to wait six months before starting to collect your judgment. Otherwise, the debtor might find an attorney who will file a motion to set the default judgment aside.

Of course, there is a potential downside to waiting six months. If the debtor owes several people money, another creditor may move quickly to grab the debtor's assets or establish priority as a secured creditor. So in balancing whether or not to wait six months, consider the following:

- Consider waiting at least 30 days before starting to collect. As more time goes by, the defendant will have a harder time winning a motion to set aside the judgment.
- Make sure the defendant was served personally with the original court summons. Go back and ask the process server exactly what happened. Also, reread the proof of service filed with the court. The defendant will have a much harder time setting aside a default if she was personally served than if the summons and complaint were left at her place of business or with someone at her residence.
- Evaluate the defendant's financial situation. Does the defendant have lots of debts and few assets? Does the defendant have a steady job that provides a good income? The better off the defendant is financially, the less you have to worry about other creditors beating you to the punch if you postpone your collection efforts.
- Think about what the defendant is likely to do. If the defendant clearly owes you the money and is not likely to go to court unless forced to, it's probably safe to go ahead with collection efforts.

b. Defendant Might Appeal

Once you were declared the winner in your lawsuit, the court should have informed you and the defendant of the date the judgment was entered, or officially filed, in court records. You are then supposed to prepare a document called Notice of Entry of Judgment and serve it on the defendant to provide formal notice that the judgment has been entered (Code of Civil Procedure § 664.5).

If the debtor was present at the trial, she has 30 days to file a notice of appeal after you serve her with a Notice of Entry of Judgment. If you fail to prepare and serve the Notice of Entry of Judgment, she has 90 days from the date the judgment was entered to file a notice of appeal (California Rule of Court, Rule 122). If the defendant wasn't present in court and a default judgment was taken against her, she is likely to file a motion to vacate the judgment (see Section A2, above) rather than appeal, if she chooses to do anything to contest the situation.

Once the judgment is entered, you are legally entitled to start collecting. You are not required to wait until the 30 or 90 day time periods expire. Nevertheless, we recommend that you wait. If you start collection activities sooner, you may push the debtor into filing an appeal. On the other hand, if you have information that other creditors are seizing assets of the debtor or that the debtor is selling a house, you'll want to act immediately.

Even if the debtor does appeal, you can go ahead with your collection activities while the appeal is pending unless the debtor furnishes the court with something called an undertaking—a security similar to a bond—for an amount up to two times the amount of the judgment (Code of Civil Procedure § 917.1).

There are benefits and risks to collecting while an appeal is pending. The benefit of grabbing assets now is that you eliminate the risk that they might no longer be available when the appeal ends—often several years down the road. The risk is that you might lose the appeal, which means you will have to pay back the money you collected, plus interest and costs incurred by the debtor as a result of the collection.

Only you can decide if the benefit outweighs the risk. You may want to go ahead with collections if the appeal really lacks merit, you are concerned that assets might disappear or other creditors might grab all the assets if you delay. If none of these are concerns for you, we recommend that you wait until the appeal has run its course and your judgment is affirmed before you begin collecting.

c. Defendant Has a Case Pending Against You

Let's say that not only did you win your case against the debtor, but that the debtor has a separate lawsuit pending against you. (Unusual, we agree, but not unheard of.) In that situation, the court that issued your judgment can issue an order called a Stay of Enforcement of the Judgment, which puts on hold your right to collect. A court might do this only if it finds that the debtor is likely to prevail in the other action, the amount in dispute in the other action is comparable to the amount of your judgment and you might not be able to pay the judgment in the other case (Code of Civil Procedure § 918.5).

3. Federal Court Judgments

If your judgment was awarded by a federal court, the defendant has 30 days to file a notice of appeal after the judgment is entered—that is, signed by the judge or clerk and recorded in the clerk's docket (Federal Rule of Appellate Procedure, Rule 4(b)). If the United States or a federal officer or agency is the defendant, the appeal period is extended to 60 days (Federal Rule of Appellate Procedure, Rule 4(a)(1)).

As with state court judgments, you are legally entitled to start collecting as soon as the judgment is entered, although you probably want to wait until the appeals period passes. Even if the debtor appeals, you can collect—but if the debtor posts a bond with the court, you will need to cease your collection efforts. You will also have to pay back the debtor, with interest and costs, if the debtor wins the appeal. If you win the appeal, you may be able to collect your judgment out of the bond (Federal Rule of Appellate Procedure, Rule 20.1).

A defendant can file a motion to set aside a federal judgment. The defendant has several grounds to bring this motion, though the most common is "mistake, inadvertence, surprise or excusable neglect" (Federal Rule of Civil Procedure, Rule 60(b)). The defendant has one year to file the motion, although winning is a real uphill battle. Most judgment creditors can continue collecting without fear that their judgments will be overturned on this ground.

B. If You Can't Locate the Debtor

If you can't find the debtor, you may have to spend some time tracking her down before you can start collecting. This is called "skiptracing" in the collections trade. You have a number of resources at your disposal.

Massive amounts of information about virtually every person in this country have been collected by many public and private organizations. Data about addresses, phone numbers, employment, criminal convictions, real estate transfers, automobile registration, business or professional licenses, credit and voting are stored in computer files. To obtain most of this information, you need only write, call or visit the appropriate office—or search the Internet. Some private records are obtainable by making a special request or by serving subpoenas. (See Chapter 6.)

This section describes resources likely to help you locate the debtor, not the debtor's assets. If you already know where the debtor is, Chapter 6 and the chapters that focus on seizing specific types of assets can help you figure out what the debtor owns.

 More information on skiptracing. If you need skiptracing ideas beyond this book, take a look at *You, Too, Can Find Anybody*, by Joseph J. Culligan (Hallmark Press). You also might take a look at *Paper Trails: A Guide to Public Records in California*, by Stephen Levine and Barbara T. Newcombe (Center for Investigative Reporting and California Newspaper Publishers' Association). While not a "how-to" book, it gives detailed information on virtually every imaginable public record available. *Public Records Online*, edited by Michael Sankey, Peter Weber & James Flowers (Facts on Demand) shows you how to use the Internet to search public records.

1. Internet

Ask any regular Internet surfer how to find a long lost friend and he'll spout off several Internet sites that search for people. Admittedly, many of these records are out of date or incomplete, but they provide a good starting point for your search. Professional debt collectors use them all, with varying degrees of success. Here are several free Internet sites that might prove helpful as you search for your missing debtor.

- www.555-1212.com: Searches phone directories
- www.argali.com: Searches white and yellow pages, reverse directories (if you know the telephone number or address only), email addresses and more. To use this page, you will have to download a program from the website (it's free).
- www.anywho.com: Searches white and yellow pages, toll-free directories and reverse directories (if you know the telephone number only).
- www.bigfoot.com: Searches white and yellow pages and email addresses.
- www.infospace.com: Searches white page directories, yellow page directories, reverse directories and email addresses.
- www.411locate.com: Searches white and yellow pages, email addresses and public

records. Some searches are free, others cost money.

- www.skipease.com: Provides links to dozens of search engines, websites and resources.
- www.bop.gov: Use the inmate locator to search the federal Bureau of Prisons to see if your missing debtor is an inmate in a federal penitentiary.
- www.searchsystems.net: Searches a variety of public records on the Internet.

If the free sites prove fruitless, you can try searching on one or more of the Internet sites that charge for their services:

- www.informus.com: This employment screening company searches driving records, criminal records and credit reports.
- www.peoplesearch.com: Searches public records, criminal records and more.
- www.peoplefind.com/Default.htm: Searches criminal records, public records, credit reports, post office boxes and more.
- www.knowx.com: Allows you to search for liens, bankruptcies and assets, as well as public records, licenses, addresses and telephone numbers.
- www.usinterlink.com: Searches for unlisted telephone numbers, cell phone numbers and addresses.

2. Telephone Directories

If you haven't already done so, call directory assistance (area code plus 555-1212) for all areas where the debtor might possibly live and ask if there is a listing.

If you get the debtor's phone number but not the address, call the number from outside the calling area so it appears on your phone bill as a long distance call. Once the bill arrives, contact your phone company. Explain that you don't recognize the number and want to find out to whom the call was made. The representative will trace the call. Usually, you will be told the name

under which the number is listed and the person's address, unless it an unlisted number.

3. Directories of Unlisted Phone Numbers

The debtor may have an unlisted phone number. Calling it "unlisted" may be a misnomer, however. Unlisted numbers don't appear in the official phone company directories. But they often show up in directories of unlisted numbers, which are compiled surreptitiously and circulate among bill collectors. You may be able to gain access to one through an auto repossessor or other person who works in the collections industry. You'll be charged as much as $100 for a copy of a directory or for the information you need. If the information is good enough, it may be worth it.

4. Crisscross Directories

The idea behind crisscross directories is that if you know only certain information about the debtor, you can fill in the missing pieces. For example, if you know the street on which the debtor lives, you can locate the exact address. If you know the address, you can get the phone number. If you know just the phone number, you can find the address. Some crisscross directories include a person's occupation and business name. You can also obtain the names, addresses and phone numbers of neighbors (or former neighbors), often a good source of information about the debtor.

Crisscross directories are available for most major metropolitan areas. You can find them in public libraries, title companies or the county tax assessor's or recorder's office. Also, most Internet search services include a crisscross directory feature.

5. Voter Registration Records

Contact the registrar of voters for the city in which you suspect the debtor lives. If the debtor has registered to vote, the listing will include the debtor's name, address, phone number, birthdate, party affiliation and date of registration. If the debtor has moved within the same county, the registrar will have the new address.

Even if the debtor isn't a registered voter, you might find contact information for relatives with the same last name—assuming the name isn't too common.

6. U.S. Post Office

If the judgment debtor has moved and left a forwarding address, the post office will provide it to you. Send a request to the post office that serves the zip code where the debtor used to live. Even if an Internet search of change of address directories came up empty, this request might

turn up something. Those directories are updated infrequently.

Sample Request for Post Office Change of Address

June 14, 20___

Postmaster
San Francisco, CA 94118

Dear Postmaster:

I am enclosing a self-addressed, stamped envelope. Please provide me with the forwarding address on file for:

Allan Weaver
234 West Street
San Francisco, CA 94118

Sincerely,

Daffodil Marcos
Daffodil Marcos

If you have a post office box number for the debtor, the post office will release the street address and phone number of the box holder only if the box is listed in the name of a business. Some post offices will give you this information over the phone, but usually you will have to request it in writing. You do not have to explain why you want the information.

The post office usually won't give out an individual box holder's address unless you provide a statement that the name, address and telephone number are needed to serve legal papers in a pending proceeding. A sample is below.

Whether this will work depends on the post office branch, and possibly on whether the person making the request is a registered process server. You may even need a court order, which is beyond the scope of this book. (Chapter 19 covers court orders.)

Sample Request For Post Office Box Holder Information

I, Daffodil Marcos, request the address of Allan Weaver, holder of P.O. Box 133 at the San Francisco, California 94118 Post Office.

Pursuant to Postal Service Regulations (Administrative Support Manual, Section 352.44e(2)), I hereby certify that litigation has commenced and the address information is necessary to effect service of court process upon the box holder and for no other purpose.

Names of all known parties: Daffodil Marcos (plaintiff), Allan Weaver (defendant)

Court: San Francisco Municipal Court

Case No.: 12345

The box holder is served in the capacity of:

[X] defendant, ☐ witness, ☐ other: _____.

The nature of this litigation is as follows: Breach of contract by Allan Weaver.

Dated: June 14, 20___

Signature:

Daffodil Marcos
Daffodil Marcos

If the post office does not have the box holder's correct address on file, you can write a letter to the postmaster letting her know—and asking her to require the debtor to update this information. According to the Domestic Mail Manual, the postmaster can terminate post office box service for a variety of reasons, including a box holder's refusal to update information on the application for a post office box (Form 1093.)

7. Credit Reports

A credit report includes a debtor's name, address, phone number, Social Security number and date of birth, as well as credit history and possibly employment information. A credit bureau might provide a copy of the debtor's credit report if you state that you need the information for a legitimate business purpose, such as collecting a debt (Civil Code § 1785.11(a)(3)(F)).

Credit bureaus typically provide credit reports to banks, credit card issuers, finance companies, mortgage lenders, landlords and other businesses that subscribe to their credit reporting services. Although credit bureaus often are unwilling to provide information to nonsubscribers, it can't hurt to ask. Check your local phone book for the phone numbers of the "big three" bureaus—Experian, Equifax or TransUnion. If you can't find a listing, check their Internet sites (www.experian.com, www.equifax.com or www.tuc.com). Most of the information on the site is about ordering your own file or becoming a subscriber. But the bureaus constantly update their pages, and you can email their customer service departments with your inquiry.

If a bureau will provide you with a copy of the debtor's credit report, you will probably have to provide a copy of your judgment or other documents showing that you're entitled to the report. You will probably also have to pay a fee of $50–$60.

Obtaining the debtor's credit report under false pretenses (such as pretending to be the debtor) is illegal. The debtor can sue you for at least $2,500 in compensatory damages, up to $5,000 in punitive damages plus costs and attorney fees (Civil Code § 1785.31).

8. Public Real Estate Records

If the debtor owns real estate in California, the tax collector or assessor's office in the county where the property is located should have the debtor's current address. This is true even if the debtor lives outside of the county. The taxing authority needs the current address to send the property tax bill. In addition, if the debtor owns more than one piece of property, the county recorder's office might show another address (where the debtor might be now) if a recorded deed was ever sent there.

9. Business Records

If the debtor owns a business that sells taxable goods (the sale of most goods in California is taxed), the statistics unit of the Board of Equalization will probably have information on the business. You can contact the Board at 916-445-0840 or www.boe.ca.gov.

If the debtor is one of the millions of Californians licensed by the Department of Consumer Affairs or another agency, location information may be easily available. Start with the Department of Consumer Affairs (800-952-5210 or www.dca.ca.gov). If another agency licenses the debtor, the Depart-

ment of Consumer Affairs can provide a referral to the correct agency. Business addresses are usually listed in these records, and sometimes you'll get a home address as well.

If the debtor is a sole proprietor, California partnership or member of a California partnership, you can search the fictitious name records at the clerk's office in the county in which the principal place of business is located. This lists the business's owners and their addresses.

If the debtor is, or owns, a California corporation, foreign corporation authorized to do business in California, California limited liability company, limited partnership or foreign general partnership authorized to do business in California, the debtor must register with the Secretary of State. You can get basic information from the Secretary of State's website, at http://kepler.ss.ca.gov/list/html. If you want more detailed information, click on the tabs at the bottom of the page—one is for corporations, the other for partnerships and limited liability companies. These tabs will lead you to instructions for requesting information by mail, including an order form, fee schedule and mailing addresses. ■

Chapter 3

Collection Practices to Avoid

State and federal laws protect debtors from unfair collection practices, including harassment and public embarrassment, by people who collect debts on behalf of others (collection agencies and collection lawyers) and by creditors collecting their own debts. Although some of these laws apply only to people collecting debts on behalf of others, we recommend that you follow them—or at least the provisions barring harassment and other unpleasant activities. Harassing a debtor is both unnecessary and counterproductive. The debtor might even sue you if your behavior turns outrageous. Imagine how mad you will be if a court tells *you* to pay money to a person who is not paying your judgment.

Most debt collection laws were designed to regulate collection activities before a creditor obtains a judgment—in fact, some of the laws bar a creditor or debt collector from threatening to sue someone unless the creditor or collector actually intends to pursue a lawsuit. You are well beyond that stage of collections. Fortunately for you, now that you have a judgment, there will be little reason to contact the debtor, except to request payments. Nevertheless, we suggest that you read this chapter, as you don't want to get sued for inadvertently violating the law.

A. Debt Collection Laws

The federal Fair Debt Collection Practices Act (FDCPA) regulates only people who are paid to collect debts on behalf of others—collection agencies and collection attorneys (15 U.S.C. § 1692 and the sections that follow). The FDCPA prohibits a collector from engaging in many kinds of behavior and also gives a debtor the right to tell a bill collector to cease communications. You are not bound by this law. While we admonish you not to harass the debtor, you are free to continue to contact the debtor even if the debtor asks you to stop. But before making yet another call or sending yet another letter, ask yourself why you

want to contact the debtor again and whether you really expect to get anything from the additional communications.

⚠ You might be subject to the FDCPA if you mislead the debtor. Even though individual creditors are ordinarily not subject to the FDCPA, there is an exception for creditors who use a false name or other deception to lead the debtor to believe that he or she is dealing with a third party debt collector. For example, if you send letters to the debtor on collection agency letterhead, you could be liable for violating the FDCPA.

The California debt collection law (Civil Code § 1788 and the sections that follow) regulates not only those who collect debts on behalf of others, but also creditors collecting their own debts— which means the law applies to you. It primarily prohibits a collector from engaging in certain kinds of behavior—most of the same activities that are barred by the federal law. The state law does not give the debtor the right to insist that you cease communications or collection activities.

If you're in doubt about a particular activity, you can look up the laws and decide for yourself whether or not it is permissible. (Chapter 23 explains how to do legal research.)

B. Common Sense

While this chapter lists specific activities prohibited by federal and state laws, don't assume you are free to do anything that isn't listed. Use these examples as a guide for the types of activities that are prohibited.

If you are honest, reasonably sensitive to the debtor's rights and interested solely in collecting your judgment, there is little possibility that you will run afoul of these laws. But if you are seeking revenge, feeling vindictive or simply hoping to make the debtor's life miserable, your actions are apt to backfire. Remember the saying: "He who seeks revenge should first dig two graves."

C. Communicating With the Debtor

If you want to contact the debtor to request payment or other information, whether in person, in writing or by phone, follow the guidelines listed here.

Phone calls. Here are some general rules if you are going to call the debtor:

- Do not call before 8 a.m. or after 9 p.m.
- Do not call the debtor directly, if he has an attorney.
- Do not call the debtor at work if you know that his employer prohibits his receiving collections calls at work.
- Do not place telephone calls without identifying yourself.
- Do not call repeatedly.
- Do not pretend you are different people on successive calls so you can call again and again.

Harassment or abuse. Do not engage in conduct meant to harass, oppress or abuse. Specifically:

- Do not use or threaten to use violence.
- Do not harm or threaten to harm the debtor, her reputation or her property.
- Do not use obscene or profane language.
- Do not threaten to publish the debtor's name as a person who doesn't pay bills.
- Do not visit the debtor and refuse to leave when asked.

False or misleading representations. Don't lie. Specifically:

- Do not claim to be a law enforcement officer or suggest that you are connected with the federal, state or local government.
- Do not falsely represent the amount owed.
- Do not claim to be an attorney or that a communication is from an attorney.
- Do not claim that you will have the debtor imprisoned or that her property will be seized, unless you intend to have the property seized.
- Do not claim that the debtor has committed a crime.

- Do not threaten to sell the debt to a third party, unless you truly intend to hire a collection agency.
- Do not send a document that looks like it's from a court or attorney or part of a legal process unless the document really is.
- Do not use a false business name.
- Do not claim to be employed by a credit bureau or collection agency.

Unfair practices. Don't use any unfair or outrageous method to collect the debt. Specifically:

- Do not add interest, fees or charges not authorized in the original agreement or by state law.
- Do not deposit a post-dated check prior to the date on the check.
- Do not solicit a post-dated check by threatening criminal prosecution.
- Do not call the debtor collect or otherwise cause him to incur communications charges.

STICKS AND STONES MAY BREAK MY BONES BUT WORDS WILL NEVER....

Sample "No-No Letter"

August 22, 20___

Dear Dan Deadbeat:

This letter will advise you that my judgment against you will stand for the rest of your life, wherever you go and whatever you do, unless you pay it off within one week.

You owe me $6,000 plus interest at the rate of 25% per year, and you're obliged to pay me in full before you make mortgage payments, buy food for yourself or feed your cat.

This judgment gives me the right to talk to your boss about you, and to let him know what a deadbeat you are. In fact, I've even set up an appointment to meet with him at the end of next week if I don't hear from you.

Why not just pay up now, before anything happens to you or your family? I'm sure you'd hate to see your microwave, stereo and car repossessed, or just happen to get smashed up.

I'm looking forward to talking with you soon, Danny-boy.

Sincerely,

Chris Meeke

Chris "you can call me knee-breaker" Meeke

D. Communicating With Others About the Debtor

In general, you cannot contact third parties about the debtor (except for the debtor's attorney or a credit bureau), unless you do so to obtain information that can help you locate the debtor.

This means that you cannot call the debtor's employer to inform her of your judgment or to ask her to put pressure on the debtor to pay.

There are two exceptions to this rule, however. First, you can contact the debtor's employer to verify employment or initiate legal collections, such as a wage garnishment. Also, if the debtor is on active military duty, you can contact the commanding officer and request assistance.

If you intend to contact a third person to obtain location information, you must give your name and state only that you are confirming or correcting location information. Here are some dos and don'ts for communications with third parties:

- Do not state that the debtor owes a debt.
- Do not contact a third party more than once unless the third party requests you to do so, or unless you believe the third party's response was wrong or incomplete and that the third party has correct or complete information.
- Do not send a postcard mentioning the judgment or indicate anything on the outside of an envelope about the debtor owing you money.
- If you write to a debtor at a place where another person is likely to open the mail, write PERSONAL or PERSONAL AND CONFIDENTIAL on the envelope.
- Do not harm or threaten to harm a person associated with the debtor, or that person's reputation or property.
- Do not tell the world how the debtor is a no-good so and so.
- Do not distribute telegrams, pictures, photographs, cartoons, tapes or other materials to embarrass the debtor for not paying the judgment.

E. Giving and Getting Information About the Debtor

As a creditor of the debtor, you may be contacted by a financial or credit agency, such as a credit bureau, bank, finance company, credit interchange club or another creditor. You are free to provide these agencies with credit or financial information about the debtor. You are not obligated to do so if you don't want to, however. If the debtor asks you not to disclose information about your judgment, you have a decision to make. Your judgment is a matter of public record and the debtor cannot bar you from talking about it. At the same time, if you talk after the debtor asked you not to, the debtor isn't likely to come forward with payment.

If you decide to talk, state facts only, such as "I obtained a judgment against Shorty's Shoe Shop six months ago. I have asked for payment three times, but have received nothing." Avoid general negative assertions, such as "Susan Leroy is a hopeless deadbeat and pathological liar and you would be nuts to do business with her." Similarly, don't make statements or conclusions you can't prove, like "Wayne Lee doesn't have very good credit." ■

Chapter 4

Creating Liens on the Debtor's Property

Collection Factor			
	High	Moderate	Low
Potential cost to you			✓
Potential for producing cash	✓		
Potential for settlement		✓	
Potential time and trouble			✓
Potential for debtor bankruptcy			✓

A lien is a legal assertion that you have a claim of a specific value against certain property. A lien changes your general judgment against the debtor into a claim for a specific dollar amount against whatever property is subject to the lien. If the debtor sells or refinances the property, you are entitled to be paid out of the proceeds.

EXAMPLE 1: Lucinda obtains a judgment against Nathan and places a lien for $10,000 on Nathan's house. Nathan wants to sell his house to Frieda. To do so, however, he must clear up any liens. Thus, Lucinda will be paid out of the proceeds so that Frieda can take ownership of the house free of any claims against it.

EXAMPLE 2: This time, Lucinda obtains a $2,000 judgment against Nathan's Rug Cleaning for damaging her Persian carpet. She places a lien against Nathan's business assets. Prospective purchasers of Nathan's Rug Cleaning or its assets—other than customers buying goods in the normal course of business—will require Nathan to pay off the lien as a condition of sale.

A lien is a passive collection device—it doesn't get you your money right away. Instead, it gives you standing as a creditor to be paid from proceeds if the property is sold or refinanced. Usually a lien will eventually produce enough cash to pay off your judgment, with post-judgment costs and interest. Collecting a judgment through liens involves little effort or expense, but it requires a lot of patience. If you think in terms of years rather than months, a lien can become, in the words of a former judge, a "little money machine."

Throughout this book, we caution against using overly aggressive collection measures that may push the debtor into bankruptcy. Placing liens is a good way to minimize this risk. After all, a lien doesn't affect the debtor's right to use and enjoy the property for the time being—it kicks in only when and if the property is sold or refinanced. Of course, if you are looking for money right now, liens won't do you much good, unless interest rates are dropping and the debtor is likely to refinance her property soon.

In addition, if many creditors are trying to collect a judgment through liens, you may find yourself at the end of a very long line. When the property sells or refinances, your pockets may be just as empty as they are today. When you record your lien, check to see whether other liens already exist on the property. If there are other liens, place yours anyway—but also give serious consideration to using some of the more aggressive strategies discussed in this book.

Property Can Be Transferred Without Removing Liens

No law requires that liens be removed before title to property is transferred. If the lien isn't paid off, it simply remains on the property and the new owner of the property has to deal with it. This means that in transfers between relatives, the new owner may take title to the property, liens and all. If the new owner wants to transfer the property to someone who will need financing or who wants clear title, however, the lien will have to be paid. In the real world, judgment liens tend to get paid off sooner or later.

⚠️ **Forcing the sale of property.** Once you place a lien, you don't have to just sit and wait to get paid out of sales or refinance proceeds. Theoretically, you can force a sale of property and get paid out of the proceeds. This is rarely cost effective, however, because of the time and expense involved.

The following types of liens are discussed in this chapter:
- real estate liens
- business property liens, and
- personal property liens.

Other Liens

Be aware of creditors with other types of liens who may stand in line to be paid ahead of you.

- **Tax lien.** This lien is created by a taxing authority, such as the IRS or Franchise Tax Board, if the debtor makes no arrangement to pay back taxes.
- **Mechanic's lien.** This lien is created by someone who worked on or supplied materials to a real estate improvement project, then was not paid.
- **Child support lien.** A parent owed child support can place a lien on the payor's property.
- **Lien on pending legal action.** If the debtor is involved in a lawsuit (other than yours), the other party to that lawsuit might record a lien. If the other party wins the case, he would be entitled to pursue payment on his already recorded lien.

A. Real Estate Liens

You can create a lien on real estate owned by the debtor by registering your judgment with the recorder's office in any county in which the debtor currently owns real estate or might acquire

it (Code of Civil Procedure § 697.340). Once recorded, a lien applies to all of the debtor's real estate in the county—plus any real estate the debtor acquires after you create the lien. For example, assume that you register your judgment in Alameda County, even though the debtor owns no property in that county when you register the judgment. If the debtor later buys a house in Berkeley (a city in Alameda County), your lien automatically will attach to the property.

It doesn't matter what court issued your judgment—a California small claims or superior court, a civil court in another state or a federal court (Code of Civil Procedure § 697.060(a)). Judgments from all of these courts can be registered to create real estate liens. You can even register a judgment obtained in a worker's compensation case (Code of Civil Procedure § 697.330).

Real estate liens won't work for everyone. For example, don't waste your time creating a real estate lien if the facts suggest that your judgment debtor is unlikely ever to own real estate. But keep in mind that liens last the length of the judgment (ten years) and can be renewed if the judgment is renewed. (See Chapter 20, Section B.) Because fortunes can change, don't be too quick to write off the lien remedy as inapplicable.

1. Limits of Real Estate Liens

As mentioned, you will be paid if the owner of the real estate sells or refinances her property—provided there is sufficient money available after the mortgage lender and anyone who has recorded a lien ahead of you is paid. For instance, if the debtor falls behind on her monthly payments and the mortgage lender forecloses on the property, your chances of collecting on the lien are low, given that a foreclosure sale rarely brings in enough to pay the amount owed to the mortgage lender.

You face another potential limitation if your real estate lien attaches to the debtor's home. California law provides homeowners with the right to exempt from collection a portion of the equity in their residence (Code of Civil Procedure § 704.720). This exemption, called a homestead, runs from $50,000 for single owners, to $75,000 for married couples, to $125,000 for elderly and disabled homeowners (Code of Civil Procedure § 704.730).

Exemption laws apply to forced collections, not voluntary sales. If you force the sale of the property—which, as we mentioned earlier, is rarely a good idea—you don't get paid until after the mortgage is paid off, the homeowner gets the exemption amount and anyone who recorded a lien ahead of you is paid. If there's enough equity in the property for you to get paid, you will. But don't count on it. Anyone with that much equity in his house isn't likely to let it be sold involuntarily.

You face another possible limitation if the debtor declares bankruptcy. The Bankruptcy Code gives debtors various ways to deal with liens in bankruptcy. One, called "lien avoidance," allows a debtor to wipe out a lien completely. Lien avoidance is available on judgment liens to the extent the lien impairs the debtor's homestead exemption. This means that if no equity remains after the mortgage (including any second mortgage) and homestead exemption are deducted, the debtor will likely be able to eliminate your judgment lien (11 U.S.C. § 522(f)).

2. How to Create a Real Estate Lien

You create a real estate lien by completing a form called an Abstract of Judgment, having the court certify its contents and then recording it in any county you choose—typically, where the debtor owns real estate or might in the future. (Chapters 6 and 23 give tips on how to find out whether and where the debtor owns real estate.)

a. Complete Abstract of Judgment

An Abstract of Judgment is a simple form affirming that a judgment was entered against the debtor on a specific date for a specific amount. A completed sample is shown below; a blank copy of the form is in the Appendix. If your judgment is for child or spousal support, use the Abstract of Support Judgment form in the Appendix. The content is essentially the same as the form shown below.

Page 1

Caption: Follow the format of your earlier court papers. Check the box labeled "Judgment Creditor." Don't check the box labeled "Amended" unless you are filing an amendment to your original abstract—see Section A2, below.

Item 1: Check the "judgment creditor" box.

Item 1a: Enter the name and last known address of the judgment debtor.

Item 1b: Enter the judgment debtor's driver's license number; check "unknown" if you don't know it.

Item 1c: Enter the judgment debtor's Social Security number; check "unknown" if you don't know it.

⚠ **If you check "unknown" for Item 1b or Item 1c, make sure you really don't know.** Check any papers you have, such as canceled checks, a lease or rental application or a credit application in your possession, or call anyone you know who might have the information. If another creditor later establishes that you had this information or could easily have obtained it, your lien may be nullified (*Keele v. Reich* (1985) 169 Cal. App. 3d 1129). If you discover the information after recording the Abstract of Judgment, you can amend it (Code of Civil Procedure § 674(6)). (See Section A2, below.)

Item 1d: Enter the name and address at which you served the judgment debtor with the Summons and Complaint in the lawsuit in which you obtained the judgment. This information is on the Proof of Service filed by you or your process server. If you've misplaced your copy of the Proof of Service, check with the clerk of the court where you filed it.

If your judgment was obtained in another state, you must have it properly entered in California to enforce it here. In Item 1d, enter the name and address at which you served the debtor with a Notice of Entry of Sister-State Judgment or the address you listed on the Statement for Registration of Foreign Support Order.

Item 1e: Leave this blank unless you're filing an amended Abstract—see Section A2, below.

Item 1f: If your judgment is against more than one defendant, and you want to impose a lien against real property owned by any of them, check the box. On the back of the form, enter the name, last known address and other requested information for each additional defendant. Be sure to fill out the caption on top of the back page.

Date and Signature: Enter the date and type your name. But don't sign yet.

Item 2a: Check this box.

Item 2b: Leave this blank.

Item 3: Enter your name and address.

Item 4: Enter the judgment debtor's name exactly as appears on the judgment.

What If the Debtor Goes By a Different Name?

If the debtor uses a name that doesn't appear in the judgment—for example, the debtor goes by several different names or has an "aka," you'll need to file a separate document, called an Affidavit of Identity. Ordinarily, you can only go after property held in the debtor's name *as it appears in the judgment.*" By filing an Affidavit of Identity, you can go after property, using a writ or abstract, that the debtor owns under a different name. Instructions for filing an Affidavit of Identity are in Chapter 1D.

Item 5a: Enter the date on which the clerk entered your judgment. This isn't the date it was filed or mailed, which may appear on the judgment. If you don't know the exact date of entry of judgment, call the court clerk.

Items 5b-5c: If you renewed your judgment prior to its expiration (see Chapter 20), put the renewal dates here.

Item 6: Enter the total amount of the judgment or renewed judgment.

Abstract of Judgement

EJ-001

ATTORNEY OR PARTY WITHOUT ATTORNEY *(Name and Address)*:   TEL NO.:

☐ Recording requested by and return to:

Lucinda Comstock   (650) 555-0010
811 Fairlawn Lane
Daly City, CA 94000

☐ ATTORNEY FOR   ☒ JUDGMENT CREDITOR   ☐ ASSIGNEE OF RECORD

NAME OF COURT: San Francisco Superior Court
STREET ADDRESS: 400 McAllister Street
MAILING ADDRESS:
CITY AND ZIP CODE: San Francisco, CA 94102-4514
BRANCH NAME:

FOR RECORDER'S USE ONLY

PLAINTIFF: Lucinda Comstock

DEFENDANT: Nathan Ickles

ABSTRACT OF JUDGMENT ☐ **Amended**	CASE NUMBER: 0000-0001
	FOR COURT USE ONLY

1. The ☒ judgment creditor ☐ assignee of record
   applies for an abstract of judgment and represents the following:
   a. Judgment debtor's

   Name and last known address

   Nathan Ickles
   17200 Mission Street
   San Francisco, CA 94112

   b. Driver's license No. and state: California 6660000   ☐ Unknown
   c. Social security No.:   ☒ Unknown
   d. Summons or notice of entry of sister-state judgment was personally served or
      mailed to *(name and address)*: Nathan Ickles
                                        17200 Mission Street
                                        San Francisco, CA 94112
   e. ☐ Original abstract recorded in this county:
      (1) Date:
      (2) Instrument No.:

   f. ☐ Information on additional judgment debtors is shown on page two.

Date: July 7, 20xx
Lucinda Comstock
_____
(TYPE OR PRINT NAME)

▶   *Lucinda Comstock*
           _____
           (SIGNATURE OF APPLICANT OR ATTORNEY)

2. a. ☐ I certify that the following is a true and correct abstract
      of the judgment entered in this action.
   b. ☐ A certified copy of the judgment is attached.
3. Judgment creditor *(name and address)*:
   Lucinda Comstock
   811 Fairlawn Ave
   Daly City, CA 94000
4. Judgment debtor *(full name as it appears in judgment)*:
   Nathan Ickles

6. Total amount of judgment as entered or last renewed:
   $ 7,250
7. ☐ An ☐ execution lien ☐ attachment lien
   is endorsed on the judgment as follows:
   a. Amount: $
   b. In favor of *(name and address)*:

[SEAL]

5. a. Judgment entered on
      (date): June 4, 20XX
   b. Renewal entered on
      (date):
   c. Renewal entered on
      (date):

   This abstract issued on *(date):*

8. A stay of enforcement has
   a. ☒ not been ordered by the court.
   b. ☐ been ordered by the court effective until
      (date):
9. ☐ This judgment is an installment judgment.

Clerk, by _____, Deputy

Form Adopted for Mandatory Use
Judicial Council of California
EJ-001 [Rev. January 1, 2002]

ABSTRACT OF JUDGMENT
(CIVIL)

Page 1 of 2
Code of Civil Procedure, §§ 488.480,
674, 700.190

Item 7: Leave this blank unless you obtained a pre-judgment attachment of the judgment debtor's property.

Items 8a-8b: Check Item 8a unless you are in the very unusual situation in which the court has ordered a stay of enforcement. In that case, check Item 8b and enter the date the stay will expire.

Item 9: Check this box only if your judgment specifies that the debtor can pay it off in installments. You can still use an Abstract of Judgment to record a judgment lien. But your lien will be only for the amount of money then due and not yet paid under the installment judgment, not for the full amount of the judgment. If the debtor doesn't pay as required under the installment judgment, the lien will gradually increase.

This abstract issued on: Leave this box blank. It's for the clerk to complete.

Clerk, by: Leave this line blank. It's for the clerk to sign.

Page 2

You will complete Page 2 only if you indicated on page 1 that you want to impose a lien against real property owned by more than one defendant. If you have no reason to complete Page 2, enter "DO NOT RECORD THIS SIDE" in the caption and leave the rest blank. When you record the Abstract of Judgment with the county recorder, you will be charged by the number of pages. You can save yourself a few dollars per abstract by indicating that you don't want Page 2 recorded.

b. Have Court Issue Abstract

Once you've completed your Abstract of Judgment, make as many copies as you need to record—that is, one for each county in which the debtor owns or might own real property. After you have made your copies, sign each one, turning them all into "originals." Then take or mail them to the court clerk to be officially "issued." If you mail the Abstracts, you can use the cover letter in the Appendix. You'll have to pay a small fee for obtaining an issued Abstract of Judgment, call the court clerk before mailing, or take your checkbook if you go in person.

The clerk will check the case file to make the information you wrote is accurate. Once she verifies the date and amount of the judgment, she will date and sign each Abstract form, stamp them with the official seal and hand (or send) them back to you. This constitutes officially issuing the Abstract of Judgment.

c. Record Abstract of Judgment

Once you have your officially issued Abstract of Judgment, take or mail it to the county recorder's office for each county in which you want to create a lien. If you have reason to believe that the debtor is in the process of selling or refinancing the property, or that other creditors may be creating liens, go in person to speed up the process. The cost varies from county to county depending on the number of judgment debtors and the number of pages being recorded. Check with the recorder for the exact amount.

The recorder may first return a conformed copy, stamped with recording information. Keep this copy until you receive back your original Abstract of Judgment, which usually takes several weeks.

Once your Abstract of Judgment is recorded, all the judgment debtor's real estate in that county has a lien on it. If the debtor acquires property later on, the lien attaches to it, assuming the lien is still effective. Ordinarily, a lien remains effective as long as a judgment is valid—up to ten years from the date of entry of judgment and renewable for ten-year periods—or until you release it, which you must do when your judgment is satisfied. (See Chapter 20.)

The county recorder is supposed to send the judgment debtor a Notice of Lien that informs her of the lien and gives her a chance to correct any mistakes on it.

Liens on Jointly Owned Property

How a lien on jointly owned real estate works depends on the form of joint ownership. To find out how property is owned, you can check the deed in the county recorder's office or hire a local title insurance company to check for you.

- **Tenancy in common.** A judgment lien attaches to the debtor's particular interest and remains attached even if the judgment debtor transfers—or leaves in a will—her ownership to someone else. Property is held as a tenancy in common if the deed doesn't specify a particular type of joint ownership.
- **Joint tenancy.** A judgment lien attaches to the judgment debtor's share of the joint tenancy and remains enforceable if the debtor transfers his share to a third party. If the judgment debtor dies, however, your lien is wiped out. The surviving joint tenants automatically take the property without the lien.
- **Community property.** A judgment lien attaches to the entire property when it is held by a married couple as community property. The lien will be enforceable against the property even if it is transferred to a third party.

d. Your Continuing Responsibilities

As the holder of a judgment lien against the debtor's real estate, you have several ongoing responsibilities.

If you move. You must file any address change with the court that issued your judgment. The debtor will need to know how to reach you so you can be paid and remove the lien. (See Chapter 1, Section E.)

If you discover that you knew or had access to the debtor's Social Security number or driver's license number. You must file an amendment to the Abstract of Judgment. Use the same form and check the box labeled "Amended" after the title. Complete the form again, adding the new information. This time, fill in line 1e, indicating the number of the original Abstract and the date you filed it. Before you sign the form, make enough copies to record the Amendment in every county where you recorded the original Abstracts. Sign each form and record them in the counties where you recorded your original Abstracts. You will retain the lien priority of the earlier Abstract (Code of Civil Procedure § 674(b)).

If the judgment is satisfied. You must quickly release the lien if your judgment is paid or settled. Failure to promptly release liens can subject you to liability for damages that result. (Chapter 22 tells you how to release liens.)

If the debtor has a common name. You may be contacted by other people who own property under that name to clarify that your debtor is not the other person. You must immediately cooperate in clearing up the confusion and must provide the clarification in writing, if requested. For instance, if your lien was recorded against the property of the wrong person, that person may provide you with proof that he is not the judgment debtor and demand that you release the lien. You then have 15 days to provide him with a release document suitable for recording (Code of Civil Procedure § 697.410(b)). If you don't, you could become liable for any damages resulting, as well as a $100 fine. And the wronged person can request a court order to release the lien. (See Chapter 22 for information on releasing liens.)

B. Business Asset Liens

If the judgment debtor is a business—whether a sole proprietor, corporation, limited liability company or partnership—you can create a lien against some of its assets. This is very easy to do. You simply register your judgment with the California Secretary of State. The lien lasts for five years, until the judgment is satisfied or until the judgment creditor removes it, whichever happens first.

> **EXAMPLE:** Nathan owned and operated a business in which he built and sold small business computer systems. Lucinda bought a lemon of a system from Nathan for $8,000 and sued him when he refused to give her a refund. By the time Lucinda got a judgment against Nathan, Nathan had liquidated the business. Lucinda knew that Nathan had been an independent businessperson and had not worked for anyone else for over 20 years. Figuring that Nathan would soon open another business, Lucinda created a judgment lien against Nathan's (future) business assets. If Nathan had not had this long history as a businessperson, Lucinda might have waited until Nathan actually went back into business before creating the lien.

A judgment lien on business assets attaches to any of the following assets that the debtor currently owns or acquires while the lien is in effect (remember, the lien lasts as long as five years):

- accounts receivable—money owed to the debtor from a transaction involving her business
- chattel paper—a document showing evidence of a monetary obligation and security interest in specific goods, such as an automobile lease
- business equipment and furniture, such as machines, tools, computers, bookcases and cash registers—if the judgment debtor is a sole proprietor, he may be able to claim some of them as exempt tools of his trade and prevent you from getting them
- farm products—crops that have been harvested
- items of inventory worth $500 or more—most of the inventory of a car dealership would qualify, but rarely would items in a book store, and

- negotiable documents of title, such as a negotiable bill of lading or warehouse receipts.

(Code of Civil Procedure §§ 697.530 and 697.510(b)).

The lien does not attach to the debtor's cars, boats or other vehicles registered with the Department of Motor Vehicles (Code of Civil Procedure § 697.530(d)(1)). It also does not apply to business fixtures that have been permanently attached to the office or building, such as a lighting system; these become part of the real estate (Code of Civil Procedure § 697.530(e)).

1. Limits of Business Asset Liens

As with other liens, a business asset lien is most likely to pay off when the business itself is sold, not when business assets are sold. But few business property assets carry title documents, so it is easy for a debtor to sell business assets without your knowing of the sale or the purchaser knowing of the lien. When assets are transferred in the ordinary course of business (bought and sold for a reasonable amount in a method acceptable to that business), any lien on them is extinguished, meaning the buyer gets it free and clear of the lien. If assets of $500 or more are transferred not in the course business, the lien will remain, but you will need a lawyer's help to enforce it. (See Chapter 23.)

Even a lien on the business itself may not yield you money. Your lien has priority only over judgment liens filed after you file your lien. If the debtor used the business as security when she bought the property or on other loans made before you file your lien, the lenders have priority over you when the business sells, as long as the lenders have has taken the steps necessary to "perfect" their security interests. They do this by filing a financing statement—called UCC1—with the Secretary of State. To find out if other liens have been filed, contact the Secretary of State's office to request Form UCC11, the National Information Request Form for California. You can call the Secretary of State's UCC division at 916-653-3516 or you can download the form and instructions from the Secretary of State's website at www.ss.ca.gov. From the Secretary's home page, click on the "California Business Portal," then go to the UCC page and click on "Forms & Fees" to find the UCC11. You can ask for a general search or you can limit your search by street address or time period. The fee for the search is $10, but the Secretary's office will also charge you copying costs for any documents it turns up. Follow the instructions that accompany the form to submit fees that will cover these costs.

In addition, you cannot create a business asset lien if you have a superior court installment judgment, unless all of the installments under the judgment have come due and the debtor has not paid them (Code of Civil Procedure § 697.510(a)). By contrast, you can use this lien if you have a small claims installment judgment, but only for the amount that is delinquent unless a court orders otherwise (Code of Civil Procedure § 697.540).

Still, it can make sense to create a business asset lien if the judgment debtor is a relatively large business with valuable assets or inventory. If the business goes bankrupt, you will be treated as a secured creditor. Furthermore, if the business needs a loan or sells, the lender or buyer will probably require the business to pay off the lien.

2. How to Create a Business Asset Lien

You create a business asset lien by completing a form called a Notice of Judgment Lien, serving a copy of it on the debtor and filing it with the California Secretary of State. If five years pass and you still have not collected your judgment, your lien will expire. You can obtain another one; however, you won't get the benefit of the earlier filing date. The effective date of the second lien will be the new filing date (Code of Civil Procedure § 697.510(c)).

a. Complete Notice of Judgment Lien

A blank copy of the Notice of Judgment Lien and instructions for filling it out are in the Appendix. A sample completed form is below. The instructions are printed on the back of the form, but two items require further explanation.

Item 3F: Enter the total of your judgment, plus accrued interest and any post-judgment costs you have incurred. (See Chapter 16 to figure out these amounts.)

Item 3G: Put the date you will mail the Notice of Judgment Lien, and then make sure you do mail it that day. If the Notice gets to the Secretary of State's office more than ten days after this date, the Secretary of State may reject the form and you'll have to refile it.

b. Serve and File the Notice of Judgment Lien

After you complete the Notice, you must have the judgment debtor served with it. Service by first class mail is sufficient. (See Chapter 21 for information on how to have documents served by mail.) Make sure the person who serves the Notice completes a Proof of Service form.

Mail the original and one copy of the Notice along with the Proof of Service to California Secretary of State, P.O. Box 942835, Sacramento, CA 94235-0001. Enclose a check made out to the Secretary of State for $10. If you file in person, you'll have to pay an additional $6 fee.

C. Personal Property Liens

It is possible to create a short-term lien against a judgment debtor's personal property—all property that isn't real estate, such as jewelry, stocks, pianos, precious metals and computers. This type of lien is created primarily to prevent the property from being transferred to avoid collection, but also to protect you if the debtor files for bankruptcy.

Notice of Judgment Lien on Personal Property

NOTICE OF JUDGMENT LIEN
FOLLOW INSTRUCTIONS CAREFULLY (front and back of form)

A. NAME & PHONE OF FILER'S CONTACT (optional)

Lucinda Comstock   650-555-0010

B. SEND ACKNOWLEDGMENT TO: (NAME AND ADDRESS)

Lucinda Comstock
811 Fairlawn Lane
Daly City, CA 94000

THIS SPACE FOR FILING OFFICE USE ONLY

1. JUDGMENT DEBTOR'S EXACT LEGAL NAME —Insert only one name, either 1a or 1b. Do not abbreviate or combine names.

1a. ORGANIZATION'S NAME

1b. INDIVIDUAL'S LAST NAME	FIRST NAME	MIDDLE NAME		SUFFIX
Ickles	Nathan			

1c. MAILING ADDRESS	CITY	STATE	POSTAL CODE	COUNTRY
17200 Mission Street	San Francisco	CA	94112	USA

2. JUDGMENT CREDITOR'S NAME– Do not abbreviate or combine names.

2a. ORGANIZATION'S NAME

2b. INDIVIDUAL'S LAST NAME	FIRST NAME	MIDDLE		SUFFIX
Comstock	Lucinda			

2c.. MAILING ADDRESS	CITY	STATE	POSTAL CODE	COUNTRY
811 Fairlawn Lane	Daly City	CA	94000	USA

3. ALL PROPERTY SUBJECT TO ENFORCEMENT OF A MONEY JUDGMENT AGAINST THE JUDGMENT DEBTOR TO WHICH A JUDGMENT LIEN ON PERSONAL PROPERTY MAY ATTACH UNDER SECTION 697.530 OF THE CODE OF CIVIL PROCEDURE IS SUBJECT TO THIS JUDGMENT LIEN.

A. Title of court where judgment was entered: _____ San Francisco Superior Court _____

B. Title of the action: __ Comstock v. Ickles _____

C. Number of this action: _____ 0000-0001 _____

D. Date judgment was entered: _____ June 4, 20XX _____

E. Date of subsequent renewals of judgment (if any): _____

F. Amount required to satisfy judgment at date of this notice: $ _7,250_ _____

G. Date of this notice: _July 7, 20XX_ _____

4. I *declare under penalty of perjury under the laws of the State of California that the foregoing is true and correct:*

Lucinda Comstock

SIGNATURE – SEE INSTRUCTION NO. 4

Dated: _July 7, 20XX_ _____
(If not indicated, use same as date in item 3G.)

FOR: _____

FILING OFFICE COPY

NOTICE OF JUDGMENT LIEN (FORM JL1) (Rev. 6/01)
Approved by the Secretary of State

Chapter 6 describes a procedure called a debtor's examination. This is a process in which you serve papers on the judgment debtor ordering him to come to court and answer questions about his income and assets (Code of Civil Procedure § 708.110). Legally, as soon as the papers are served on him, a lien attaches to the debtor's non-exempt personal property and remains for a year (Code of Civil Procedure § 708.110(d)). For information on what property is exempt, see Chapter 13. You can renew the lien by serving a new debtor's examination papers.

If the debtor sells or gives away personal property subject to this lien, you may be able to take it from the new owner if you can track it down. If a third party bought the property at or near its fair market value, and had no knowledge of your lien, you may be out of luck (Code of Civil Procedure § 697.610 (a)). The lien may also give you an advantage over other creditors if the judgment debtor files for bankruptcy more than 90 days after the lien takes effect. (See Chapter 17.)

If the Debtor Appeals

If the debtor files an appeal, you should wait until the appeal is decided before creating liens. You are prohibited from recording an Abstract of Judgment for 30 days after judgment is entered and while a small claims appeal is pending (Code of Civil Procedure § 116.810). And for other judgments, creating liens while an appeal is pending could mean that you'll be stuck with significant costs later on if the defendant wins. See a lawyer before creating liens while an appeal is pending.

Chapter 5

Getting the Debtor to Pay Voluntarily

Collection Factor			
	High	**Moderate**	**Low**
Potential cost to you	✓		
Potential for producing cash	✓		
Potential for settlement	✓	✓	
Potential time and trouble	✓		
Potential for debtor bankruptcy	✓		

➡ **You might be able to skip this chapter.** This chapter focuses on steps you can take to try to get the debtor to pay voluntarily in cash or kind. People whose goal is to preserve a personal, business or family relationship with the debtor often take this approach, resorting to forced collection methods only if absolutely necessary. You might also read this chapter if you know the debtor has no money and you want to explore alternatives to cash payment. However, if neither of these is true for you and your gut tells you that getting the debtor to pay voluntarily is highly unlikely, you can probably skip ahead to Chapter 6.

*A*t first glance, it may seem hopelessly optimistic to think that the debtor you have sued will now pay you without further legal struggle. But it is a real possibility.

Before you obtained your judgment, you had only your own conviction that you were entitled to money. The debtor may have disputed the amount or even the existence of the debt. Or, the debtor might have known that she owed you money, but also known that you couldn't force collection until you had a judgment. Now you have that judgment. You can subject the debtor to forced collection for at least ten years from the date you obtained your judgment—and you can even renew the judgment after the ten years expire. Imagine what this will do to the debtor's credit rating—and what a powerful incentive it can provide for voluntary payments.

A. Ask for Your Money

Once the debtor's time to appeal has expired (see Chapter 2), remind the debtor that the judgment is due. Depending on your relationship with the debtor and your own comfort level, you can do this in a letter or phone call. If the debtor is likely to greet a phone call angrily or is a business with which you have no personal contact, send a letter. If you do call, note the date, time and content of the conversation. This type of documentation can be valuable if the debtor later accuses you of harassment.

The debtor should already know about the judgment, even if you obtained it by default. But the debtor might not know about it, or at least might not know the exact amount. The debtor may be ignoring the situation, including the court papers. So when you contact the debtor, have these three goals in mind:

- to let the debtor know you are serious about collecting
- to inform the debtor exactly what she owes you, and
- to leave the channels of communication open so you can try to work something out without resorting to forced collection methods.

Your first contact is not likely to produce immediate payment unless you are dealing with a reputable business or individual who refused to pay before your lawsuit because of a genuine dispute concerning the merits of your claim. Instead, most debtors who have ignored your previous efforts to work things out or have reneged on promises to pay will probably continue the pattern. So view your call or letter as an opening to negotiate. Your tone should be firm, yet polite.

For example, let's say that you obtained a judgment against a local grocer. You call and say something like this: "Hello, Ms. Aquino? This is Robert Bridge … I am the man who obtained the judgment against you in small claims court for $800. I'm calling to find out when I can expect to receive payment."

If the debtor is willing to talk to you, try to pin her down to specifics—for example, full payment by a specified date, eight equal payments on the 15th of each month, payment in goods or services or some other arrangement satisfactory to you. If the debtor tries to put you off, come back with a counteroffer, such as, "I will accept part now and the rest in a post-dated check that I can cash in two weeks," or "How about a $200 payment each month, with the first check dropped by my office today?" Except in unusual circumstances, insist on being paid at least some money now, even if the debtor gives you a song and dance about having no money. Even a small payment starts the process and gets the debtor thinking in terms of paying you what she owes. Getting a debtor over this psychological hump is very important.

You may wish to ruffle the debtor's feathers a little and suggest that you "really don't want to start formal collection methods," but it's usually better, during your first contact, to stick to a softer approach. There will be time for heaviness later, if necessary.

If you write rather than call, include a statement that you'd like to settle the matter amicably. If you know that the debtor is having financial problems that make immediate payment in full difficult, let the debtor know that you can be flexible if the debtor gets in touch with you promptly to work out a payment plan in good faith.

Below are two sample letters. The first is a brief reminder to a small businessperson who lost a judgment to another small businessperson in a relatively routine matter. It is the sort of letter you might send if a debtor hasn't paid but has obvious assets and will probably cooperate. The second letter assumes the same situation, with the very important difference that the creditor knows the judgment debtor is experiencing significant financial difficulties.

Sample Reminder that Payment is Due

July 9, 20___

Mr. Dan Franklin
Franklin Printing Company
1 East Street
San Francisco, CA 94110

Re: *Papers-a-Plenty v. Franklin Printing Company*

Dear Dan:

This is a reminder that I have not yet received payment of the final judgment of $3,500 which I was awarded on June 5, 20___, in Small Claims Court case #845-23499 in San Francisco. Can you please send your payment now, so I can close this matter?

I appreciate your prompt attention to this matter, and look forward to receiving your payment within the next ten days. Please feel free to contact me about arranging a schedule for payments if you cannot pay the judgment in full at this time.

Sincerely,

Brenda Samek

Brenda Samek
President, Papers-a-Plenty

Sample Reminder that Payment is Due When Debtor Has Financial Problems

July 9, 20___

Mr. Dan Franklin
Franklin Printing Company
1 East Street
San Francisco, CA 94110

Re: Papers-a-Plenty v. Franklin Printing Company

Dear Dan:

As you know, Papers-a-Plenty has a judgment against you for $3,500 in Small Claims Court case #845-23499 in San Francisco for goods supplied. This is a legal debt and I expect payment in full.

I understand that you have recently experienced some difficult financial times. While my strong preference is to collect the judgment promptly, I am willing to do so in a way that will leave you in the best financial condition possible under the circumstances. Accordingly, I am open to a regular payment plan to take care of this matter over the next few months.

In addition, let me say that I honestly feel our difficulty in getting together to resolve this matter prior to this judgment was due in part to your financial pressures. For this reason, I am open to discussing working together on future projects, once the judgment is paid.

I hope we can work out a plan for you to pay off the judgment amicably. I look forward to hearing from you within the next ten days.

Sincerely,

Brenda Samek

Brenda Samek
President, Papers-a-Plenty

B. Send a Final Demand Letter

If your first call or letter doesn't produce a satisfactory response within ten days, follow up with a more formal, written demand. Face up to the fact that your initial goodwill and positive rewards approach didn't work, and emphasize the arsenal of legal weapons you have available to collect if voluntary payment isn't promptly forthcoming. Your detailed knowledge about your legal rights may convince a debtor to pay rather than avoid you.

To emphasize your tougher stance, start your formal demand letter with the words "Final Notice." Then be forceful, but don't violate any collection laws. (See Chapter 3.) Let the debtor know generally that you can make her life unpleasant. Don't mention that you might deplete cash assets, such as a bank account; this is apt to prompt the debtor to change banks and hide her money.

Below is a sample. (Legal citations tell the debtor that you know what you're talking about.)

After you send a letter like this, the debtor may contact you. Sometimes the debtor mainly wants to tell you why he hasn't paid. Even if you believe you are being fed a line, it normally pays to be patient enough to open up communications. If you hear a debtor out, you sometimes get paid sooner.

EXAMPLE: Janice didn't appear in court when Jim sued her for refusing to pay for work he had done. After Jim got the judgment, he wrote asking for payment. Janice called Jim to explain in a long-winded way that she hadn't paid because she had had some objections to how Jim had done the project, and also because one of her big clients hadn't paid her—which was probably the real reason. Jim listened sympathetically but reminded Janice that she had never raised any objections about his work, either personally or in court, and that he was entitled to be paid under the judgment. After complaining a bit more,

Final Notice

August 21, 20___

Ms. Susan Hernandez
P.O. Box 123
San Jose, CA 98765

Dear Ms. Hernandez:

As you know, I received a judgment against you for $6,164 in the San Jose Municipal Court on June 19, 20___. I wrote to you on July 20, 20___ requesting payment and offering to set up a payment schedule. I have not heard from you.

This judgment is final. Accordingly, I hereby request that you pay it in full immediately. When I receive full payment, I will file a Satisfaction of Judgment with the court, which will close the matter.

It is in your best interest to get this matter taken care of as quickly as possible. A judgment will remain on your credit record for up to seven years. An unpaid judgment can interfere with your ability to get credit.

I have the right to garnish your wages (Code of Civil Procedure § 706.010), seize your car (Code of Civil Procedure § 700.090) and put a lien your house (Code of Civil Procedure § 700.180). If I am forced to undertake these or other forced collection methods, you will be liable for the cost, as well as the original judgment and post-judgment interest.

If I don't receive full payment within ten days, I will begin forced collections.

Sincerely,

Martin Wing

Martin Wing

Janice finally admitted it, and paid up. Jim is convinced that listening patiently to Janice's face-saving explanation for the delay speeded up the collection process.

The Debtor's Credit Rating

Credit reporting agencies have employees who comb legal filings looking for information to add to consumers' files, such as judgments, divorces and convictions. Under federal law, negative information, including court judgments, can stay on a credit report for up to seven years. The debtor may not realize this. It behooves you to let the debtor know, and we include such information in the sample "final notice."

Some debtors may not care because their rating is already so bad that your judgment won't make much difference. But most people know that bad credit can affect their ability to get a credit card, take out a loan, rent an apartment or buy a house or car.

Let the debtor know that credit bureaus hire companies that routinely check public records, including court records, and add that information to their database. Also let the debtor know that as soon as the judgment is paid, you will file notice with the court, and that her credit report will be updated to show that the judgment has been satisfied.

C. Negotiate an Installment Plan

The debtor may try to work out an installment payment arrangement, claiming that he can't afford to pay the full amount now. You will need to use your best judgment in assessing what the debtor tells you. Do you think he really has financial difficulties? Or is he simply trying to delay paying you?

Take the initiative. Suggest a payment plan that works for you. How do you know what that might look like? Start by assessing the likelihood of success if you force collections. For example, if the debtor is working at a decent job and you could easily garnish his wages, you have the leverage to insist on fairly rapid and substantial payments.

Be wary of a debtor who proposes to pay nothing now, with the first payment to start in a few weeks or months. You are not apt to see a cent. Also, the debtor probably expects you to be a fairly tough bargainer and may make a first offer he thinks you will reject. Start your bargaining from a high end and give yourself room to move down.

Of course, there are exceptions to every rule. If you feel the debtor is sincere and has some financial problems that will clear up soon, consider waiting a short but reasonable time. For example, if the debtor is paid infrequently—such as an inventor who receives patent royalties—you may agree to wait until he expects his next payment.

1. Installment Payment Agreement

If the debtor agrees to make installment payments, draw up an agreement. A letter can do the trick—for example, "If you pay $325 per month for seven months beginning February 1, 20__, I will not actively seek to execute on the judgment except for recording an Abstract of Judgment." Send two signed copies of your letter to the debtor; ask that she sign one and return it to you and keep the other copy for her records. Keep the signed letter in your files, but don't file it with the court. If the debtor defaults on the agreement, immediately proceed to forced collections. Below is a sample letter.

Another—more legalistic—approach involves getting something called a Stipulation of Payment to the Judgment. Formal stipulations need to be approved by the judge and, if the debtor fails to keep her word, you must obtain court approval to end the stipulation and initiate formal collection activities. This is too much work.

Sample Installment Agreement

September 13, 20__

Jane Lee
11232 First Street
Oakdale, CA 93221

Dear Ms. Lee,

This letter confirms your agreement to pay me $250 per month by the first of each month until you fully pay off the $1,900 judgment, plus post-judgment costs and interest, which I obtained against you on June 3, 20__ in Small Claims Court case number 854.

As long as you make these payments, I will not undertake the collection remedies available to me under California law, other than recording an Abstract of Judgment against your real estate. If you fail to make a payment within five days of the due date, however, this agreement will immediately become null and void, and I may proceed with available legal remedies to obtain the full balance due.

Please sign a copy of this letter and return it to me in the enclosed envelope, along with a completed Income and Expense Statement.

Sincerely,

_9/13/xx_	_Preston Wiley, III_
Date	Preston Wiley, III

Agreed to:

_____	_____
Date	Jane Lee

2. Income and Expense Statement

A collection agency usually requires a debtor who wants to make installment payments to fill out a form indicating the debtor's assets, income and expenses. The agency uses the information to decide whether or not to accept the proposal to pay in installments and if so, in what amount. You can ask for the same information as a condition of any settlement, but don't insist on it. Many debtors will pay your debt, but don't want to give you all that private information. However, if the debtor returns the completed form and later defaults on the agreement, you will have information you can use to collect.

We provide a blank Income and Expense Statement in the Appendix.

D. Accept Less Than the Judgment as Full Payment

Suppose the debtor offers to pay you a portion of the judgment immediately if you agree to waive the rest. Your first response may be "no way." You went to the trouble of getting your judgment, and you want to be paid in full. But think again. Collections experts can tell you that taking a hard line may get you nothing.

1. Four Considerations

Before rejecting or accepting partial payment, consider these four factors.

a. Likelihood of Collecting the Full Judgment

If the debtor has income or assets you believe can satisfy your judgment, don't compromise. On the other hand, you aren't likely to collect on your own from a financially strapped debtor with no visible means of support. In that situation, it probably makes more sense to take the proverbial bird in the hand than to try to catch the two in the bush.

b. Value of Your Time

When comparing a partial payment to the full amount, remember that collecting the full judgment will take time—and that time is money. For instance, assume you are self-employed and value your time at $40 an hour. If it will take you 30 hours to collect your judgment, you have to subtract $1,200 from your judgment to determine its actual value to you. Under this approach, you should reject an offer by the debtor to pay you $1,000 on a $3,000 judgment. You'd have to spend 50 hours collecting—20 hours more than you think it would take—before the offer would pay out. On the other hand, an offer of $2,000 on the judgment makes sense. It translates into 25 hours of collecting—five hours fewer than you think it would take to collect the full amount.

c. Possibility of Losing More Money

Consider the debtor's assets and income. Could you easily collect the full judgment, or will it be tough to get your hands on the debtor's property? If you spend money on futile collection techniques —going after empty bank accounts and cars with no value—you're just throwing good money after bad. In this situation, it's probably better to take a reduced amount than to risk coming up empty-handed.

d. Your Desire to Get the Last Dime

Remember the prayer that asks for the vision to seek what is possible, the courage to accept what isn't and the wisdom to know the difference? That's the strategy we suggest you use in collecting your judgment. On the other hand, you may be just so angry at the judgment debtor that you will to do whatever it takes to collect every penny owed. You have that right, and it's up to you to weigh how much time and trouble you are willing to expend to achieve it. But keep in mind the words of one collections professional: "You'll have two choices. Either learn to take what you can with a smile, or go after every last nickel and be pissed off when you come up short."

2. How a Partial Payment Offer Is Made

In California, if you receive a partial payment check containing the language "cashing this check constitutes payment in full," you can cross out the language and collect the balance (Civil Code § 1526). When enacting this law, the legislature also created a procedure allowing debtors to settle debts for less than the full amount. Here's how.

1. The debtor must send you a letter stating that she intends to send you a partial payment check—also called a restrictive endorsement—to cover the full amount.
2. You have 15 days to state any objection.
3. If you don't object, the debtor can send you a check for the partial payment with a letter stating that the check constitutes payment in full.

E. Respond to the Debtor's Claims of "No Money"

What if the debtor really doesn't have the means to pay your judgment? You have three ways of approaching this problem. The first is to try to help the debtor find money. The second is to see if the debtor can offer something besides money that you will accept as payment. The third is simply to forget about ever collecting and to expend your energy in a more creative way.

1. Help the Debtor Find Money

Debtors often have more ways to pay than they originally think. You can help them identify potential resources. Most of the sources listed below apply to debtors with personal or small business debts, though some are more appropriate to one than the other. Some resources may be adequate to pay you in full, while others will help the debtor pay in installments.

When you mention some sources of cash, the debtor may resist. She may not want to touch a particular asset. Or she may not want to ask friends, relatives or her boss for a loan—because she doesn't want to take on another obligation or is reluctant to talk about her financial problems. But you have a judgment and are in a fairly strong position to persuade her to tap one or more of these resources. If you hit resistance in one area, suggest an alternative. If she repeatedly turns you down, ask her to suggest sources for payment. The trick is to get the debtor involved in the problem-solving process, on the theory that if she really wants to find the money to pay you, she will.

This process can have an important side benefit. Even if you don't get cash, you might collect valuable information about the debtor's assets that you can use if you have to force collections.

Some of our suggestions may seem inappropriate or naive. They are neither. There is no way to predict which suggestion will touch a nerve with a particular debtor. Please suspend your disbelief; do not reject any suggestion out of hand. Go through each one with the debtor until you find one that works.

Deposit accounts. This may seem too obvious. After all, if the debtor has money in the bank, he wouldn't claim to be broke, would he? Leaving aside the fact that some debtors lie, others simply don't think of funds that they have earmarked for special purposes. You are entitled to be paid before the debtor's family goes on its next vacation, buys Christmas presents or spends other nonessential money.

Retirement accounts. Many people have thousands of dollars in retirement accounts—IRAs, Keoghs or 401(k) plans—which can be withdrawn, although subject to penalties and the loss of interest. Because of the cost involved, the debtor may not consider these funds available. If you offer to take slightly less than the full amount to help offset the penalty for early withdrawal, you may get paid.

Investments. The debtor may not think of securities as a source of ready cash. In fact, debtors sometimes conveniently forget they have these resources. Even a debtor who remembers her investments may resist selling because they provide a feeling of security. Suggest that the debtor keep the securities and use them as collateral to take out a bank loan—or better yet, a margin loan from the broker—to pay you.

People who actively play the stock market often have large cash reserves on deposit with their broker so that stock transactions can be instantly carried out with a telephone call. This is a source of money for payment.

Income tax refunds. The debtor may be awaiting a tax refund, which can be given to you as a relatively painless way of satisfying all or part of the judgment. This approach works best in the first several months of the calendar year, just before the refund comes from the IRS or California Franchise Tax Board.

Personal loans. Ask the debtor to borrow the money to pay you. If he's a member of a credit union, suggest he check there first. Credit union loans tend to have good terms (low interest rates). Credit unions may also be more willing to lend money because they usually insist that the loan be repaid through paycheck withholding.

Another source for a personal loan is a bank or savings and loan. Even a debtor with financial problems may qualify, especially if he has a car he can pledge as collateral or has a longtime relationship with a particular bank.

Home equity loans. If the debtor owns real estate, she may qualify for an equity loan. This suggestion is most appropriate if the debtor owes you a substantial amount of money and hasn't already encumbered the property with second or third deeds of trust.

Credit card cash advance. Virtually everyone—even destitute debtors—have credit cards. So suggest that the debtor take a cash advance on a MasterCard, Visa or other account.

Insurance policies. Whole life insurance policies have a cash value. Usually, a debtor can borrow against this value. In addition, if your judgment is based on a tort (personal injury) claim, the debtor's homeowner's or renter's policy may cover it.

Pay advance. Sometimes, the debtor's employer will advance money against a salary or other money the debtor is entitled to receive, such as a bonus or extra pay for overtime. Even a debtor who doesn't want others to know about the judgment may be willing to request an advance if the alternative is a wage garnishment. But be careful not to threaten a wage garnishment if you don't intend to, or cannot, implement one.

Loans from friends or relatives. Family or close friends may make a loan to the debtor, although many debtors resist the idea, out of pride or shame. But this reaction often doesn't make much sense. Wouldn't you want to help a good friend or relative who truly needs it? If the answer is yes, perhaps you can think of a way to help the debtor overcome his reluctance to ask.

Selling personal possessions. Selling unwanted household or office items can be an excellent and often painless way for the debtor to raise funds. A successful garage sale can raise several hundred dollars or more. Ask the debtor about items he might not need and can sell. For instance, you might say something like, "Is there some older office equipment you aren't using very much, since you bought the new computer?" Or "Why don't you put your video camera up for sale? You aren't using it anymore anyway. If you sell it now, you'll still get good value, but if you hold it a year or two, it will lose most of its value."

Investors or new business partners. If the debtor has a basically sound business that is struggling, bringing in an investor is an obvious way to raise funds. The additional capital might even give the business an infusion of management skill.

If the debtor is receptive and you know something about his business, suggest ways for him to do this. For example, personal friends or others in the same type of business who might not agree to make a simple loan might be willing to extend an investment, if they think the business has a chance of making them some money. (*How to Write a Business Plan,* by Mike McKeever (Nolo) gives information on how to organize and write a business plan for potential investors.)

Hobbies. If the debtor has a hobby, he may be able to get money from it. For example, a person who is a whiz with cameras might get jobs photographing parties or weddings. Someone who has a way with dogs might offer a dog sitting service. The possibilities are almost endless.

Rental income. Can the debtor rent out part of his house or business building?

Help the debtor find work. If the debtor is unemployed, a good way to get paid is to help her find work. If you have a business, you may even hire her in exchange for a promise to pay—this is viable only if you and the debtor have a decent relationship and the debtor has skills you can use. If you hire the debtor, pay her what you'd pay anyone else doing that job, but insist that you be given a reasonable amount each pay period as an installment payment against the debt—10% to 20% of the total pay is a fair amount. If the debtor is self-employed and you can make use of her services, negotiate to pay a lower than normal rate. Keep track of the difference until the judgment is paid off.

Sometimes, just keeping in touch with the debtor is a way to help her find work.

EXAMPLE: Lisa got a judgment against Farley, a former business associate, who was having financial difficulties. Lisa agreed to accept a small payment each month. After Farley made one payment and missed one, Lisa ran into him at a business event, spoke to him privately and reminded him of their agreement. Farley reconfirmed the agreement, paid for several months and then dropped out of sight. When he resurfaced, Lisa reminded him of the debt. Farley explained that his consulting business was kaput and he had no income. Lisa got an idea about a job he might bid on and called him. Farley made the bid, got the job, thanked Lisa and resumed making payments. We think the moral of this story is not only that it often produces better results to help people who are down on their luck rather than simply dunning them, but that it almost always pays in the long run to stay in touch with people who owe you significant amounts of money.

Another possible source of money is an extra part-time job. If the debtor is receptive but needs help finding a job, be ready to offer suggestions.

2. Barter for Goods or Services

If the debtor is not likely to have enough money to pay you a meaningful amount any time soon, think of non-monetary ways he can satisfy your judgment. One way is to accept goods or services instead of money. Although it's rare today, not too long ago entire communities operated on a barter, rather than cash, basis. A carpenter might have little cash but could trade carpentry work for food, shelter and even medical care. There is no reason why you can't encourage the debtor to embrace barter.

Perhaps the debtor owns equipment or furniture that you could use—or you know someone you could give it to.

EXAMPLE: Tanya was owed money by a former client, Melanee. Melanee had to move several thousand miles away, and suggested that Tanya take her furniture as full payment. At first Tanya refused, not having any use for somewhat battered furniture. Then, realizing her daughter was planning to move into her first apartment and had nothing, she agreed. It wasn't as good as full payment, but it was much better than getting nothing from a person who was likely to be judgment-proof for years to come.

We don't suggest that you take the debtor's property with the idea of selling it and crediting the debtor with the proceeds. The price you get will probably be far less than the debtor expects, which may mean another hassle. Either agree to accept specific property in exchange for a specific credit, or insist that the debtor sell the property and give you the proceeds.

If you consider barter, be flexible. What can the debtor reasonably offer you? What are you willing to accept? Agricultural produce, canned goods, artworks, handicrafts, camping gear, furniture, sports equipment, electronic equipment or photographic equipment are among the items a debtor may offer you. If the debtor has a business, maybe he has a conference table and chairs, desk, file cabinet or computer.

If the judgment debtor has nothing tangible to give you, he may be able to provide some service. These could be anything from lessons—such as music, art, computer repair or tennis—to home or car repairs. We are suggesting specific, finite services. We are not suggesting that the judgment debtor work for you on an ongoing basis without pay.

Any agreement you come up with needs to be spelled out in writing. Be precise on what the debtor will do in order to satisfy all or part of the judgment. Clearly describe the goods or services to be received as barter. Also, specify what happens if the debtor doesn't fulfill his end of the agreement so he understands that you will force collections if he doesn't comply. Make sure the debtor is credited with partial payment for any partial performance. Finally, be sure the debtor states that he has entered into the agreement knowingly and freely, and fully understands what it says.

A sample agreement is below. When the debtor fulfills his part of the bargain, it's your legal obligation to file a Satisfaction of Judgment with the court. (See Chapter 22.)

Sample Agreement For Payment By Barter

Judgment Creditor Raul Maquez ("Judgment Creditor") and Judgment Debtor Hiya Ito ("Judgment Debtor") agree as follows:

1. The judgment referred to in this agreement was obtained by Judgment Creditor against Judgment Debtor, entered in the Solano County Small Claims Court on April 23, 20___, Case # 123, plus post-judgment costs which have been incurred, and accrued interest.

2. Judgment Debtor agrees to provide the following goods and services to Judgment Creditor, valued at a total of $700, toward satisfaction of the judgment, costs and interest:

   a. One hour-long jujitsu lesson per week for ten consecutive weeks, beginning September 6, 20___ ($250, or $25 per lesson).

   b. One used Yamaha electronic keyboard, model Y315 ($200).

   c. One used oak computer workstation ($250).

3. In consideration for this agreement, Judgment Debtor understands that this judgment held against her by Judgment Creditor will be considered ☐ fully satisfied, or ☒ satisfied for the amount described in paragraph 2.

4. Judgment Debtor understands that if she fails to deliver the goods and/or services described in paragraph 2 within one week of the date Judgment Debtor signs this agreement, this agreement will immediately become null and void at the Judgment Creditor's option, and the judgment can be enforced against Judgment Debtor to obtain the balance due on the judgment, less the value of any item or part of any item described in paragraph 2 that Judgment Debtor has already paid or provided to Judgment Creditor.

Judgment Debtor and Judgment Creditor have entered into this agreement knowingly and freely, and fully agree to its terms.

Agreed to by:

_____   _____
Date   Judgment Creditor

_____   _____
Date   Judgment Debtor

Chapter 6

Determining What the Debtor Owns

*U*nless the debtor agrees to pay you voluntarily (see Chapter 5), the collection method that is most likely to yield money quickly is seizing the debtor's assets. This isn't hard to do—as long as you know what assets the debtor has and where to find them.

If you have no idea what the debtor owns, you may be able to find out by using one or more of the procedures described in this chapter. They are designed to help you discover general information about the debtor's assets, income and expenses. Later chapters provide methods for locating specific types of assets.

If You Want To Find	Go To:
Bank and deposit accounts	Chapter 8, Section A
Where the debtor works	Chapter 9, Section B
Debts owed to the debtor by others	Chapter 10, Section B
Motor vehicles	Chapter 12, Section B
Real estate	Chapter 14, Section B

A. Debtor's Statement of Assets

If your judgment was issued by a small claims court, a special information collection method is available to you. Once the judgment is entered, the clerk must give the debtor a form called a Statement of Assets, which the debtor has to complete and return to you within 30 days. If the debtor files a motion to vacate or an appeal, he doesn't have to return the form to you until 30 days after losing his motion or appeal. Check with the small claims advisor or clerk about the procedure.

Unfortunately, few judgment debtors complete the form. If that happens to you, you can file a motion asking the small claims court judge to hold the debtor in contempt of court for failing to complete and return the form.

If you received a completed Judgment Debtor's Statement of Assets, you'll have information about the debtor's occupation, employer, income, bank accounts, vehicles and other personal property.

B. Family Court Records

If the debtor recently divorced or went through a support modification proceeding, the court file in that case probably contains valuable information about her assets. In most divorce and support cases, parties must submit detailed income and expense statements giving information about their finances. In addition, a divorce judgment often specifies which items of property each spouse gets in the divorce.

These court files are public records. To review a particular file, you must visit the court clerk's office. You need to find out the case number of the divorce or support proceeding. Ask the clerk where you can find the list of active or recently active case names. Once you find the right case, write down the case number. Give it to the court clerk to obtain the case file. Review and copy down information about bank account numbers, retirement plans, employment, real estate, cars and whatever else looks helpful. Ask the clerk how you can make copies if there's too much information to write down. You cannot take the court file, or any documents in the file, out of the clerk's office.

C. Schedule a Debtor's Examination

As a judgment creditor, you can require the judgment debtor to appear in court and answer questions about his income and assets (Code of Civil Procedure § 708.110(a)). This procedure is called a "debtor's examination." The purpose is to provide you with a way to find out about assets that could be used to satisfy your judgment.

This is a fairly simple procedure. You fill out a form, have a copy personally served on the judgment debtor and file the original with the court. The judgment debtor must then show up in court and answer your questions. If you want the debtor to bring documents for your examination, such as bank statements, stock certificates, deeds and pay stubs, you can have him served with an additional form called a Subpena Duces Tecum.

If the debtor doesn't cooperate, you can ask the supervising official (typically a judge or discovery commissioner) to order him to appear. If he still doesn't show up, the supervising official can issue a bench warrant or order him to court to explain why he shouldn't be held in contempt of court. But erase any visions of having the debtor arrested for contempt of court. While debtors have a nasty habit of not showing up for debtor's examinations, courts are often too busy to care.

You can also order third parties to appear at a debtor's examination to answer questions or provide documents for you to review—but only if you believe those third parties possess personal property belonging to the judgment debtor or owe the debtor at least $250 (Code of Civil Procedure § 708.120 (a)).

⚠ Don't examine the debtor in writing. Instead of conducting a debtor's examination, you can send written questions called interrogatories to the debtor (Code of Civil Procedure § 708.020). The procedure costs very little and is easier than conducting a debtor's examination. But it also gives him time to figure out how to hide assets. In addition, debtors rarely fill them out. Collection professionals almost never use interrogatories and we recommend against them. If the debtor is willing to give you information, send an income and expense statement for him to complete and return to you instead. (See Chapter 5, Section C2.)

1. Determine the Proper Court for Debtor's Examination

The proper court for conducting the debtor's examination is usually, but not always, the court in which the money judgment was entered—called the "judgment court." You can use the judgment court if the judgment debtor:

- lives or has a place of business in the same county as the judgment court, or
- lives or has a place of business within 150 miles of the judgment court.

If neither of these conditions applies, you must move the examination to a court in the same county as the debtor's residence or place of business (Code of Civil Procedure § 708.160).

To conduct a debtor's examination in a different county from the judgment court, follow these steps (Code of Civil Procedure § 708.160):

1. Find the court in the county where the debtor lives or has a place of business.
2. Fill out the debtor examination form. (See Section C3, below.)
3. Obtain an Abstract of Judgment from the judgment court. (See Chapter 4.)
4. Prepare a declaration showing that the judgment debtor lives or has a place of business in the county where examination is being sought. (See the sample declaration, below.)

5. Mail or take all of these papers to the new court along with the appropriate filing fee—probably under $20 (call ahead to find out the amount).

➡ If the debtor lives far away. It is usually a waste of time and money to conduct an examination if you have to travel a long way to do it. As mentioned, debtors often don't show up, and courts are often too busy with other matters to protect your right to conduct the examination. Consider doing your own investigation along the lines suggested in subsequent chapters on specific types of assets, or hiring an investigation agency if the judgment is large enough to warrant the cost. (See Chapter 23, Section C2.)

2. Schedule the Examination

Before you complete the examination form, contact the court clerk to set a date and place for the exam. The clerk will tell you when debtors' examinations are scheduled at that courthouse and will let you know the next available date.

Some courts let you select the date; others assign you a particular date. Either way, make sure the date is far enough in the future to allow you to get the form issued from the court and get the debtor personally served at least ten days before the examination. As a general rule, you should allow at least 20 days for service, which means that you shouldn't schedule the debtor's examination sooner than 30 days from when you start the process. It isn't uncommon to have an examination date set for six to eight weeks after the process is initiated.

3. Complete the Form: Application and Order for Appearance and Examination

A few courts have their own forms, so before you start typing, call the court clerk and ask whether the court has its own form or uses the Judicial Council's Application and Order for Appearance and Examination form. If you use a local form, modify these instructions as needed. A sample completed form and instructions follow. You can find a blank copy of the form in the Appendix.

Page 1

Caption: Follow the format of your earlier court papers. Check the box labeled "Enforcement of Judgment." Check the appropriate box to indicate whether you want the judgment debtor or a third person to appear.

Item 1: Enter the name of the person you want to appear.

Item 2a or 2b: Check the correct box depending on whether you want the debtor to appear or you want a third party to appear. If you want both, you must complete two separate forms.

Item 2c: Leave this box blank.

Rectangular box: Enter where and when the examination will be held.

Item 3: We recommend that you have a professional (sheriff, marshal or registered process server) carry out the service, in which case you'd leave this blank. If you use someone else, put his name here. (See Section E, below, for more on service.)

Item 4: Check "judgment creditor" and insert the same name you put in Item 1, above.

Item 5: Check "judgment debtor" if you want to examine the debtor. If you want to examine a third party, check "third person" and attach a declaration showing that the third party possesses property worth more than $250 belonging to the debtor. You need not specify how you learned this—you can state that your knowledge is based on information and belief, although we suggest that you provide as much detail as you can (Code of Civil Procedure § 708.120(a)). Below is a sample declaration. Type it up, double-spaced, on numbered pleading paper.

Application and Order for Appearance and Examination

AT-138, EJ-125

ATTORNEY OR PARTY WITHOUT ATTORNEY (Name, state bar number, and address):

Frank Starlet
77 Pinecomb Court
Napa, CA 94559

TELEPHONE NO.: 707-555-1207   FAX NO.:
ATTORNEY FOR (Name): In Pro Per

NAME OF COURT: Superior Court of California
STREET ADDRESS: County of Napa
MAILING ADDRESS: P.O. Box 880
CITY AND ZIP CODE: Napa, CA 94559
BRANCH NAME:

PLAINTIFF: Frank Starlet

DEFENDANT: Courtney Horn

FOR COURT USE ONLY

APPLICATION AND ORDER FOR APPEARANCE AND EXAMINATION

[X] **ENFORCEMENT OF JUDGMENT**   [ ] **ATTACHMENT (Third Person)**
[X] **Judgment Debtor**   [ ] **Third Person**

CASE NUMBER:

000-0002

ORDER TO APPEAR FOR EXAMINATION

1. TO (name):   Courtney Horn
2. YOU ARE ORDERED TO APPEAR personally before this court, or before a referee appointed by the court, to
   a. [X] furnish information to aid in enforcement of a money judgment against you.
   b. [ ] answer concerning property of the judgment debtor in your possession or control or concerning a debt you owe the judgment debtor.
   c. [ ] answer concerning property of the defendant in your possession or control or concerning a debt you owe the defendant that is subject to attachment.

   Date: August 1, 20XX   Time: 9 am   Dept. or Div.: 1   Rm.: 100
   Address of court [X] shown above   [ ] is:

3. This order may be served by a sheriff, marshal, registered process server, **or** the following specially appointed person (name):

Date: _____   _____
                                          JUDGE OR REFEREE

This order must be served not less than 10 days before the date set for the examination.
IMPORTANT NOTICES ON REVERSE

APPLICATION FOR ORDER TO APPEAR FOR EXAMINATION

4. [X] Judgment creditor   [ ] Assignee of record   [ ] Plaintiff who has a right to attach order
   applies for an order requiring (name): Courtney Horn   to appear and furnish information
   to aid in enforcement of the money judgment or to answer concerning property or debt.
5. The person to be examined is
   a. [X] the judgment debtor.
   b. [ ] a third person (1) who has possession or control of property belonging to the judgment debtor or the defendant or (2) who owes the judgment debtor or the defendant more than $250. An affidavit supporting this application under Code of Civil Procedure section 491.110 or 708.120 is attached.
6. The person to be examined resides or has a place of business in this county or within 150 miles of the place of examination.
7. [ ] This court is **not** the court in which the money judgment is entered or (attachment only) the court that issued the writ of attachment. An affidavit supporting an application under Code of Civil Procedure section 491.150 or 708.160 is attached.
8. [X] The judgment debtor has been examined within the past 120 days. An affidavit showing good cause for another examination is attached.

I declare under penalty of perjury under the laws of the State of California that the foregoing is true and correct.

Date: June 2, 20XX

Frank Starlet   ▸ *Frank Starlet*
_____   _____
(TYPE OR PRINT NAME)   (SIGNATURE OF DECLARANT)

(Continued on reverse)

Form Adopted for Mandatory Use
Judicial Council of California
AT-138, EJ-125 [Rev. July 1, 2000]

**APPLICATION AND ORDER
FOR APPEARANCE AND EXAMINATION**
(Attachment—Enforcement of Judgment)

WEST GROUP
Official Publisher

Code of Civil Procedure,
§§ 491.110, 708.110, 708.120

Sample Information and Belief Declaration

I, Frank Starlet, declare as follows:

1. I obtained a judgment against Courtney Horn from the Napa County Superior Court on January 10, 20___, in case #0000-0002.

2. The balance due on the judgment is $6,000, plus accrued interest and post-judgment costs.

3. My neighbor, Roscoe Kline, is a former business associate of Courtney Horn. On several occasions, Courtney Horn and I attended social functions given by Mr. Kline. At these functions, Ms. Horn told me several times that she owns a variety of original paintings, valued at approximately $12,000. I am informed and believe that these paintings are in the possession of her agent, Arnold Florsheim.

4. Ms. Horn also told me that these paintings are the primary items of value she owns.

I declare under penalty of perjury under the laws of the State of California that the foregoing is true and correct.

6/2/xx   *Frank Starlet*
Date   Frank Starlet

DECLARATION OF FRANK STARLET

Item 6: Leave this blank, but read it to make sure you are filing in the right court.

Item 7: Check this box only if the court where you want the examination conducted is not the one that issued the judgment. In that situation, go back and read Section 2, above.

Item 8: Leave this blank if this is the first time you have tried to examine the judgment debtor or if you examined him more than 120 days ago. If you examined him within the last 120 days, check this box and attach a declaration stating your good reason for another examination (Code of Civil Procedure § 708.110 (c)). A sample is below.

Sample Declaration for Examination Within 120 Days

I, Frank Starlet, declare as follows:

1. I obtained a judgment against Courtney Horn from the Napa County Superior Court on January 10, 20___, in case #0000-0002.

2. The balance due on the judgment is $6,000, plus accrued interest and post-judgment costs.

3. My neighbor, Roscoe Kline, is a fomer business associate of Courtney Horn. On several occasions, Courtney Horn and I attended social functions given by Mr. Kline. Several times Ms. Horn told me that she owns a variety of original paintings, valued at approximately $12,000. I am informed and believe that these paintings are in the possession of her agent, Arnold Florsheim.

4. Ms. Horn also told me that these paintings are the primary items of value she owns.

5. On May 15, 20___, I conducted a third party debtor's examination of Arnold Florsheim to discover more about Courtney Horn's paintings. Mr. Florsheim told me that he returned the paintings to Courtney Horn in January 20___.

6. Although fewer than 120 days have elapsed since my last examination of Courtney Horn, I need to conduct another examination to discover the location of the paintings.

I declare under penalty of perjury under the laws of the State of California that the foregoing is true and correct.

6/2/xx   *Frank Starlet*
Date   Frank Starlet

DECLARATION OF FRANK STARLET

At the bottom, type your name and the date, and sign the application.

Page 2

If you want to examine a third party, complete Item 2 in the box titled "Appearance of a Third Person." In capital letters, fill in the amount of money you think the person owes the debtor, or describe the property you believe is in the third party's possession.

4. Have Court Issue Order

Take or send the completed Application and Order for Appearance and Examination to the court to be signed by a judge. Once the form is signed, the court clerk will return either the original form or a certified copy to you to be served on the judgment debtor.

If you will be sending in the form, make four photocopies of the original. Send the original and three photocopies (keep one for yourself) to the clerk of the court along with a self-addressed stamped envelope and a cover letter explaining that you want the order issued and returned to you—you will find a generic cover letter in the Appendix. Call first to find out the filing fee.

A Debtor's Examination Creates a Personal Property Lien

An important added benefit to ordering the judgment debtor in for a debtor's examination is that you automatically create a lien on the debtor's personal property the instant the Application and Order for Appearance and Examination is served on him (for more information, see Chapter 4C). The lien attaches to the debtor's non-exempt personal property and lasts for a year. You can renew the lien by personally serving a new Application and Order for Appearance and Examination.

D. Obtain a Subpena Duces Tecum

A Subpena Duces Tecum is a form you can serve on the debtor or a third party if you want her to bring certain documents to the court for you to examine. If you do this, the judgment debtor or third party will have pertinent documents with her at the examination—which makes it much harder to repeatedly answer "I don't know" to your questions.

If you decide to obtain a Subpena Duces Tecum, do it at the same time as you get the Application and Order for Appearance and Examination.

1. Complete the Form

Call the court to find out if it uses its own form or the one adopted by the California Judicial Council. Also, ask if the court pre-issues subpenas—that is, provides blank forms with the court's seal on them (often photocopied). If the court uses its own form or pre-issues them, obtain the form from your court. A sample completed form and instructions follow.

Caption: Follow the format of your earlier court papers. Check the box labeled "Duces Tecum."

The People of the State of California, to (Name): Enter the name of the judgment debtor or the third party you are examining.

Item 1: Enter the date, time and place of your scheduled debtor's examination, listed on the Application and Order for Appearance and Examination.

Item 2: Check "c." You are asking the debtor or third party to produce the documents at the examination.

Item 3: Enter your name and telephone number. This identifies you as the contact person if the person being examined has questions.

Item 4: This states that witness fees and mileage must be paid upon service if requested then, and before the proceeding if requested later. Thus,

Civil Subpena

ATTORNEY OR PARTY WITHOUT ATTORNEY *(Name and Address)*:	TELEPHONE NO.:	FOR COURT USE ONLY
Frank Starlet 77 Pinecomb Court Napa, CA 94559	707-555-1207	

ATTORNEY FOR *(Name)*: In Pro Per

NAME OF COURT:	Superior Court of California
STREET ADDRESS:	County of Napa
MAILING ADDRESS:	P.O. Box 880
CITY AND ZIP CODE:	Napa, CA 94559
BRANCH NAME:	

PLAINTIFF/PETITIONER: Frank Starlet

DEFENDANT/RESPONDENT: Courtney Horn

CIVIL SUBPENA [X] Duces Tecum	CASE NUMBER: 0000-0002

THE PEOPLE OF THE STATE OF CALIFORNIA, TO (NAME):

Courtney Horn

1. **YOU ARE ORDERED TO APPEAR AS A WITNESS in this action at the date, time, and place shown in the box below UNLESS you make a special agreement with the person named in item 3:**

a. Date: August 1, 20XX	Time: 9 am	[X] Dept.: 1	[ ] Div.:	[X] Room: 100
b. Address: 825 Brown St. Napa, CA 94559				

2. AND YOU ARE
   a. [ ] ordered to appear in person.
   b. [ ] not required to appear in person if you produce the records described in the accompanying affidavit and a completed declaration of custodian of records in compliance with Evidence Code sections 1560, 1561, 1562, and 1271. (1) Place a copy of the records in an envelope (or other wrapper). Enclose your original declaration with the records. Seal them. (2) Attach a copy of this subpena to the envelope or write on the envelope the case name and number, your name and date, time, and place from item 1 (the box above). (3) Place this first envelope in an outer envelope, seal it, and mail it to the clerk of the court at the address in item 1. (4) Mail a copy of your declaration to the attorney or party shown at the top of this form.
   c. [X] ordered to appear in person and to produce the records described in the accompanying affidavit. The **personal attendance** of the custodian or other qualified witness and the production of the original records **is required** by this subpena. The procedure authorized by subdivision (b) of section 1560, and sections 1561 and 1562, of the Evidence Code will not be deemed sufficient compliance with this subpena.

3. **IF YOU HAVE ANY QUESTIONS ABOUT THE TIME OR DATE FOR YOU TO APPEAR, OR IF YOU WANT TO BE CERTAIN THAT YOUR PRESENCE IS REQUIRED, CONTACT THE FOLLOWING PERSON BEFORE THE DATE ON WHICH YOU ARE TO APPEAR:**
   a. Name: Frank Starlet   b. Telephone number: 707-555-1207

4. **Witness Fees:** You are entitled to witness fees and mileage actually traveled both ways, as provided by law, if you request them at the time of service. You may request them before your scheduled appearance from the person named in item 3.

DISOBEDIENCE OF THIS SUBPENA MAY BE PUNISHED AS CONTEMPT BY THIS COURT. YOU WILL ALSO BE LIABLE FOR THE SUM OF FIVE HUNDRED DOLLARS AND ALL DAMAGES RESULTING FROM YOUR FAILURE TO OBEY.

Date issued:

. . . .   ▶ _____
         (TYPE OR PRINT NAME)   (SIGNATURE OF PERSON ISSUING SUBPENA)

                                                             _____
         (See reverse for proof of service)   (TITLE)

Form Adopted by Rule 982
Judicial Council of California
982(a)(15) [Rev. January 1, 1991]   **CIVIL SUBPENA**   WEST GROUP Official Publisher   Code of Civil Procedure, §§ 1985, 1986, 1987

if the subpena is directed to a third party, your server must be prepared to pay the fees and mileage on the spot.

Leave the bottom of the front and the back blank. They will be completed later.

2. Complete the Declaration for the Subpena

A Subpena Duces Tecum is not valid unless it is accompanied by a declaration in which you state that you believe the records you want are in the possession of the person you are subpenaing, and that the records are material to your efforts to collect your judgment (Code of Civil Procedure § 1985(b)).

To prepare a declaration, use lined paper with numbers down the left side (called pleading paper). In your declaration, you must state why you want the person to produce these materials and why you think they are relevant to your case. A sample is below.

Attach to your declaration an Exhibit A—a list of the documents you want the person to bring to court. You can assume that he possesses any document that would normally be in his possession. For instance, you can request that the judgment debtor bring ledgers and statements for his bank accounts, stock certificates issued in his name, bonds owned by him, deeds to real estate he owns and certificates of title to his automobiles. A sample Exhibit A, below, contains a basic list of documents you might want to request.

There's no court charge for issuing a Subpena Duces Tecum unless you have to transfer the examination to another court. (See Section C1, above.)

Sample Declaration for Subpena Duces Tecum

I, Frank Starlet, declare as follows:

1. I obtained a judgment against Courtney Horn from the Napa County Superior Court on January 10, 20___, in case #0000-0002.

2. The balance due on the judgment is $6,000, plus accrued interest and post-judgment costs.

3. I am scheduling a debtor's examination of Courtney Horn for August 1, 20___, at 9 am in Dept. 1 of this Court. So that Courtney Horn can provide information I need to levy on her property, she will need to bring certain materials with her to the debtor's examination.

4. I believe that Courtney Horn has in her possession or under her control the documents or copies of the documents listed in the attached Exhibit A, as well as any other documents which provide information about her assets.

5. These materials are needed to enforce this judgment.

6. These materials are relevant to this case because they contain information which I need to levy on the judgment debtor's property in order to satisfy this judgment.

I declare under penalty of perjury under the laws of the State of California that the foregoing is true and correct.

_6/2/xx_	_Frank Starlet_
Date	Frank Starlet

DECLARATION OF FRANK STARLET

Exhibit A: Documents Requested in Subpena Duces Tecum

Exhibit A: Documents Requested in Subpena Duces Tecum

1. Passbook, ledger and statements for bank, credit union and savings and loan checking, savings, money market and mutual fund accounts for previous year.

2. Stock certificates, certificates of deposit and bonds for investments held currently or during previous year.

3. IRA, Keogh, 401(k) or other pension fund statements.

4. Pay stubs of judgment debtor and judgment debtor's spouse.

5. Receipts for property owned by judgment debtor or judgment debtor's spouse but held by third parties.

6. Insurance policies.

7. Any trust instrument under which judgment debtor is trustee or beneficiary.

8. Copies of child or spousal support order, if judgment debtor pays or receives support.

9. Deeds to real estate; deeds of trust.

10. Title certificates to motor vehicles.

11. Title certificates to personal property other than motor vehicles.

12. General ledger for business debtor or independent contractor.

13. Promissory notes payable to judgment debtor or judgment debtor's spouse evidencing debts owed by others.

14. Invoices for goods and services delivered by judgment debtor or judgment debtor's business to third parties.

16. Bills of sale for property sold within previous three months.

16. Patents, copyright certificates, trademark registration certificates, royalty contracts for books, music, film, computer software, art, etc.

17. Leases signed by judgment debtor as a landlord or a tenant.

18. Copies of canceled checks paid by tenants (if judgment debtor is landlord).

19. Copies of current occupational licenses or certifications.

20. Applications for credit made within previous three years.

21. Receipts for funds placed in escrow.

22. Bankruptcy papers, if petition filed within previous six years.

23. Pawnbroker receipts.

24. Determination of eligibility and award for Social Security, disability, unemployment, workers' compensation or other public benefit.

25. Copies of judgments against judgment debtor, copies of judgments that judgment debtor has against another party, copies of recent court papers filed in any cases in which judgment debtor or judgment debtor's business or spouse is a party.

3. Have Court Issue Subpena

Unless you are using a form that already has the court's seal on it, follow the procedures described in Section C4, above, for obtaining an Order of Examination from the court, but instead request that a Subpena Duces Tecum be issued. If you're obtaining the subpena at the same time as the Application and Order for Appearance and Examination, you can send or bring these to the court together.

E. Have the Documents Served

You must now find someone to serve the Application and Order, and any Subpena Duces Tecum, on the judgment debtor or third party. Both documents must be served at least ten days before the hearing date. And the documents must be served correctly to establish a personal property lien. (See Section C4, above.)

Serving papers is covered in Chapter 21. This section provides a few additional details.

1. Who Can Serve the Papers

Unless a judge signs an order allowing service by an individual, the Application and Order for Appearance and Examination must be served by a sheriff, marshal or registered process server. An individual may serve the Subpena Duces Tecum without the court's permission. If you want to move quickly, hire a registered process server.

2. Type of Service Required

An Application and Order for Appearance and Examination and any Subpena Duces Tecum must be personally served—on either the debtor or a third party. If you have a third party served, you must also serve the debtor with a copy by mail (Code of Civil Procedure § 708.120(b)(2)).

3. Witness Fees

Any third party is entitled to be paid a witness fee for appearing at an examination. The fee includes both mileage (currently 20¢ a mile) and an appearance fee of $35 (Code of Civil Procedure § 2020(f) and Government Code § 68093).

Your server must offer to pay a third party at the time of service. If the witness doesn't take the money, be ready to pay her at the hearing. Also be prepared to reimburse her for photocopying the documents requested in the Subpena Duces Tecum, at the rate of 10¢ per page.

Witness Fees for the Judgment Debtor? Some judges have held that, because the judgment debtor is not really a witness to the proceeding (instead, he or she is a party), you don't have to pay the debtor witness fees. Still, it might be a good idea to pay fees anyway. If you pay by check and the debtor deposits your check into his or her bank account, you will know the debtor's bank account number—which will make it much easier to levy on the debtor's bank account (see Chapter 8 for more on collecting from bank accounts.)

4. Complete a Proof of Service and File Forms

After the debtor or third party is served but before the examination, you must complete a Proof of Service form indicating how and when the debtor or third party was served. A Proof of Service for the Application and Order for Appearance and Examination form appears in the Appendix. The Proof of Service for the Subpena Duces Tecum is on the back of that form.

After you complete the Proof of Service forms, file them, along with the original or certified copy of the Application and Order for Appearance and Examination and the original Subpena Duces Tecum, with the court clerk. If you serve only the Application and Order for Appearance and Examination, complete only that Proof of Service and file it with the original or certified copy of the form.

> ⚠️ **File the forms on time.** The documents usually must be filed with the court at least five business days before the examination is scheduled, although some courts require only three days and a few will accept the forms the day of the examination. Whatever the deadline is, make sure you meet it—otherwise, the clerk may cancel the examination and you will have to start over.

F. Prepare for the Examination

Before you appear at the examination, call the court clerk to make sure it is still scheduled. The examination may have been taken off the court calendar if the proof of service wasn't filed on time, or if the judgment debtor or third party wasn't personally served at least ten days before the scheduled date. Either way, you'll have to start over. If your sole purpose was to establish a lien (Chapter 4, Section C), you don't need to refile and serve the documents if the debtor was served properly.

In planning for the examination, make a list of questions to ask. Confine yourself to questions that you really need answered; don't rattle off a list of irrelevant or unnecessary questions. If you unnecessarily repeat yourself or waste time, the debtor or third party may walk out or ask the supervising official to cut the examination short. Make each question count.

We provide a checklist of possible questions in the Appendix. Before the examination, review the list, crossing out questions that don't apply or to which you already know the answer.

One question you should always ask the debtor is how much cash he has on him, because you can ask the judge to order the debtor to turn the cash over to you right on the spot. There is no specific legal authority for this, but it is a common technique that most judges endorse. The judge won't necessarily order it verbally; you need to prepare a written order for the judge to sign. A completed sample is below; a blank form is in the Appendix.

G. Conduct the Examination

It is common for judgment debtors not to show up for an examination. (See Section H, below.) For the moment, however, let's assume that your debtor does appear.

The examination is usually scheduled for a courtroom and then moved elsewhere. When you arrive at the actual location, you'll find a commissioner, referee or judge present, along with a bailiff. When your name is called, the debtor is briefly sworn in and agrees, under penalty of perjury, to answer your questions truthfully. You and the debtor are then directed to an area where you can discuss the matter privately, with the supervising official nearby.

If you served a Subpena Duces Tecum, ask the debtor for the documents. Examine each document before you begin asking your questions; some of your questions will be answered by the documents, and other questions will be suggested by them. Then ask your unanswered questions.

If the debtor failed to bring the documents, won't answer your questions or isn't responding honestly or thoroughly, ask the supervising official for help. If necessary, the official (if he isn't a judge) can ask the judge to take action. Usually, a little assistance of this type will get the debtor to cooperate. But if he still refuses when ordered by the judge, the judge can cite him for contempt of court, fine him and even jail him.

Whatever the debtor says, don't come off like a hostile adversary maliciously asking embarrassing and personal questions. Present yourself as someone trying to help the debtor find money to pay you. The debtor may may not be paying you because she doesn't have the money or has put other obligations first. (Chapter 5 suggests ways that the debtor can come up with money to pay your judgment.) If you explain that you need to

Order for Delivery of Property After Examination (Page 1)

1 Frank Starlet

2 77 Pinecomb Court

3 Napa, CA 94559

4 (707) 555-1207

5 Appearing in Pro Per

6

7

8   Superior   COURT OF CALIFORNIA

9   COUNTY OF _____ Napa _____

10

11 Frank Starlet _____ ,) Case No. ____ 000-0002 ____
                    Plaintiff,   )
12 vs.   ) ORDER FOR DELIVERY OF
) PROPERTY AFTER EXAMINATION
13 Courtney Horn _____ ,) [CCP Section 708.205]
                    Defendant.   )
14   ) Examination Date: __ Aug. 1, 20XX __
) Time: __ 9 a.m. __
15 _____   ) Place: __ Dept. 1, Rm 100 __

16

17 The examination of ____ Courtney Horn _____

18 (judgment debtor or third person) was conducted on the date and at the time set forth above. It appearing from

19 this examination that:

20   [X] the judgment debtor has an interest in property in the possession or under the control of

21 __ judgment debtor _____ (judgment debtor or third person); OR

22   [ ] a third person owes the judgment debtor $_____ (or property described as follows:

23 _____

24 _____),

25 and that the property described above is not exempt from enforcement of a money judgment:

26   IT IS ORDERED THAT ____ Courtney Horn _____

27 (judgment debtor or third person) shall [X] immediately/ [ ] within _____ days of entry of this order

28 deliver to __ Frank Starlet _____

ORDER FOR DELIVERY OF PROPERTY AFTER EXAMINATION   1

Order for Delivery of Property After Examination (Page 2)

1 (judgment creditor or levying officer of _____ County at

2 the following address: _____ ,

3 California) the property: _$85.00 cash_ _____

4 _____

5 which shall be applied toward the satisfaction of the judgment entered in this action on

6 ___ January 10, 20XX _____ (date).

7

8 DATED:

9

10 _____

11 Judge/Commissioner of the ___ Superior ___ Court

12

13

14

15

16

17

18

19

20

21

22

23

24

25

26 ////////

27 ////////

28 ////////

ask some questions to work out a reasonable payment plan, she may open up. Another reason not to be pushy during this examination is that it could nudge the judgment debtor into declaring bankruptcy.

If the Judgment Debtor Brings an Attorney

Don't be concerned if the debtor shows up with an attorney. Simply explain that you want to arrange a voluntary payment plan that the debtor can honor. In other words, approach the attorney in the same way you would approach the debtor to get answers to your questions. Then, proceed to ask your questions.

The attorney will let the debtor know whether or not he should respond. As long as your questions are reasonable, there is no reason the debtor shouldn't answer. If the attorney puts up resistance that seems unreasonable, ask the supervising official to explain your situation to the judge. The judge may ask the attorney to direct the debtor to answer questions that the judge feels are appropriate.

Facing an attorney gives you one benefit: if you do work out a settlement and the debtor reneges, you can nag the attorney rather than the debtor. Attorneys tend to be easier to find—and less emotionally involved in the situation—than their debtor clients.

H. If the Debtor Doesn't Sh

If a debtor fails to show up, most judges simply set another date for the debtor's examination. Usually, the court will notify the debtor of the new date. But ask about this; sometimes, you are responsible for service the notice. If the debtor doesn't show up the second time, you can apply and pay for the court to issue a bench warrant. Ask the court clerk to provide you with an application form. The fee may be $50 or more.

If the judgment debtor is arrested on the bench warrant, the debtor will have to post bail to be released pending a future appearance on the warrant. You should be notified of the date set for the appearance on the warrant. If the judgment debtor appears at the hearing on the warrant, you can ask the judge to sign an order turning the bail over to you (see Chapter 19) or ask the judge to order the bail be paid directly to you. ■

Chapter 7

Obtaining a Writ of Execution

A Writ of Execution (or simply a Writ) is a key tool for forcing collections. The phrase "Writ of Execution" conjures up visions of black-hooded hangmen presiding over medieval scaffolds. But today's Writs take a completely different form—and could probably benefit from a name change. A Writ is simply authorization from the court to seize the debtor's income (wage garnishment) or assets (levy).

Obtaining a Writ of Execution is easy. The debtor won't even know you've done so, until you actually use it to seize the debtor's income or assets.

As explained in Chapter 2, you'll want to wait until certain periods expire before initiating forced collections. For instance, if you are seeking a Writ of Execution on an out-of-state judgment, you usually can't obtain a Writ until 30 days after the debtor is served with the Notice of Entry of Sister-State Judgment. Once all time periods have passed, however, it doesn't mean you should run to court to get your Writ. A Writ of Execution lasts only 180 days from the date of issuance. Although you can get a new one (Code of Civil Procedure § 699.510), it's still easier to wait until you've identified specific assets you hope to seize, then get your writ.

⚠ Know the local rules. Some courts require you to file an extra form with your Writ of Execution. In Los Angeles County Superior Court, for example, you must file an Application for Writ of Execution. Get these additional forms from the court clerk.

A. Complete the Writ of Execution Form

A Writ of Execution form is in the Appendix. You will need one for each county in which you are going after assets.

A court will issue only one Writ per county at a given time, and a Writ can be used for only one asset at a time. If you want to seize more than one asset in the same county, you must do so sequentially, not simultaneously. After the levying officer seizes (or attempts to seize) asset X, he must return the Writ to the court. Then you can request that he pursue asset Y, using the same Writ. If the Writ expires (remember, it lasts only 180 days), you will need a new one to go after assets in that county.

If you anticipate needing more than one Writ, you can save yourself some time by taking the following steps:

1. Complete page 1, except for Item 1 and Items 11–20, and page 2 (if applicable).
2. Make one photocopy of the partially completed form for as many Writs as you think will need.
3. Complete Item 1 and Items 11–20 for each Writ.

Follow the rest of our instructions for each Writ. A sample is below.

Caption: Follow the format of your other court papers. Check the Execution (Money Judgment) box.

Other Kinds of Writs

A Writ of Possession is normally obtained in eviction actions, when a landlord sues to recover possession of the premises from the tenant. It is also used in actions where a secured creditor seeks judicial authority to repossess personal property. A Writ of Sale is issued on a judgment for sale of real or personal property.

Item 1: Enter the name of the county in which the assets are located.

Item 2: Leave this as is.

Item 3: Enter your name exactly as it appears in the judgment and check the judgment creditor box. You are an assignee of record only if someone gave you the right to receive her judgment.

Item 4: Enter the judgment debtor's name exactly as it appears in the judgment, and the debtor's last known address. If there's a second judgment debtor, list her name and last known address below the first debtor. If there are more than two, check the additional judgment debtors box, turn over the sheet, check box 4 on page 2 and enter the additional judgment debtors' names and addresses. You must list all judgment debtors in each Writ, even if those other judgment debtors own no property in this county.

Item 5: Enter the date on which your judgment was entered—you'll find it on the judgment or the Notice of Entry of Judgment. If you don't know the date, call the court clerk or look in the court file. If you converted a sister-state judgment to a California judgment, enter the date the California judgment was entered.

Item 6: Check this box only if you have renewed your judgment before its ten-year expiration. If so, fill in the renewal dates. (See Chapter 20.)

Item 7: If you contacted a third party who has a security interest in the debtor's property—such as a dealer who is still owed money under a car loan—that third party may have requested that you send him a notice of sale if you decide to seize and sell that property. If so, check box 7b, turn over the sheet, check box 7 on page 2 and enter the third party's name and address. Otherwise, check box 7a.

Item 8: Skip this unless you have amended your judgment to add additional judgment debtors. If you have, check box 8, turn over the sheet, check box 8 on page 2 and enter the new debtors' names and addresses. If you *originally* obtained judgment against more than one defendant, this item does not apply—unless you've added even more defendants since obtaining your judgment.

Item 9: Skip this item.

Item 10: Check this box only if you obtained a judgment against someone in another state and turned it into a California judgment. (We don't cover this procedure in this book.)

Item 11: Enter the full amount of the judgment, including court costs and interest accrued before judgment. This sum is on the judgment or the Notice of Entry of Judgment.

Item 12: If you are getting a Writ for the first time, leave this blank unless you are filing a Memorandum of Costs at the same time. Filing a Memorandum of Costs may alert the judgment debtor that you are planning to force collections, because you must send her a copy of these papers. If you want to surprise the debtor, plan on claiming costs and interest later—you can do so up to two years after they were incurred. If you decide to file the Memorandum of Costs now, you usually must do so at least two weeks before a Writ is issued. If you previously filed a Memorandum of Costs, enter any collections costs and accrued interest recorded on that form. If you've filed more than one, enter the cumulative total. (The Memorandum of Costs is covered in Chapter 16.)

Item 13: Add Items 11 and 12 and enter the sum here.

Item 14: Enter the total amount of money you have received toward the judgment. (See Chapter 16 for a worksheet to keep track of payments.) Also credit the value of services or goods you've received under any barter agreement. (See Chapter 5, Section E2.)

Item 15: Subtract Item 14 from Item 13 and enter the difference.

Item 16: If you haven't filed a Memorandum of Costs and you are proceeding shortly after obtaining your judgment, leave this blank. The levying officer will probably add the interest. If enough time has elapsed since you obtained your judgment to make the interest significant, file a Memorandum of Costs and enter the amount here. If you've already filed a Memorandum of Costs, enter the post-judgment interest you recorded there.

Item 17: Enter the fee for issuance of the Writ of Execution. The court clerk can tell you the amount.

Item 18: Total up Items 15, 16 and 17 and enter it here.

Item 19a: Multiply the amount in Item 15 by 0.0002739 to get the daily interest rate and enter it here.

Item 19b: Leave this item blank unless either of the following are true:

- you work for a public agency trying to recover costs that a court waived because of the agency's public status, or
- the court originally waived your filing fee or other court costs because of your indigency, and the judgment states that the waived fees are to be recovered from the judgment debtor.

If Item 19b applies, enter the amount waived.

Item 20: Check this box only if you plan to ask the levying officer to collect different amounts from more than one debtor. If so, get out a blank piece of paper, type "Attachment 20" at the top and state the amounts for each debtor.

Back of Form: If you filled out Item 4, 7 or 8 on the back, add the case name (such as *Ng v. Smith*) and the case number at the top. Otherwise, leave this blank.

B. Have Court Issue Writ

Each Writ of Execution must be issued by the court clerk for that county. For each Writ, make three photocopies, plus one copy for each additional judgment debtor. Copy both sides, even if page two is blank. Put one copy away for safe-keeping.

Take the original and remaining copies to the court clerk's office. You will give all of them to the clerk; she will affix the official seal of the court and put the date of issuance on the Writ. If you mail the original and copies, ask that the Writ of Execution be issued and mailed to you. (A generic cover letter is included in the Appendix.)

C. What to Do With Your Writ

After you obtain your Writ, you must decide which assets you want to go after. Chapter 1 has a chart listing the types of assets typically available for collection. Remember that the Writ lasts only 180 days and generally cannot be used to go after more than one asset simultaneously (although

some counties will let you, because the levying officer keeps the original Writ and serves copies on whomever you instruct the officer to levy against).

Although specific counties and levying officers work differently, the general procedure is the same. You contact a levying officer, give him the original Writ and indicate which assets you would like him to go after. Once he seizes (or is unsuccessful at seizing) the asset, he will hold onto the Writ until the 180 days expire. Some levying agents return original Writs to the court instead. Your preference is that he keep the Writ—and you can ask him to do so if he doesn't. (In your cover letter, state that you want the Writ held for its entire life, absent a 100% successful levy.) Why do you want him to keep it? So he can use it again before the 180 days expire. If, however, he prematurely returns the Writ, you can obtain a new one.

If the levy satisfies your judgment, the levying officer will automatically return the Writ to the court.

As soon as the levying officer attempts a levy or wage garnishment, a personal property lien automatically applies against the asset the officer is to seize and remains for two years (Code of Civil Procedure § 697.710). (See Chapter 4, Section C.)

What if you overcollect? If you limit your collection efforts to one county, you don't have to worry about overcollecting. The levying officer should make sure that you receive no more than you are entitled to under the Writ. If, however, you give Writs to levying officers in two or more counties, there is a risk that you'll be overpaid. Rather than holding off on collecting in more than one county, collect what you can and promptly return any surplus to the levying officer, who will return it to the judgment debtor.

After you collect all the money due you, immediately instruct the levying officers to return to the court any Writs of Execution in their possession.

Writ of Execution

ATTORNEY OR PARTY WITHOUT ATTORNEY *(Name and Address):*	TELEPHONE NO.:	FOR RECORDER'S USE ONLY

☐ Recording requested by and return to:

Thuy Ng
308 Marshall Ave.
Bakersfield, CA 93300

TELEPHONE NO.: 805-555-9931

☐ ATTORNEY FOR ☒ JUDGMENT CREDITOR Pro Per ☐ ASSIGNEE OF RECORD

NAME OF COURT: Kern County Superior Court
STREET ADDRESS: 1415 Truxton Avenue
MAILING ADDRESS: Bakersfield, CA 93301
CITY AND ZIP CODE:
BRANCH NAME:

PLAINTIFF: Thuy Ng

DEFENDANT: Leslie Smith

WRIT OF	☒ EXECUTION (Money Judgment) ☐ POSSESSION OF ☐ Personal Property / ☐ Real Property ☐ SALE	CASE NUMBER: 0000-0003

FOR COURT USE ONLY

1. To the Sheriff or any Marshal or Constable of the County of:
Kern
You are directed to enforce the judgment described below with daily interest and your costs as provided by law.

2. To any registered process server: You are authorized to serve this writ only in accord with CCP 699.080 or CCP 715.040.

3. *(Name):* Thuy Ng
is the ☒ judgment creditor ☐ assignee of record
whose address is shown on this form above the court's name.

4. Judgment debtor *(name and last known address):*

Thuy Ng
47049 Hollywood Way
Bakersfield, CA 93300

☐ additional judgment debtors on reverse

5. Judgment entered on *(date):* Nov. 11,20XX
6. ☐ **Judgment renewed** on *(dates):*

7. Notice of sale under this writ
a. ☒ has not been requested.
b. ☐ has been requested *(see reverse).*
8. ☐ Joint debtor information on reverse.

[SEAL]

9. ☐ See reverse for information on real or personal property to be delivered under a writ of possession or sold under a writ of sale.
10. ☐ This writ is issued on a sister-state judgment.
11. Total judgment . . . . $ 4,811
12. Costs after judgment (per filed order or memo CCP 685.090) . . . . $ 0
13. Subtotal *(add 11 and 12)* . . . . $ 4,811
14. Credits . . . . $ 0
15. Subtotal *(subtract 14 from 13)* . . . . . $ 4,811
16. Interest after judgment (per filed affidavit CCP 685.050) . . . . $ 0
17. Fee for issuance of writ . . . . $ 7
18. **Total** *(add 15, 16, and 17)* . . . . $ 4,818
19. Levying officer:
(a) Add daily interest from date of writ *(at the legal rate on 15)* of . . . . . $ 1.31
(b) Pay directly to court costs included in 11 and 17 (GC 6103.5, 68511.3; CCP 699.520(i)) . . . . $
20. ☐ The amounts called for in items 11-19 are different for each debtor. These amounts are stated for each debtor on Attachment 20.

Issued on *(date):*	Clerk, by _____, Deputy

— NOTICE TO PERSON SERVED: SEE REVERSE FOR IMPORTANT INFORMATION. —

(Continued on reverse)

Form Approved by the
Judicial Council of California
EJ-130 [Rev. January 1, 1997*]

WRIT OF EXECUTION

Code of Civil Procedure, §§ 699.520, 712.010, 715.010
WEST GROUP
Official Publisher
* See note on reverse.

Chapter 8

Collecting From Deposit Accounts

Collection Factor			
	High	Moderate	Low
Potential cost to you		✓	✓
Potential for producing cash	✓		
Potential for settlement		✓	
Potential time and trouble		✓	
Potential for debtor bankruptcy		✓	

This chapter shows you how to locate and collect from deposit accounts—savings, checking, money market and mutual fund accounts in banks, savings and loans or credit unions. We also show you how to look for cash or other liquid assets, such as securities and gems, in safe deposit boxes. For convenience, we use the term "bank" to refer to banks, savings and loans and credit unions.

If you can find this kind of money—and it is not exempt under California's debtor protection laws—you are miles ahead in the collection game. What do we mean by exempt? Legally, the judgment debtor is allowed to keep cash that she received from certain sources, such as Social Security. No matter how large your judgment, if the debtor can prove that the money came from exempt sources, you cannot take it. But the debtor must file a form called a Claim of Exemption with the levying officer who collected the money—and debtors rarely do so. If she doesn't file the form, you can go after the funds without worrying about where they came from. If she files a Claim of Exemption and the court rules that the money is exempt, you'll have to return it.

➡️ **You might be able to skip Section A.** If you know the judgment debtor's bank account number, skip to Section B, below. If you need to find deposit accounts, read Section A.

A. Finding Banks and Account Numbers

A levying officer cannot seize the money in a bank account or the contents of a safe-deposit box unless he has the name of the bank, the branch, the exact name on the account and the account number. Some levying officers can get the job done without the account number, but your chances of collecting are better if you can provide it.

⚠️ **Be discreet.** If the debtor gets a whiff that you are closing in on a deposit account, she will surely move it. Then you'll have to start from scratch.

1. Check Your Papers

You can easily find the debtor's bank and account number if you have a copy of a check written by the debtor, which may be the case if you had a business relationship. You may also have this information on a credit application or other form you had the debtor complete.

2. Ask the Debtor

If you haven't done so already, schedule a Debtor's Examination, following the procedures described in Chapter 6. At the exam, you can ask the debtor about her bank accounts—and you can ask the debtor to bring copies of bank statements, using a Subpena Duces Tecum.

3. Write Debtor's Business a Check

If the debtor is or has a business, have a friend buy some goods or services and write a check for the purchase. When the debtor deposits your friend's check, the debtor's bank will stamp the check. You can examine the check once it comes back to your friend to identify the bank and possibly the account number. If your friend doesn't routinely get his canceled checks, he can request a copy of a specific check from his bank for a small fee.

If you are unable to interpret the back of the check, call or take it to a branch of the bank where it was deposited and ask for help.

4. Ask Business Associates

People with whom the debtor does business may be willing to share account information with you, if you can provide them with help they need. Technically, sharing information about the debtor with third parties is a legal no-no, but no one is likely to complain. Limit your contacts to people in your business network who you are pretty sure will be sympathetic to your situation and won't immediately call the debtor and tip him off.

5. Check Government Records

If the debtor runs a business, you may be able to find bank account information from public records. For example, if the debtor has applied for a Seller's Permit, he was required to list banks and account numbers on the application. To access these records, contact the Board of Equalization at 800-400-7115. And if the debtor has been involved in other lawsuits, court records and filings in those cases may include banking information.

B. Figuring Out if the Funds Are Exempt

As mentioned, some of the money in a deposit account may be exempt. If you try to levy on an account containing exempt cash, it is up to the debtor to file a Claim of Exemption with the court and prove that the money came from an exempt source. Few debtors file such a claim. Even if the

debtor does, it's possible that the debtor has some exempt money but mixes it with non-exempt money and cannot prove that the money grabbed by the levying officer came from the exempt source. In such a situation, you can oppose the debtor's Claim of Exemption. Also, if your judgment is for child support, most exemptions won't apply. (See Chapter 15 for information on opposing a Claim of Exemption.)

The following is a list of sources of cash deposited in bank accounts that the debtor may claim as exempt. The debtor can exempt these monies only if they are held in personal—not business—accounts.

- **Wages:** The debtor may exempt up to 75% of her wages. If the debtor's wages were garnished prior to the deposit, however, the ungarnished amount is fully exempt (Code of Civil Procedure § 704.070(b)).

- **Public benefits:** The debtor may exempt 100% of Social Security, veterans', welfare, unemployment and workers' compensation benefits. Funds of up to $2,000 for one debtor or $3,000 for two debtors directly deposited by the Social Security Administration are automatically exempt. Funds of up to $1,000 for one debtor or $1,500 for two debtors directly deposited by the welfare department are automatically exempt. The debtor does not have to file a Claim of Exemption for amounts that are automatically exempt. Excess amounts may also be exempt, but the debtor will have to file a Claim of Exemption for that portion (Code of Civil Procedure § 704.080).

- **Retirement plans:** The debtor may exempt public and private retirement benefits, including IRAs and Keoghs, with one exception. If the debtor periodically receives the proceeds of a private retirement plan, those proceeds are exempt only to the same extent as wages (Code of Civil Procedure §§ 704.110(d) and 704.115).

- **Insurance proceeds:** The debtor may claim as exempt 100% of disability and health insurance benefits, matured (paid out) life insurance proceeds needed to support the debtor and the debtor's family and loan proceeds of up to $8,000 for an unmarried debtor and $16,000 for a married couple on an unmatured life insurance policy. The debtor may generally claim as exempt homeowner's insurance proceeds up to six months after received or up to $1,900 on an auto insurance policy if the vehicle was lost or stolen (Code of Civil Procedure §§ 704.010, 704.100 and 704.720).

- **Personal injury awards:** The debtor may claim as exempt personal injury and wrongful death awards to the extent they are necessary to support the judgment debtor and the judgment debtor's family, with one exception. If you are a healthcare provider with a judgment for services rendered in connection with the injury or death, the funds may not be claimed as exempt (Code of Civil Procedure §§ 704.140 and 704.150).

- **Financial aid:** The debtor may exempt funds received for financial aid to attend an institution of higher learning (Code of Civil Procedure § 704.190).

- **Miscellaneous:** Other sources of income a debtor may claim as exempt: up to $1,000 paid to an inmate (Code of Civil Procedure § 704.090), benefits paid in order to relocate (Code of Civil Procedure § 704.180) and union benefits paid during a labor dispute (Code of Civil Procedure § 704.120).

C. Levying on Joint and Business Accounts

If the account is in the debtor's name alone—whether the debtor is a business entity or an individual—the entire account will be subject to your levy. If the account belongs to the judgment debtor and his spouse, the entire account will be subject to your levy, but the spouse will have an opportunity to object to the levy.

EXAMPLE 1: The judgment is against Stewart Kingfish. The account is in the name of Stewart Kingfish. You may levy against the entire account.

EXAMPLE 2: The judgment is against Stewart Kingfish, Inc., a California corporation. You may levy against any account carrying the name of Stewart Kingfish, Inc. You may not levy against an account belonging to Stewart Kingfish unless you amend the judgment to name him as an individual.

EXAMPLE 3: The judgment is against Stewart Kingfish as an individual. The account is in the name of Stewart Kingfish, Inc., a solely owned corporation. You may not levy against the corporate account unless you amend the judgment to name the corporation as a defendant.

EXAMPLE 4: The judgment is against Kingfish and Kingfish, a California partnership. You may levy against a Kingfish and Kingfish partnership account. If your judgment is against Stewart Kingfish, one of the partners, you may not levy against the account without a special order of the court called a "charging" order. This book does not cover charging orders.

EXAMPLE 5: The judgment is against Stewart Kingfish as an individual. The account is in the name of Kingfish Consultants, an individual proprietorship owned by Stewart Kingfish. You may levy against the Kingfish Consultants account if you provide the levying officer with a certified copy of the fictitious business name statement filed by Stewart Kingfish.

If the account is in the name of the judgment debtor's spouse, either alone or with others, you may levy on it. But you must provide the levying officer with a declaration showing that the parties are married (Code of Civil Procedure

§ 700.160(b))—a sample declaration appears in Section D, below. The spouse and any third parties will have the opportunity to object to the levy.

If the account is in the name of the debtor and someone else not his spouse, you may not levy on the other person's share of the funds. Most deposit accounts are presumed to be held in joint tenancy—the presumption is that each account holder owns an equal share of the account. For example, if the debtor holds the account with two other people, you can assume his share is one-third, and that's the amount on which you may levy. In some cases, the bank will turn over an entire joint account, figuring it is up to the non-debtor to object.

Because of the need to protect the rights of non-debtors, you may be required to post a bond for twice the amount on which you are seeking to levy. If so, check with a title insurance company or bonding company. The bond normally costs between 2% and 4% of its face amount. This cost is not recoverable from the bonding company, but you can recover it from the judgment debtor by claiming the amount on a Memorandum of Costs. (See Chapter 16.)

D. How to Levy on Bank Accounts and Safe-Deposit Boxes

To levy on an account, you must first obtain a Writ of Execution. (See Chapter 7.) If there are accounts in more than one county, you will need a Writ for each county. Once you have your Writ, follow these steps.

1. Determine Your Timing

If you plan to levy on a checking account, timing is important. The amount of money in it probably fluctuates a lot during the month. Unless you time the levy carefully, the account may not have enough funds to make your efforts cost-effective.

If you plan on levying on a savings account or the contents of a safe-deposit box, timing is less of an issue.

You can find out how much money is in the debtor's checking account at any given time by calling the bank and asking if a check for X amount will clear. If the answer is no, call back later and ask if a check for slightly less will clear. Keep trying until you find an amount that will clear. Before long, you'll get a rough idea of the balance in the account. By making several calls, you should figure out when the balance is highest —often around the 1st of the month. This is especially true now that many paychecks and government checks are directly deposited into accounts.

If you move to levy when the account balance is low, you not only collect little money, but also alert the debtor to your efforts. He will almost certainly move his account. There is an old saying: "If you shoot at the Emperor, don't miss." In the same manner, when you levy on a bank account, count on doing it only once.

The levying officer will normally need a little lead time before making the levy. Therefore, you will want to deliver your instructions well in advance of when you want the actual levy to occur. Check with the levying officer to find out how far in advance he will need your papers; some may have a backlog.

Large judgments normally can't be satisfied in full by levying on a checking account. The best you can do is to get as large a portion as possible of the money you are owed. If you have a $2,500 judgment and levy on $800 in a checking account, you'll probably need to use other collection efforts to go after the rest.

2. Provide Instructions for Levying Officer

To find the levying officer for a given county, call the sheriff's office and ask if it levies on civil money judgments. If not, ask if another public official does. If the local levying officer doesn't levy on bank accounts, is backlogged or has a reputation for inefficiency, consider hiring a registered process server. (See Chapter 21.) We generally recommend against using a registered process server because of the potential for complications and cost, but you may have little choice.

When you find the right person, call and find out the fee, how many copies of the Writ are needed and whether the office has local instruction forms for you to use. Prepare your instructions for the levying officer using his form or the Instructions to Levying Officer form letter in the Appendix. Provide as much of the following information as possible:

- name, branch and street address of the financial institution
- account number
- a statement that you are seeking personal property
- name or names in which the account is held, and
- when to serve the levy—specifically, a request that the levy be held until you phone in a request for it to be served on the bank; if the levying officer is unwilling to hold the Writ for your phone call, specify the day and time of enforcement in your instructions.

If you want the levying officer to seize more than one account, prepare separate instructions and provide separate Writs for each seizure. For example, if you want the levying officer to grab the debtor's savings account in bank X and the debtor's checking account in bank Y, prepare two sets of instructions and be prepared to pay separate fees for each. Remember—if you collect more than the total balance due on your judgment, you must return the surplus.

If the account is held under the name of the debtor's spouse, you will have to complete a declaration to that effect so that the levying officer can seize the account. A sample declaration appears below.

Safe-Deposit Boxes

When levying on a safe-deposit box, the levying officer is faced with several choices. She can:

- ask the judgment debtor to voluntarily open the box
- forcibly open the box if the judgment debtor refuses to cooperate, or
- require you to obtain a seizure order from the court allowing the box to be opened (see Chapter 19, Section A1).

If the safe deposit box must be forcibly opened, the bank will require you to post a deposit (usually $50–$100) to cover the costs.

A safe-deposit box typically contains items such as insurance policies, stock certificates, bonds, title certificates, jewelry and/or cash. Some or all will be seized by the levying officer. Cash and bonds can be given to you outright; tangible items such as jewelry must be stored and sold by the levying officer. For this, you will need to post a large deposit to cover storage and sales costs. If you don't want this property sold—it may not be worth it—the levying officer will return it to the judgment debtor.

The judgment debtor can file a Claim of Exemption for certain items. (See Chapter 15.)

A sample Instructions to Levying Officer form letter is below. Make the necessary copies of the Writ and your instructions (and your declaration, if the account is held in a spouse's name), keeping one set for your records. Then mail or bring the documents and fee to the levying officer.

Sample Instructions to Levying Officer

October 19, 20___

Sheriff, Santa Cruz County:

Enclosed please find an original and three copies of a Writ of Execution and a check for $25.

Please serve the Writ of Execution and levy against any bank accounts and safe-deposit boxes belonging to Stewart Kingfish at National Bank of Commerce, 567 Andrews Avenue, Santa Cruz. One known account number is: 034-731078. Please collect from any other accounts owned by Stewart Kingfish at that branch. Please send any funds collected to me at 566 Oceanview Terrace, Carmel, CA 90000.

Please hold this Writ until I notify you by phone that I want it served, and then levy that same day or as soon thereafter as possible. [Or, Please perform this levy between the third and sixth day of the month.]

If you levy on a safe-deposit box, ask the judgment debtor to open it voluntarily. If the box contains personal property other than cash that must be stored and sold, contact me first for further instructions. Contact me for further instructions before using force to open any safe-deposit box. All property being sought in this Writ is personal property.

Sincerely,

Juanita Pope

Juanita Pope

Sample Declaration to Levy on Bank Account Held in Spouse's Name

I, Juanita Pope, declare as follows:

I obtained a judgment against Stewart Kingfish from the Santa Cruz County California Superior Court on April 28, 20XX, in Case Number 003-0004.

I have knowledge of and believe to be true that Judgment Debtor Stewart Kingfish is married to and was married to Denise Kingfish, SSN# 555-55-5555, at the time the judgment was awarded.

California Code of Civil Procedure § 700.160(b)(2) allows levies against deposit accounts in the name of a spouse.

I swear under penalty of perjury under the laws of the state of California that the foregoing is true and correct.

_12/03/xx_	_Juanita Pope_
DATE	JUANITA POPE

3. Serve Notice of Levy

The levying officer uses the Writ and your written instructions to fill out a Notice of Levy, which he serves on the person in the institution in charge of the debtor's account. The debtor gets a copy. Any other debtor listed in the judgment should also receive a copy.

The Notice of Levy includes the amount necessary to satisfy the judgment. It also advises the institution that it has up to ten days to oppose the levy and that the funds must be frozen in the interim. If the bank objects—which is unlikely, unless the account is virtually empty—we suggest that you drop the matter or consult a lawyer. If the debtor files a Claim of Exemption opposing the levy, you must set a court hearing where the merits of the levy can be decided by a judge. (See Chapter 15.)

4. Distribute Proceeds

Once the levying officer collects the proceeds of the levy, he will disburse them to you. There may be a delay, but it shouldn't be too long. If you're concerned that you've fallen through the cracks, call the levying officer. ■

Chapter 9

Collecting From Wages

Collection Factors			
	High	**Moderate**	**Low**
Potential cost to you			✓
Potential for producing cash	✓		
Potential for settlement	✓		
Potential time and trouble		✓	
Potential for debtor bankruptcy	✓		

*I*f the debtor is working, you may be able to intercept up to 25% of his wages (up to 50% for child or spousal support) to satisfy your judgment. This process is called a wage garnishment. You can garnish wages relatively quickly and cheaply if:

- the debtor receives a regular wage—that is, he is not self-employed
- the debtor's pay is above the poverty line
- other wage garnishments aren't already in effect, unless your wage garnishment is for child or spousal support, and
- the debtor does not quit the job, contest the garnishment or file for bankruptcy.

A wage garnishment requires little effort on your part. You give the levying officer information about where the judgment debtor works, provide a Writ of Execution (Chapter 7) and pay a modest fee. Then you simply wait; the levying officer collects money from the employer and gives it to you. You can end the wage garnishment if you and the judgment debtor make an agreement about payment of the judgment. If the judgment debtor is married, you can garnish his spouse's wages, but you need a court order (Code of Civil Procedure § 706.109).

A wage garnishment is often a strong impetus for a debtor to make arrangements to pay off a judgment—many people want to avoid the embarrassment and inconvenience of having their salary reduced. Also, despite a federal law that bars an employer from firing an employee whose wages are garnished due to a single judgment, most employees believe that a garnishment won't win them brownie points with their bosses. And the law does not bar an employer from firing an employee whose wages are garnished to pay more than one judgment.

But instead of inducing the debtor to settle, a wage garnishment could have the opposite effect—pushing a debtor to quit her job or worse, file for bankruptcy. The loss of part of a paycheck, coupled with having an employer know about her financial problems, may cause a debtor to look for a quick solution to relieve the pressure. If you choose to garnish wages, remember that you walk a fine line between making great progress on collecting your judgment and closing off any possibility of collecting.

The debtor probably won't go bankrupt or quit his job if the judgment isn't for very much, he is a well-established member of the community without other debt problems, he owns his own well-established business or he owns real estate with significant equity.

A. Limits on Wage Garnishments

Under federal law, you cannot garnish more than 25% of the debtor's disposable income. There is an additional protection for low-income people. A wage earner must be left with a weekly wage equal to 30 times the current federal minimum wage—which is currently $5.15. (The California minimum wage is $6.75.) This means that the debtor gets to keep the first $154.50 per week; you can garnish 25% of the excess (15 U.S.C. § 1673(a)(1); Code of Civil Procedure § 706.050).

If your judgment is for child or spousal support, you can garnish at least 50% of the judgment debtor's take home pay after the first $154.50 per week. A judge has the discretion to increase that to as much as 60% if the debtor is not currently supporting a child or spouse (15 U.S.C. § 1673(b); Code of Civil Procedure § 706.052(c)).

You face some additional limitations—or at least potential obstacles—in a few situations.

1. Debtor Is Already Subject to Another Garnishment

You cannot garnish wages if they are already being garnished by another creditor, unless (1) the first garnishment takes less than 25% of the debtor's disposable income, or (2) you have a judgment for alimony or child support. Support judgments receive first wage garnishment priority, and as mentioned, can be used to grab up to 60% of the judgment debtor's net earnings. If neither exception applies, the employer will reject your garnishment and you will have to apply again when the previous creditor's garnishment ends.

2. Debtor Needs the Money for Basic Support

The debtor has the right to object to your garnishment on the ground that she needs the money for her own support or the support of a spouse or children (Code of Civil Procedure § 706.052(a), (b)). The debtor makes this objection by filing a Claim of Exemption, explained in Chapter 15. The debtor cannot use this exemption if the debt underlying the judgment was for food, shelter, medical care or another necessary of life (Code of Civil Procedure § 706.051(c)). Even if the debt is for something else, a debtor rarely wins this argument, unless she has extraordinary expenses or earns little more than the minimum wage.

3. Debtor Is a Federal Employee or in the Military

You can garnish the wages of most federal employees, including someone on active military duty, but the process may prove cumbersome (5 U.S.C. § 5520a). (You can't garnish the wages of a seaman, longshoreman or harbor worker. But see Chapter 19 for possible use of an assignment order.)

You must serve the federal agency for which the employee works with an Application for Federal Employee Commercial Garnishment, a copy of which is in the Appendix. You must serve it personally or by certified or registered mail, return receipt requested. You will likely choose service by mail because the offices to direct service for many federal agencies are in Washington, D.C.

Below is a completed sample copy of the Application for Federal Employee Commercial Garnishment and instructions on how to complete it. A blank copy is in the Appendix and available at www.opm.gov/forms.

Title and address of employing agency's designated agent: Enter the name and address of the director of personnel for the agency where the debtor works. This is where you will send the documents. A government publication called the Code of Federal Regulations (CFR) contains an appendix listing the address and phone number for every federal agency, indicating the appropriate official to receive your papers. The CFR is available at a law library or large public library—you want to look at 5 CFR 581.501, Appendix A (most employees), or 5 CFR 582.501 (certain military employees). You can also look up the CFR at www.access.gpo.gov/nara/cfr/cfr-retrieve.html. You'll be asked to enter the Title (5), Part (581 or 582) and Section (501).

Once you have the address and phone number, call the office to verify the address and to find out exactly what forms—and how many copies—the agency needs.

Item A1: Enter the debtor's name.

Item A2: Enter the debtor's birth date. If you don't know, write "unknown."

Item A3: Enter the debtor's Social Security number. If you don't know, write "unknown."

Item A4: Enter the name of the federal agency for which the debtor works, the debtor's title (or job description) if you know it and the address, including zip code, where the debtor works.

Item A5: Enter the debtor's last known home address.

Application for Federal Employee Commercial Garnishment

APPLICATION FOR FEDERAL EMPLOYEE COMMERCIAL GARNISHMENT

Approved by OMB
3206-0229
Approval Expires
08/31/99

Date Received in Office of Designated Agent

INSTRUCTIONS

1. Federal law, 5 U.S.C. § 5520a, provides for the commercial garnishment of the pay of Federal employees.
2. Each garnishment order or similar legal process in the nature of garnishment must be delivered to the agency's Designated Agent. (See 5 CFR Part 582 Appendix A and 5 CFR Part 581 Appendix A for the lists of Designated Agents to receive legal process.)

3. Employing agencies will generally begin to disburse amounts withheld from employee-obligor's pay within 30 days of receipt by Designated Agent.
4. Employing agencies will **not** modify compensation schedules or pay disbursement cycles in responding to legal process.
5. 31 CFR Part 210 governs funds remitted by Electronic Funds Transfer.
6. See reverse side for Public Burden Statement.

Title and Address of Employing Agency's Designated Agent

Dept. of Agriculture, Forest Service
Director–Personnel Management
900 RP–E
P.O. Box 96090
Washington, DC 20090-6-90

Note: Service of legal process **may** be accomplished by certified or registered mail, return receipt requested, or by personal service only upon the agent to receive process as explained in 5 CFR 582.201, or if no agent has been designated, then upon the head of the employee-obligor's employing agency.

A. EMPLOYEE IDENTIFICATION - 5 U.S.C. § 5520a requires sufficient information to enable the employing agency to identify the employee-obligor. Please provide as much of the information in items 1 through 5 as possible.

1. Full Name of Employee-Obligor

Cedric Lopez

2. Date of Birth

March 2, 1962

3. Employee/Social Security Number

123-45-6789

4. Employing Agency, Component, and Employee's Official Duty Station/Worksite Address and ZIP Code

Department of Agriculture
Forest Service
2400 Washington Ave.
Redding, CA 96001

5. Home Address or Current Mailing Address and ZIP Code

127 Laurel Street
Project City, CA 96000

6. For Agency Use

B. CASE INFORMATION

1. Name of Court and Case Number in Garnishment Order

Shasta County Superior Court
000-00004

2. Garnishment Amount

$ 25% of net earnings until judgment is satisfied

3. Legal process expiration date (if time limited)

September 17, 20XX

4. Is there a dollar amount or percentage limitation under the applicable law of the jurisdiction where the order has been issued that will result in a lower amount to be garnished than would otherwise be applicable under the Consumer Credit Protection Act, 15 U.S.C. § 1673? ☐ Yes ☒ No   If Yes, provide a citation and a copy of the applicable provision:_____

5. Does the law of the jurisdiction where this legal process is issued have a "one order at a time" rule that precludes employers from garnishing more than one order at a time?
☒ Yes ☐ No

6. Does the law of the jurisdiction where this legal process is issued provide for the garnishment of interest amounts that are not reflected on the order or in item number B2?
☒ Yes ☐ No

C. AUTHORIZED PAYEE IDENTIFICATION

1. Full Name of Person Authorized to Receive Payment, as it appears on Court Order

Lester Brand

2. Address of Authorized Payee, including ZIP Code

194 Calico Ave
Redding, CA 96000

3. Daytime Telephone - Area Code and Number

530-555-1860

4. Signature of Authorized Payee, Creditor, or Creditor's Representative, and Date Signed

Lester Brand

D. ELECTRONIC FUNDS TRANSFER (if available)

If you wish to request that the funds be remitted by electronic funds transfer rather than by paper check, please complete items D1 through D5.

1. Name and Address of Authorized Payee's Financial Institution

2. Depositor (Payee) Account No. and Title

3. 9-Digit Routing Transit No. of Authorized Payee's Financial Institution (Verify with Financial Institution)

Type of Account: ☐ Checking ☐ Savings

4. Name and Title of Authorized Payee's Representative

5. Signature of Authorized Payee's Representative and Date Signed

U. S. Office of Personnel Management

Optional Form 311 (March 1997)

Item A6: Leave this blank.

Item B1: Enter the name of the court that issued your Writ of Execution, such as "Shasta County Superior Court," and the case number.

Item B2: If you know the debtor's monthly net earnings, calculate 25% of those earnings and enter that figure here. Otherwise, cross off the dollar sign and enter "25% of net earnings until judgment is satisfied."

Item B3: Enter 180 days (six months) from the date the Writ was issued.

Item B4: Check the "no" box.

Item B5: Check the "yes" box.

Item B6: Check the "yes" box.

Items C1-C4: Enter the requested information about yourself.

Items D1-D5: If you would like the money directly deposited into your bank account—rather than mailed to you—enter the requested information. Otherwise, leave these blank.

Once you send the form, the agency is supposed to begin the garnishment within 30 days—but your garnishment will be subject to all other garnishments served before that date. Child and spousal support garnishments always get first priority.

4. Debtor Receives Public Benefits or Payments From Pension Plan

Social Security benefits can never be garnished. Unless your judgment is for child or spousal support, you can't garnish unemployment insurance, workers' compensation awards, relocation benefits or disability or health insurance benefits. Garnishing payments made from a retirement plan also is very difficult. Most retirement plans contain "anti-alienation" provisions barring the plan administrator from paying anyone except the plan holder or beneficiary, such as a spouse. If the debtor receives these benefits, you may be better off looking elsewhere for payment.

B. How to Garnish Wages

Before you can garnish wages, you must obtain a Writ of Execution directed to the county where the debtor is employed. (See Chapter 7.) Once you have the Writ, follow the steps below.

1. Locate Debtor's Workplace

To garnish the debtor's wages, you need her employer's name and address. Skip to Section B2, below, if you have this information and have called to verify it. If you don't have a clue about the debtor's employment, here are some suggestions for tracking it down.

Don't violate the debt collection laws. When speaking with others, avoid mentioning your judgment. (See Chapter 3.)

- **Debtor's examination:** You can request that the debtor appear in court and answer questions concerning her employment at a debtor's examination. (See Chapter 6.)
- **Debtor's statement:** If you are collecting a small claims judgment, the debtor is supposed to file a debtor's statement within 30 days, which should include the name of his employer. (See Chapter 6.)
- **State employment:** If you think the debtor may work for the state, go to the website of California's Department of General Services, Telecommunications Division, at www.cold. ca.gov/state_employees.asp. Here, you can type in someone's name and find out whether he or she works for a government agency. If the person works for the state, this site will give you contact information. You can also get this information over the phone, by calling 916-657-9900.
- **Unions:** The debtor may belong to a union; check with a local branch. If you are asked

why, and you believe the union won't cooperate if you tell the truth, have a good explanation ready. Possibly say you are trying to contact the person about employment, or that you previously worked with the person and just got back into town. You'll find a list of labor unions in your phone book under "Labor Organizations."

- **Debtor's friends and neighbors:** The debtor's friends or neighbors may provide you with information about where the debtor works.

When you believe you have located the debtor's place of employment, verify it by calling the work number. You can either ask if the debtor works there or ask to speak to the debtor. Or, if you don't want to speak to the debtor, call when he may not be there (lunchtime) and ask to speak with him. You should either be told, "he's out to lunch" or "no one by that name works here."

Using pretexts. In Chapter 3, we urge you not to violate debt collections laws—and misrepresenting yourself is a technical violation. Many professional debt collectors routinely get information by misrepresenting who they are, however. As long as the collector isn't abusive and doesn't harass, this kind of misrepresentation is an accepted part of the bill collector's landscape. You may need to employ it to collect from the most elusive debtors.

2. Complete Application for Earnings Withholding Order

You may be able to skip ahead to Section C. Once you know where the debtor works, you must fill out some forms to begin the wage garnishment. If the debtor works for the federal government, you must use a form entitled Application for Earnings Withholding Order (Section A3, above). You can skip ahead to Section C after completing the form.

You must give the levying officer instructions for serving the wage garnishment papers on the debtor's employer. A sample completed form and instructions are below. A blank copy is in the Appendix.

Caption: Follow the format of your previous court papers. Leave the box for the levying officer's file number blank if you haven't levied on this debtor in this county before. If you have, the number is on those papers. Put that number in the box.

To the sheriff or any marshal or constable of the county of: Enter the county where the debtor is employed.

Item 1: First, enter your name as it appears in the judgment. Then in the box on the left, enter the name and street address of the debtor's employer. In the box on the right, enter the debtor's name exactly as it appears in the judgment and the debtor's home address (or last known address). If you know the debtor's Social Security number, include it.

Item 2: Check 2a if you want the money paid to you. If you want the money paid to someone else, check 2b and enter that person's name, address and telephone number.

Item 3a: Enter the date the judgment was entered.

Item 3b: Leave this blank unless you have agreed with the debtor that he can pay less than the full judgment. If so, put the amount you agreed to here. Also, if you have received any money toward the judgment since you obtained the Writ, subtract that amount from the total shown in Item 18 of the Writ of Execution and put the difference here.

Item 4: Check this box if you are seeking to collect a judgment for spousal or child support.

Item 5: If you have special instructions to the levying officer, check this box and enter the instructions. Attach an additional page if you need more space. Example of special instructions include the following:

- At work, the debtor uses a name different than what is on the judgment.
- You are seeking less than 25% of the debtor's net income. You might garnish less

Application for Earnings Withholding Order (Wage Garnishment)

ATTORNEY OR PARTY WITHOUT ATTORNEY *(Name and Address)*:	TELEPHONE NO.:	LEVYING OFFICER *(Name and Address)*:
Lester Brand 194 Calico Ave Redding, CA 96000	530-555-1860	

ATTORNEY FOR *(Name)*: In Pro Per

NAME OF COURT, JUDICIAL DISTRICT OR BRANCH COURT, IF ANY:

Shasta County Superior Court

PLAINTIFF: Lester Brand

DEFENDANT: Cedric Lopez

APPLICATION FOR EARNINGS WITHHOLDING ORDER (Wage Garnishment)	LEVYING OFFICER FILE NO.:	COURT CASE NO.: 0000-0004

TO THE SHERIFF OR ANY MARSHAL OR CONSTABLE OF THE COUNTY OF   SHASTA
OR ANY REGISTERED PROCESS SERVER

1. The judgment creditor *(name)*:   Lester Brand

requests issuance of an Earnings Withholding Order directing the employer to withhold the earnings of the judgment debtor (employee).

Name and address of employer

Tree Trimmers, Inc.
1234 Main Street
Redding, CA 96000

Name and address of employee

Cedric Lopez
127 Laurel Street
Project City, CA 96000

Social Security Number *(if known)*:

2. The amounts withheld are to be paid to
   a. [X] The attorney (or party without an attorney) named at the top of this page.
   b. [ ] Other *(name, address, and telephone)*:

3. a. Judgment was entered on *(date)*:   January 8, 20XX
   b. Collect the amount directed by the Writ of Execution unless a lesser amount is specified here:
   $

4. [ ] The Writ of Execution was issued to collect delinquent amounts payable for the **support** of a child, former spouse, or spouse of the employee.

5. [ ] Special instructions *(specify)*:

6. *(Check a or b)*
   a. [X] I have not previously obtained an order directing this employer to withhold the earnings of this employee.
   —OR—
   b. [ ] I have previously obtained such an order, but that order *(check one)*:
   [ ] was terminated by a court order, but I am entitled to apply for another Earnings Withholding Order under the provisions of Code of Civil Procedure section 706.105(h).
   [ ] was ineffective.

Lester Brand
....
(TYPE OR PRINT NAME)

▶ *Lester Brand*
_____
(SIGNATURE OF ATTORNEY OR PARTY WITHOUT ATTORNEY)

I declare under penalty of perjury under the laws of the State of California that the foregoing is true and correct.

Date: March 17, 20XX
......Lester Brand..
(TYPE OR PRINT NAME)

▶ *Lester Brand*
_____
(SIGNATURE OF DECLARANT)

Form Adopted by the
Judicial Council of California
982.5(1) [Rev. January 1, 1993]

APPLICATION FOR EARNINGS WITHHOLDING ORDER
(Wage Garnishment)

WEST GROUP
Official Publisher

CCP 706.121

if you previously garnished the debtor's wages, he filed a Claim of Exemption and the court determined a certain amount to be exempt.

Item 6: Check a if you have not previously garnished the wages of the debtor. Check b if you previously obtained an order to garnish the judgment debtor's wages from this employer. Then check the first box if you attempted a wage garnishment before, but it was terminated by a court order. (You cannot serve another Earnings Withholding Order until 100 days after service of the first one or 60 days after it was terminated, whichever is later.) Check the second box if your wage levy was ineffective—for example, another wage garnishment had priority over yours.

Type or print your name and sign the form twice. Also, enter the date you sign the form.

3. Provide Instructions for Levying Officer

To find the levying officer for a county, call the sheriff's office and ask if it levies on civil money judgments. If not, find out who does and call to find out the fees and how many copies of the Writ and Application are required.

Make the necessary copies—keeping a set for your records—and mail or take the documents and correct fee to the levying officer. A letter of instructions to the levying officer is provided in the Appendix. If you go in person, take your checkbook or cash for payment.

Sample Letter of Instructions

December 19, 20___

To the Sheriff, County of Yolo:

Enclosed please find an original and three copies of a Writ of Execution, an original Application for Earnings Withholding Order and a check in the amount of $_____ to cover your fees.

Please proceed with a wage garnishment according to the Application for Earnings Withholding Order.

Please hold the original Writ of Execution for its entire 180-day duration or until the judgment has been satisfied, unless I contact you and instruct you differently.

Sincerely,

Ben Klein

Ben Klein

Based on the information in your instructions, the levying officer prepares an Earnings Withholding Order. He then serves it and an Employer's Return form on the employer or an agent in charge of the office or payroll. The levying officer also delivers to the debtor a copy of the Writ and information about his legal options.

4. Wait for Employer to Complete Return

The employer is legally required to complete an Employer's Return and mail it back to the levying officer within 15 days. The levying officer will forward it to you. Note on your calendar to watch for a copy of the Employer's Return about four to six weeks after you send instructions to the levying officer. If you don't get a copy, ask the levying officer what is happening with your garnishment.

On the Employer's Return, the employer:

- corrects any wrong information about the debtor's name and address
- indicates whether the debtor is still employed and if so, the earnings in the last pay period, and
- states when the debtor is paid—such as every two weeks or monthly.

In addition, the employer must notify the debtor of the Earnings Withholding Order at least ten days before the garnishment is to begin so the debtor can:

- see an attorney
- work out an agreement with you, or
- file a Claim of Exemption.

If the debtor doesn't file a Claim of Exemption or work out an arrangement with you, the employer will begin sending a portion of the debtor's wages to the levying officer each pay period. The levying officer in turn forwards the payments to you.

If you decide to lift or modify the garnishment before your judgment is paid in full, you must send a Notice of Termination or Modification of Earnings Withholding Order to the employer, the debtor and the levying officer instructing him how to proceed.

5. If Employer Does Not Cooperate

If the employer doesn't return the Employer's Return form and carry out the order, you can sue the employer to recover the amount that should have been withheld, as well as any attorney's fees you spend in this effort. You can also sue an employer who interferes with a wage garnishment, for example by accelerating or deferring payments to the judgment debtor. An employer could even be subject to criminal prosecution if she doesn't comply.

Fortunately, it is seldom necessary to go this far. After you double-check with the levying officer to make sure he has not received the Employer's Return, call or write the employer and find out what's wrong. Let her know that you

have the right to sue her. This usually produces the form. See the sample letter, below.

Sample Letter to Uncooperative Employer

January 29, 20__

Nina Hart
Downlow Corporation
1000 Industrial Street
Yolo, CA 95000

Re: *Ben Klein v. Twila Imenez*

Riverside Municipal Court Case No. 12345

Dear Ms. Hart:

On December 19, 20__, I sent instructions to the Yolo County sheriff to proceed with a wage garnishment in the above-referenced case. They have informed me that they served you at Downlow Corporation with an Earnings Withholding Order on January 2, 20__.

By law, you were required to complete and forward the Employer's Return to the sheriff within 15 days after service, and to comply with the wage garnishment unless you filed a formal objection.

There are serious legal penalties for refusing to comply with a wage garnishment. You could be found liable for the amount due and owing on the judgment, and you could be subject to a separate lawsuit.

Rather than taking more formal steps at this time, I would appreciate it if you would immediately complete and return the Employer's Return to the sheriff, and comply with the wage garnishment as required by law.

Sincerely,

Ben Klein

Ben Klein

cc: Sheriff, Yolo County (Officer's File No. 1000)

If the employer still doesn't cooperate and you don't want to sue, you can bring him in for a debtor's exam. (See Chapter 6, Section C.)

It is possible that an employer will send back the Employer's Return, but object to the wage garnishment. If this happens, the levying officer will send you a copy and ask you for further instructions. Common objections include:

- the debtor does not work there any more
- the debtor's wages are already being garnished by someone else, or
- the debtor works as an independent contractor, not an employee.

If the debtor no longer works for that employer, and you can find a current employer located in the same county as the former employer, you can send another Application for Earnings Withholding Order to the levying officer along with a new fee. The levying officer can use the same Writ of Execution. If the debtor's wages are already being garnished, you have to wait for that garnishment to end before yours take effect. If the other one lasts more than six months (180 days), you'll have to get a new Writ. If the debtor is an independent contractor, instead of a wage garnishment, you can do a third-party levy (Chapter 10) or assignment (Chapter 19).

6. If Debtor Files Claim of Exemption

The debtor can contest your wage garnishment by filing something called a Claim of Exemption with the levying officer. In this form, the debtor states that she is contesting the wage garnishment and gives her reasons for doing so. When the officer receives the Claim of Exemption, he will mail you a copy, along with a financial statement completed by the debtor and a document called Notice of Filing of Claim of Exemption. (Claims of Exemption are covered in Chapter 15.)

7. Get Your Money

If the debtor doesn't object to your wage garnishment or you win the Claim of Exemption hearing, the employer sends the money to the levying officer, who disburses it to you. Don't expect your money right away—delay is common. While you can call the levying officer to make sure your case hasn't fallen through the cracks, be patient. Levying officers often transmit collected funds in lump sums, rather than distributing them as they are collected.

Make sure you keep track of all money collected, as well as any costs incurred by you. We discuss this in Chapter 16.

If the employer receives an order of higher priority—such as for child or spousal support—your wage garnishment will be put on hold for up to two years; after that it will automatically terminate (Code of Civil Procedure § 706.032(a)(2)).

If your judgment is satisfied except for costs and interest, you can seek a final Earnings Withholding Order to recover those costs and interest (Code of Civil Procedure § 706.028).

If the debtor leaves her job, the order will automatically terminate after a 180-day period during which no money is withheld (Code of Civil Procedure § 706.032(a)(1)). If the debtor changes jobs, you can file for another garnishment with the new employer. ■

Chapter 10

Collecting From Money or Property Owed to Debtor

Collection Factors

	High	Moderate	Low
Potential cost to you		✓	
Potential for producing cash		✓	
Potential for settlement		✓	
Potential time and trouble	✓		
Potential for debtor bankruptcy			✓

One potential source of funds for satisfying your judgment is money that other parties owe the debtor. You can demand that these funds be paid directly to you instead of to the debtor (Code of Civil Procedure § 700.170). There are a few exceptions, however. For example, unless you have a judgment for child or spousal support, you can't go after debts owed the judgment debtor by the government, including tax refunds (Code of Civil Procedure § 699.720(a)(5)).

Common types of debts third parties may owe a debtor include:

- accounts receivable, if the debtor is a business
- money due for services rendered—for example, if the debtor is a professional, consultant or independent contractor or works on commission
- judgments obtained by the debtor against a third party, and
- loans made by the debtor to a third party.

Third parties may also have, at least temporarily, property that belongs to the judgment debtor. For instance, a gallery may have a craftsperson's works on consignment. Generally, for a levying officer to levy on property held by a third party, the property must be someplace that is open to the public. If it isn't, you must obtain a Seizure Order from a court to let the levying officer enter a private place to get the property. (Seizure Orders are covered in Chapter 19.) Getting a Seizure Order can be a bit complicated; we generally don't recommend it unless the amount of your judgment justifies the effort and your other attempts to collect have not been successful.

To collect your judgment out of money or property owed the debtor, the levying officer sends a levy notice to the third party, directing that person to pay the levying officer instead of the debtor. This kind of levy is a one-shot affair. You cannot request an ongoing levy, like with a wage garnishment. You can keep returning to the third party for payment, however. So if you know that the debtor is an independent contractor working mainly for Curry Company, each month you can levy on the money due the debtor from Curry Company.

There is one way to maintain an ongoing "levy." If the debtor receives regular payments from a third party—such as royalty payments or certain government benefits—you can request a court order for something called an assignment, in which the debtor assigns her right to receive these payments to you. The up side is that you don't have levy the money owed the debtor each month—it's automatically paid to you through the assignment. The down side is that you must obtain a court order. (Assignment Orders are covered in Chapter 19.)

A. Locating Money or Property Owed Debtor

To initiate a levy on money or property held by third parties, you first need to figure out who and where they are and what they owe the debtor. Below are common types of money or property others might owe the debtor. If you contact anyone directly, follow the collection guidelines in Chapter 3.

1. Independent Contractor Receipts

For our purposes, an independent contractor is someone who works for herself and does not have a formal employer–employee relationship with the person for whom she does projects or other work. If the debtor has a steady income as an independent contractor, it can be a great source for collecting your judgment.

Independent contractors include people who:

- work for a business as outside salespersons on commission
- are artists or writers who do projects on contract
- freelance their work for larger companies—such as consultants, or
- do home repair or garden maintenance on a regular or semi-regular basis.

Carpenters, stoneworkers, plumbers, painters, pool service companies, roofers, electricians, housecleaners, writers and many others fall into the category of independent contractors. Some of them, especially consultants, may be incorporated, in which case you would have to levy on the business instead. (See Chapter 11.)

It may be obvious for whom the debtor does work. A commissioned sales rep may have a business card identifying a principal supplier; a writer or artist may list major accounts on a publicity brochure.

In other situations, you may have to do some searching. You could ask a friend to pose as a potential employer and call the debtor for current references—that is, the people the debtor currently does work for. Or, people you know who know the debtor may give you this information in the course of a casual conversation. You might even follow the debtor a few mornings to see where he goes.

A more formal way to get this information is to conduct a debtor's examination, along with a Subpena Duces Tecum, asking for copies of statements and books showing accounts receivable. (See Chapter 6.) If these methods fail, consider hiring an investigator. (See Chapter 23, Section C.)

2. Accounts Receivable—Businesses

Accounts receivable are money that customers owe a business for goods or services provided. For instance, a printing business is often owed large sums for printing jobs, a wholesaler for goods supplied a retailer and a clothing manufacturer for goods distributed to stores. Or, the debtor may work out of her home selling mail-order products. While you cannot use a levy to collect from the business itself (see Chapter 11 on how to collect from a business), if you know the names of customers who have made purchases but haven't yet paid, you can levy on the money due. In many businesses, payment is not expected until 30 to 90 days from the date of the invoice.

To find out the names of such customers, call the business and pose as a potential customer. Ask for the names of customers as references. When you call the customers, ask what they have purchased from the debtor in order to estimate how much they are likely to owe. Do not state that you have a judgment or anything that would damage the debtor's business or personal reputation.

3. Accounts Receivable— Professional Services

If the debtor provides professional services as a lawyer, accountant, financial planner, doctor, acupuncturist, therapist, dentist or other professional, his clients or patients may be good sources of money. You'll want to find clients or patients with whom the debtor has a regular and ongoing relationship. Although your levy will be good for only one payment intercept, if you find someone who sees the professional regularly (such as a therapist's patient), you can return each week or month with another levy. If the client or patient is a major and steady source of income for the debtor, intercepting one payment may quickly lead the debtor to pay the debt in full or negotiate a payment plan.

If the payments are steady and large enough, consider obtaining an Assignment Order from a court. (See Chapter 19.) Under an Assignment Order, you will receive the payments from the third party as they become due until your judgment is satisfied or you cancel the assignment. You won't have to levy on each payment.

If you know the name of a regular, major client of the judgment debtor, levying on that person's payments may make sense. But don't invade anyone's privacy to find out the names of patients or clients.

4. Security Deposit

If the debtor is a renter, her landlord probably holds a security deposit. While no specific statute authorizes a levy on a tenant's security deposit and no court of appeals has reviewed the issue yet, several statutes read together may been interpreted as providing that authority: See Code of Civil Procedure §§ 695.010 and 699.710 and Civil Code § 1950.5(d).

5. Rent Payments

If the debtor is a landlord of either commercial or residential property, finding out the names of renters is usually not difficult. You can ask the debtor in a debtor's examination (Chapter 6). You could use a reverse directory, which lists the names of people who have phone numbers at a particular address. (See Chapter 2, Section B4.) You could visit the property and read the tenants' names on the mailboxes or business signs.

Several California communities have rent control ordinances that require landlords of covered units to register their units and provide information about the tenancies. If the debtor owns residential property in a community with rent control laws, the rent control agency should have information about the debtor's building.

6. Debtor's Securities

If the debtor owns stock, how you get it depends on how the stock ownership is physically represented. If a stockbroker holds the certificates for the debtor, you can use the levy described in this chapter against the branch office of the stock brokerage firm. If ownership is manifested in stock certificates held by the debtor, you can levy against the certificates themselves as tangible personal property. (See Chapter 13.) If the stock ownership is represented only in the computer database of the company issuing the stock, you can use the levy procedure outlined in this chapter against the company's California headquarters. If the headquarters are out of state, you will need to obtain an Assignment Order directed to the judgment debtor. (See Chapter 19.)

7. Debtor's Property or Money

Finding out who has possession of the debtor's property or money can be difficult. If you know the debtor or his associates well, however, you may be able to get this information through casual conversation. Or you might be able to track down some potential third parties from what you know about the debtor. For example, if the debtor has appointed a money manager to handle his funds, that person could be reached through a third-party levy. The same goes for a friend who is keeping personal property for a debtor.

Furthermore, if the debtor is a craftsperson, artist or small publisher, he might have some books or artworks on consignment with a bookstore or gallery. A third party would be legally responsible for turning over to you any payments due the debtor at the time of the levy. You could also levy against the property itself, but the fees, storage costs and sales costs associated with levies on tangible personal property usually make a levy counterproductive. (See Chapter 13.)

If you suspect that the debtor has hidden valuable assets by transferring them to third parties, and your attempt to levy against this property fails because the third party claims ownership, you still may be able to get the assets. However, you'll have to bring a separate lawsuit against the third party—a process well beyond the scope of this book.

B. How to Levy on Money or Property Held by Third Parties

Before you can levy on money or property held by a third party, you must obtain a Writ of Execution directed to the county in which the third party is located. (See Chapter 7.) Once you have the Writ, follow the steps below. If the business headquarters are in another state, you will not be able to levy against it and instead will have to obtain an Assignment Order directed to the judgment debtor. (See Chapter 19.)

1. Prepare Levying Instructions

To find the levying officer for a county, call the sheriff's office and ask if it levies on civil money judgments. If not, find out who does, then call to find out the fees and how many copies of the Writ are required. If you are levying against money only, you could use a process server to speed up the process. (See Chapter 21.)

a. Money Owed to Debtor

To levy on money owed to the debtor by a third party, include the following in your instructions:
- the third party's name and address
- the amount of money you believe the third party will owe the debtor at the time the levy is made, and
- when you want the levy to be made—near the end of the month is often good, as it is likely to be when the maximum amount will be owed.

Sample instructions are below.

Sample Instructions to Levying Officer for Money Owed

June 6, 20____

Re: Ross Toshi v. Shirley Jacks

To the Sheriff, County of Marin:

Enclosed please find an original and ____ copies of a Writ of Execution and a check in the amount of $_____ to cover your fee.

Please serve the Writ of Execution and levy against any money due and owing judgment debtor Shirley Jacks by the third party, Careful Cat Catering, 100 Siamese Street, Sausalito, CA.

Shirley Jacks should be owed approximately $1,100 by Careful Cat Catering for deli items delivered but not yet paid for. Please execute this levy sometime during the week of June 23, 20____.

Please call me if you have any questions.

Sincerely,

Ross Toshi

Ross Toshi
415-555-7888

---

b. Tangible Personal Property Held by Third Party

Tangible personal property is all property, except real estate, of a physical nature—that is, property that you can actually touch. Examples are pianos, jewelry, cameras, computers, stereos, furniture and stamp collections. Examples of intangible personal property are copyrights and trademarks.

To levy on tangible property held by a third party, you must instruct the levying officer to take, store and sell the property. You will have to pay the regular levy fee as well as a substantial deposit—probably several hundred dollars—to cover the associated costs. Sample instructions are below.

Sample Instructions to Levying Officer for Property Held

June 6, 20____

Re: Ross Toshi v. Shirley Jacks

To the Sheriff, County of Alameda:

Enclosed please find an original and ___ copies of a Writ of Execution and a check in the amount of $_____ to cover your fee.

Please proceed to levy on (remove, store and sell) the following tangible personal property belonging to Shirley Jacks, which is in the possession of Miguel Fast:

- One Steinway baby grand piano, and

- Full set of 12 crystal goblets.

This property is located at the Space Studio of Miguel Fast, 2001 Space Street, Berkeley, CA. The Space Studio is generally open to the public.

Please keep me informed as to the status of this levy. I would like to attend the sale, so let me know when that will be.

Please call me if you have any questions.

Sincerely,

Ross Toshi

Ross Toshi
415-555-7888

2. Provide Instructions to Levying Officer

Send the fee, your instructions and the original and copies of your Writ to the levying officer. The levying officer will serve the third party with copies of your papers, a Notice of Levy and a form called a Memorandum of Garnishee. The judgment debtor will be mailed a Notice of Levy.

Unless the third party has a good reason for refusing to turn over the money or property, she must give the levying officer what is due or belongs to the debtor at the time of the levy. She must also complete and return the Memorandum of Garnishee to the levying officer within ten days of receiving it.

a. If Third Party Doesn't Comply

A third party who does not turn over the money or property sought in the Writ must explain in the Memorandum why he won't or cannot comply. One common reason is that someone else already served a levy and has rights to the money ahead of you. Or the third party might state that he doesn't owe anything to the debtor or doesn't hold property for the debtor. Or the obligation might be due but not yet payable. If the levying officer receives a Memorandum of Garnishee, you will be sent a copy. We generally don't recommend pursuing the matter if the third party objects—unless the amount at stake justifies hiring a lawyer.

There are penalties for failing to comply with a levy—assuming the third party is able to comply and simply does not. If you sue the third party, he may be ordered to pay you the lesser of the following:

- the value of the judgment debtor's interest in the property or the amount of the payments you are seeking to levy, or

- the amount required to satisfy the judgment.

The court can also require the third party to pay your attorney's fees (Code of Civil Procedure § 701.020).

Fortunately, it is seldom necessary to go this far. An informed third-party debtor commonly pays after being reminded of her obligation to do so. You can help this process along with a letter along the lines of the sample provided.

Sample Letter Reminding Third Party of Levy

July 10, 20___

Re: Ross Toshi v. Shirley Jacks
    Marin County Municipal Court Case
    No. 12345

Miguel Fast
2001 Space Street
Berkeley, CA

Dear Mr. Fast:

On June 6, 20___, I sent instructions to the Alameda County sheriff to proceed with a levy on property that you have in your possession belonging to Shirley Jacks. The specific property in question is a Steinway baby grand piano and a full set of 12 crystal goblets.

The sheriff has informed me that you were personally served with levying papers on June 13, 20___, but you have not stated any objection on the Garnishee's Memorandum or turned the property over to the sheriff . By law, you were required to complete and forward the Garnishee's Memorandum to the sheriff within ten days after receiving it, and to comply with the levy unless you filed a formal objection.

For refusing to comply with a sheriff's levy, you could be sued and found personally liable for the amount due on the judgment. I do not want to take such steps. I would appreciate it if you would immediately complete and return the Garnishee's Memorandum to the levying officer, and comply with the levy as required by law.

Sincerely,

Ross Toshi

Ross Toshi

cc: Sheriff, Alameda County
    (Officer's File No. 1000)

b. If Debtor Objects

The judgment debtor might file a Claim of Exemption. If this happens, see Chapter 15.

3. Get Proceeds From Levy

The levying officer ultimately disburses the money or sales proceeds to you. Don't expect the money right away—delay is common. While you can call the levying officer to make sure your case hasn't fallen through the cracks, be patient. Levying officers often transmit collected funds in lump sums, rather than distributing them as they are collected.

Make sure you keep track of all money collected, as well as any collection costs you incurred. We discuss how to do this in Chapter 16. ■

Chapter 11

Collecting From a Business

Collection Factors—Levying on Cash Coming Into Business			
	High	Moderate	Low
Potential cost to you			✓
Potential for producing cash	✓		
Potential for settlement	✓		
Potential time and trouble		✓	
Potential for debtor bankruptcy			✓

Collection Factors—Levying on Assets of Business			
	High	Moderate	Low
Potential cost to you	✓		✓
Potential for producing cash	✓		
Potential for settlement	✓		
Potential time and trouble		✓	
Potential for debtor bankruptcy		✓	

*I*f you have a judgment against a going business—whether it's a limited liability company, corporation, partnership or sole proprietorship—you can have the levying officer collect using any of the following methods:

- make a one-time seizure of cash and checks in the cash register—called a till tap
- stay at the business for a day or longer, collecting cash and checks as they come in—called a keeper, or
- seize personal assets of the business and sell them.

These procedures are available only if the business entity is a named defendant in the judgment. If your judgment is against the debtor as an individual, you probably will need a court order to levy on the business—even if the individual owns it lock, stock and barrel.

These procedures have a coercive effect: Most business owners would rather pay your judgment than face the prospect of a sheriff standing by the cash register or seizing business assets. One sheriff reported great success in extracting payments by calling debtor businesses and describing what the levying officer would do: "Do you really want one of my deputies, with his police special on his hip, standing next to your cash register all day making your customers nervous?" In most cases, business owners facing these types of collection efforts find a way to pay the judgment voluntarily.

A. Levying Against Cash Receipts or Business Assets?

Most judgment creditors opt to levy against cash receipts rather than going for business assets. Before you make a choice, however, you should understand how each method works.

1. Levying Against Cash Receipts

As we mentioned, you can seize cash and checks on a one-time basis (till tap) or by having a sheriff stand at the cash register all day (keeper). There are some restrictions, however.

- You cannot levy against receipts received by a home-based business without a court order. (See Chapter 19.)
- You cannot levy against credit card receipts or receipts for sales that are not yet final, such as a down payment or layaway deposit.
- Some levying officers refuse to collect checks because of the problems involved in getting them cashed. You might deal with this by asking the levying officer to have the debtor endorse the checks over to you.

a. Till Tap

If you request a till tap, the levying officer makes a single trip to the business and picks up all the cash and checks in the cash register or cash box. This is a quick way of going after business receipts and you can request one as often as you want—but you have to prepare new levy forms each time. If the business owner keeps his money in his wallet or a locked safe, a till tap probably won't work.

You must pay fees in advance—currently, sheriffs charge about $85 for a till tap. If the levying officer can't tap the till—for example, because the business is closed—you may get some of the deposit back. You are entitled to collect the levying officer's fee, as well as the judgment, out of the till tap.

b. Keeper

If you request a keeper, the levying officer (usually a deputy sheriff) remains at the business and collects all cash and checks that come in. This is a great way to collect from a retail establishment. A keeper is also a good way for you to find out about the assets of the business, because you can instruct the levying officer to inventory the equipment, furniture and merchandise.

A keeper can be authorized to remain on a business's premises in daily increments, up to ten days. After that, the assets or inventory must be seized and sold. In the real world, a keeper stays until he has collected the balance specified in your Writ, plus the amount needed to cover the levying officer's costs. A keeper may choose not to stay if the debtor expressly objects. In that case, however, the levying officer is permitted to immediately seize, store and sell business assets (Code of Civil Procedure § 700.070).

You have three choices when you request a keeper.

- **An eight-hour keeper.** This is your least expensive option.

- **A 24- or 48-hour keeper.** The longer the keeper stays, the more it will cost you. A 24- or 48-hour keeper makes sense if you're dealing with a business that has unusually long hours or operates around the clock, such as a convenience store.

- **An open-ended keeper (up to ten days).** If your judgment is fairly large and the business does not take in enough cash each day to satisfy the judgment in a day or two, be prepared for a long-term keeper, if you can afford it. But be aware that with an open-ended keeper, you runner a greater risk of driving the debtor out of business or into bankruptcy.

The levying officer has a right to collect potential costs in advance; you will probably have to deposit as much as a few hundred dollars for an eight-hour keeper and much more than that for a ten-day keeper. Part of this deposit may be refunded if the costs don't run that high. And these costs may be recovered by the keeper or in a subsequent levy.

2. Levying Against Business Assets

Having business assets seized and sold is expensive, time consuming and economically risky. The forced sale of property typically brings only a small percentage of its true market value. You must pay substantial costs up front for conducting an inventory, transporting and storing the assets and holding the sale. Also, the property you try to seize and sell may already be serving as security for other debts (which get paid before you), or may be exempt from sale. Therefore, we don't recommend levying against business assets unless:

- you have a hefty judgment and are certain that the sale will bring in significantly more than the cost of having the property seized, stored and sold, or

- you want to acquire the property for your own use.

B. How to Levy Against Cash Receipts

Before you can levy against cash receipts, you must obtain a Writ of Execution directed to the county where the business is located. (See Chapter 7.) Once you have the Writ, follow the steps below.

1. Obtain Till Tap and Keeper Information

To find the levying officer for a county, call the sheriff's office and ask if it levies on civil money judgments. If not, find out who does. Then call and find out the fees for a till tap versus the different kinds of keepers, whether the levying officer has his own form and how many copies of the Writ are required.

Once you speak to the levying officer, decide which type of levy you want to use—till tap, eight-hour keeper, 24-hour keeper or open-ended keeper.

2. Provide Levying Officer With Instructions

If the levying officer does not provide a form, use the samples below as guides. A blank Instructions to Levying Officer form letter is in the Appendix. If you believe the business is likely to have a substantial amount of cash on hand at a certain time, instruct the levying officer to visit then.

Sample Letter of Instructions

March 24, 20___

Re: Anya Stoynoff v. Sloan Wells

To the Sheriff, County of San Diego:

Enclosed please find an original and ___ copies of a Writ of Execution and a check for your fee in the amount of $_____.

You are hereby instructed to seize cash and checks—ask the judgment debtor to endorse the checks over to me—in the possession of the following business to satisfy the sum specified in the accompanying Writ of Execution.

Sloan's Soup Shop
234 West Street
San Diego, CA 94118
619-555-8888

Please levy on or before 3 p.m. on a Friday—Sloan Wells makes weekly deposits at approximately 3:30 p.m. on Friday afternoons. Thank you.

Sincerely,

Anya Stoynoff

Anya Stoynoff
619-555-2343

Here are sample instructions for an eight-hour keeper. If you want a longer keeper, modify this sample to change the time the keeper is to last. Be sure to direct the levying officer to inventory the premises.

Sample Letter of Instructions

March 24, 20__

Re: Anya Stoynoff v. Sloan Wells

To the Sheriff, County of San Diego:

Enclosed please find an original and ____ copies of a Writ of Execution and a check for your fee in the amount of $_____.

You are hereby instructed to place an eight-hour keeper at the following business by virtue of the accompanying Writ of Execution.

Sloan's Soup Shop
234 West Street
San Diego, CA 94118
619-555-8888

In addition, please make an inventory of the personal property in Sloan's Soup Shop, including all equipment, appliances, machinery and utensils used for food preparation, silverware and china, linens, catering supplies and all other personal property on the premises.

Please call me if you have any questions.

Sincerely,

Anya Stoynoff

Anya Stoynoff
619-555-2343

After you type up the instructions, make the necessary copies of the Writ and instructions for the levying officer, plus one set for your file. Send the original and copies of the Writ along with your instructions and fees to the levying officer for the county where the debtor's business is located. If you are levying against money only, you could use a process server to speed up the process. (See Chapter 21.)

3. Get Your Money

The levying officer will proceed with your instructions. He may advise you about the outcome of the levy. If there was any problem with the levy— for example, the business is in a private home or has moved—he should contact you.

Once the levying officer has collected the proceeds of the levy, he will disburse them to you. Don't expect your money right away—delay is common. While you can call the levying officer to make sure your case hasn't fallen through the cracks, be patient. Levying officers often transmit collected funds in lump sums, rather than distributing them as they are collected.

Make sure you keep track of all money collected, as well as any costs incurred by you. We discuss how to do this in Chapter 16.

C. How to Levy Against Business Assets

If you decide to seize the assets of a business, the levying officer will hire a moving company, at your expense, to pick up the property, store it and conduct a sale. As costly and time consuming as it is, seizing business assets has extreme coercive value—the debtor may pay all or part of the judgment just to avoid the seizure.

Not all business property can be seized to pay off your judgment; some is off-limits. But that's the business owner's concern, not yours. You should instruct the levying officer to seize everything. The levying officer might decide not to take certain property. You have little practical alternative but to rely on his judgment.

The levying officer is likely to steer clear of the following kinds of property:

- Property found on the business premises that is not as a part of the business—that is, property that is owned by the debtor as an individual—and is exempt by law. For example, the business owner's personal motorcycle is at the business when the levying officer arrives. The motorcycle cannot be seized as a business asset, and the owner may claim it as an exempt motor vehicle. (See Chapter 12.)

- Exempt business assets—the debtor can claim up to $5,000 of tools, materials or equipment (Code of Civil Procedure § 704.060).

- Property that doesn't belong to the business—that is, items borrowed or leased from a third party, such as computers and copying machines.

- Inventory held on consignment, such as works by local artists.

- Partnership property, unless it actually belongs to the debtor. If it does not, you will need a Charging Order from the court to seize it—such orders are beyond the scope of this book.

- Inventory, furnishings, equipment and other items subject to a security interest that has been perfected through filing a financing statement with the Secretary of State. (See Chapter 4, Section B.)

- Property located in a private home, unless the debtor consents to, or a court issues an order permitting, the entry or seizure (Code of Civil Procedure § 699.030). Judges are reluctant to issue such an order unless you have exhausted other methods of collection, the judgment is big enough to justify your reaching a little further than is normally permitted or the debtor conducts a substantial business out of her home. If you feel you have a basis for collecting from a business in a private home, you must obtain a Seizure Order from the court where you obtained your judgment. (See Chapter 19.)

EXAMPLE: If Joanne, the debtor, does some professional writing out of a room in her house, this would not justify a court order allowing you to enter and seize property. On the other hand, if Joanne uses a substantial part of her home for a suite of offices, has clients coming and going on a regular basis, and has several employees, a court might allow a levying officer to enter. This might also hold true if you could show that the debtor is conducting a substantial mail order business from her home.

If you decide to go after the assets of a business, you must obtain a Writ of Execution directed to the county where the business is located. (See Chapter 7.) Once you have the Writ, follow the steps below.

1. Obtain Levying Information

To find the levying officer for a county, call the sheriff's office and ask if it levies on civil money judgments. If not, find out who does and call that person. Ask about the procedure for seizing and selling personal assets of a business, whether the levying officer has her own form, any deposit required and how many copies of the Writ are required.

2. Provide Levying Officer With Instructions

If the levying officer does not provide a form, use the below sample as a guide. A blank Instructions to Levying Officer form letter is in the Appendix. These instructions require the levying officer to give you an estimate of the potential cost of seizing the assets. This gives you a chance to back away from this remedy if it appears too expensive. They also let the levying officer seize less than all of the assets if, in his judgment, the amount seized will be sufficient to satisfy your judgment.

Sample Letter of Instructions

March 24, 20___

Re: *Anya Stoynoff v. Sloan Wells*

To the Sheriff, County of San Diego:

Enclosed please find an original Writ of Execution and ____ copies and a check for your fee in the amount of $_____.

You are hereby instructed to seize, advertise for sale and sell by virtue of the accompanying Writ of Execution the following business personal property: all money, debts, credits and effects, all goods, wares, merchandise, stock in trade, equipment, inventory, fixtures and furniture in possession or under the control of the following:

Sloan's Soup Shop
234 West Street
San Diego, CA 94118
619-555-8888

Please place a keeper in charge for a 48-hour period. As soon as possible, please inventory the premises, obtain an estimate of the moving and storage costs, and contact me at the telephone number below before taking further action. If I desire to continue with the levy, and no settlement with the judgment debtor has been made, this is your authority to remove enough property or merchandise from the premises to satisfy the amount of the claim specified in the Writ of Execution.

Finally, if a sale will be held, please advise me in advance so I can attend.

Sincerely,

Anya Stoynoff

Anya Stoynoff
619-555-2343

After you type up the instructions, make the necessary copies of the Writ and instructions for the levying officer, plus one set for your file. Send the original and copies of the Writ along with your instructions and fees to the levying officer for the county where the debtor's business is located.

3. Get Your Money

The levying officer will follow your instructions and proceed with a keeper or the seizure and sale of business property. He may contact you to ask you to post further fee deposits, to let you know the outcome of the levy or to tell you about any problem with the levy—for example, that the business lacks seizable assets or has moved.

If the debtor wants to object, she can file a Claim of Exemption. (See Section C4, below.) You must oppose it if you want the sale of the seized property to proceed. If the debtor doesn't file a Claim of Exemption or loses at the hearing, the levying officer will sell the property. He will notify the debtor at least ten days in advance and post other notices in the city or district, telling where and when the sale will take place.

Such sales are rare, because they are expensive to conduct and produce so little money. At this stage, the debtor is likely to work out a settlement to get the property back. Up until the actual sale, the debtor can settle with you—paying you the balance owed on the judgment, all collections costs and interest.

If the levying officer proceeds with a sale, you can attend. You can even buy the business assets without affecting your judgment. The levying officer will pay you out of the money you spend on the business. You might also use your judgment as credit in the bidding process (ask the levying officer about this). In this case, you would have to put up cash only if you bid higher than the unsatisfied amount of your judgment.

After the sale, the levying officer will turn over the proceeds to you, up to the balance of your judgment, less any fees and costs you still owe the levying officer for conducting the sale. If anything is left over, it goes back to the debtor.

4. If Inappropriate Property Is Seized

If the business is open to the public and not located in the debtor's home, the levying officer can seize just about anything he finds there. The levying officer can assume the debtor owns or is in charge of everything present, unless the debtor shows him evidence to the contrary. The officer will use his judgment in deciding if the evidence is convincing.

A debtor who wants to get back any seized property or protest the levy must file a Claim of Exemption with the levying officer within ten days, giving a reason why this property should not have been taken—for example, because the property belongs to someone else or is exempt. If a third party wants to claim ownership of property seized in the levy, it can object to the levy. If either the debtor or a third party objects to your levy, you will be notified and given an opportunity to oppose the objection. (See Chapter 15.) ■

Chapter 12

Seizing a Motor Vehicle

Collection Factors

	High	Moderate	Low
Potential cost to you	✓		
Potential for producing cash			✓
Potential for settlement		✓	
Potential time and trouble		✓	
Potential for debtor bankruptcy			✓

*Y*ou are permitted to go after a debtor's motor vehicles to satisfy a judgment. This includes a debtor's car, truck, motorcycle, boat, plane or recreational vehicle.

Motor Home Versus Mobile Home

Motor homes are considered vehicles—and can be seized using the methods in this chapter. But mobile homes are considered real property, not vehicles (see Chapter 14 for information on seizing real property). How can you tell the difference? Generally, a motor home is capable of routinely traveling the roads (it has wheels) and must be registered with the Department of Motor Vehicles (DMV). By contrast, a mobile home is usually attached to the ground permanently or semi-permanently and does not travel the roads unless it is being moved. A mobile home need not be registered with the DMV.

To the uninitiated, going after a debtor's motor vehicle to satisfy a judgment might sound like a good idea. In reality, however, forcing the sale of a motor vehicle usually nets little or no cash for the judgment creditor unless one of the following is true:

- the vehicle is valuable and the debtor has substantial equity in it—that is, the debtor owns it pretty much free and clear from loans
- you want the vehicle for your own use—if so, you can force a sale and buy the vehicle yourself, or
- you think that going after the vehicle will coerce the debtor into settling with you.

A. Limitations on Vehicle Levies

As mentioned, going after a debtor's vehicle is often fruitless. This section outlines some of the reasons why.

1. Debtor May Not Own Vehicle

If the vehicle is relatively new and in good condition, there's a good chance that the debtor still owes a bundle to a lender—such as a car dealer or bank. If so, that lender must be paid off before you. Because forced vehicle sales rarely net what the vehicle is worth, don't expect any money to be left over for you. If the debtor doesn't owe a lender on her car, it may be because she's leasing it—which means she doesn't own it. In that case, you are out of luck.

2. Vehicle May Not Be Worth Much

If the judgment debtor owns the vehicle free and clear—it's paid off and not leased—it may be an older model worth too little to warrant the cost of sale. You can find out the value of a vehicle by checking the *Kelley Blue Book*. You can find it in a library, bookstore or AAA office, or online at www.kbb.com.

3. Vehicle May Be Partially Exempt

If you seize a debtor's only motor vehicle, the debtor is automatically entitled to an exemption of $1,900. This means that after the sale, the debtor will receive $1,900 of the proceeds before you get a penny. If the debtor owns more than one vehicle, he may still be entitled to the $1,900 exemption, but he must come forward and claim it (Code of Civil Procedure § 704.010). If the debtor uses the motor vehicle in his business for more than just commuting, he may be entitled to exempt $4,000 (Code of Civil Procedure § 704.060(d)(1)). In short, you will receive cash from the sale of a motor vehicle only if the debtor's equity in the vehicle is substantially over the applicable exemption amount.

If you want to seize a boat or RV that is the debtor's principal residence, he may be entitled to claim a homestead exemption. (See Chapter 14.) If so, your chances of realizing any proceeds from a forced sale are almost nil.

4. Vehicle Will Sell for Far Less Than Value

Anyone who has sold a used vehicle knows that what it fetches depends greatly on how it is sold. For example, a car that can be sold for $5,000 through a newspaper may bring in only $2,500 as a trade-in.

Cars seized to satisfy a judgment are sold by the levying officer at an auction, which tends to bring in even less than a trade-in does. As a general rule, auctioned vehicles sell for about half of their Blue Book value.

5. Vehicle Levies Are Expensive

Seizing, storing and selling a vehicle can cost up to $1,500 or more. These costs must be deposited with the levying officer *in advance* of the levy. If the levy is unsuccessful or doesn't produce any

money, you will have thrown a lot of good money after bad—although you may be able to recover these costs if you satisfy your judgment from other assets.

EXAMPLE 1: Rory obtained a $2,100 small claims judgment against Terry. Rory had Terry's Honda Prelude seized and sold, after paying the levying officer a $1,100 deposit. At auction, the car sold for $10,000, even though its market value was probably closer to $18,000. Out of the $10,000, the legal owner of the Honda, Gulp Bank, was paid the amount still due on the note, or $7,700. Next, Terry received his $1,900 exemption, leaving $400. After deducting the costs of seizure, storage and sale ($400), the sheriff gave Rory $800 of his deposit back. Rory ended up losing $300 out of pocket as a result of the levy.

EXAMPLE 2: Joshua obtained a $5,000 judgment against Berta. Berta owned an RV which she kept at her mother's house except when she used it for vacations. Joshua did a little asking around and determined that the RV had a market value of $5,000. He had it seized and sold by the sheriff. It sold for $2,500 and the costs of seizure, storage and sale amounted to $1,000. Joshua realized $1,500 from the sale.

6. You May Need a Court Order

Normally, a vehicle can be seized only if it is in a public place, such as a street. If the debtor keeps it in a garage or other private place, you must first get a Seizure Order from the court. (See Chapter 19.)

B. How to Levy on a Vehicle

Before you can levy on a vehicle, you must obtain a Writ of Execution directed to the county where the vehicle is located. (See Chapter 7.) Don't assume that a vehicle is in the same county as the debtor's residence. Rather, find out where the vehicle is physically located—for instance, it might be in a public parking garage near where the debtor works. Once you have the Writ, follow the steps below.

1. Get Vehicle Information

To initiate a levy, you will have to provide the levying officer with a description of the vehicle, the license plate or vehicle ID number (VIN), and the approximate location of the vehicle. You will also need to make sure that the debtor is the legal owner or co-owner so you don't initiate a levy on a leased vehicle.

Here are some ways to get vehicle information:
- Debtor's Examination and Subpena Duces Tecum (Chapter 6)—to avoid arousing the debtor's suspicion, try to ask questions about the vehicle in a routine manner, not as though you are seeking to levy on it
- Debtor's Statement of Assets (Chapter 6, Section A)
- court records (Chapter 6, Section B), and
- data search firms, asset tracing firms and investigators (Chapter 23, Section C).

Another source of information is the Department of Motor Vehicles (DMV), which maintains information on all vehicles registered in California. If you send a request to the DMV for information on a registered motor vehicle, DMV will send a copy of your request to the vehicle's owner, who will have ten days to object to your request. Unless you are planning to serve the debtor with legal papers, the debtor's objection is likely to be upheld. (If you are planning to serve the debtor, see Chapter 21.)

If you decide to contact the DMV anyway, you need to complete Form INF-70R, Vehicle Registration Information Request. You can use it to request information about what cars, boats, trucks, RVs and motor homes are registered under the name of the debtor. You can also find out information about the legal owners of vehicles. This search currently costs $5.

To obtain a copy of form INF-70, visit or call a local DMV office or request a copy from DMV by calling 800-777-0133. Send the completed form and fee to DMV, Office of Information Services, Public Operations, Unit G-199, P.O. Box 944247, Sacramento, CA, 94244-2470. You can find more information at the DMV's website, at www.ca.dmv.gov.

As you complete the form, keep in mind that the DMV checks for an exact match of the name you provide. If you specify John Markford, but the judgment debtor's vehicles are registered under Jon Markford, the DMV search may turn up a blank. If the name is very common, you may want to submit several requests with variations of the debtor's full name (John P. Markford, John Paul Markford, J.P. Markford, J. Paul Markford). You must pay for each name search, however.

2. Determine Debtor's Ownership in Vehicle

Once your DMV information request is sent back to you, look on the printout for the legal owner, or L/O. The registered owner is indicated by the code R/O. If the debtor is neither the legal owner nor the registered owner, you have probably reached a dead end.

Legal Owners, Registered Owners and Lienholders

People typically purchase new vehicles by making a down payment and obtaining a loan for the balance. The lender retains legal title to the vehicle until the loan is paid off. Accordingly, when the vehicle is registered with DMV, the registration shows the purchaser as the registered owner and the lender as the legal owner. DMV records remain this way until the legal owner files a release after full payment of the loan.

Until the vehicle is paid off, the legal owner is normally entitled to repossess the vehicle if the registered owner defaults on payments. If the vehicle is sold to satisfy other debts, the legal owner is entitled to be paid the full value of the outstanding loan first. The legal owner can also ask the court to prevent the vehicle from being sold and have the property released to the registered owner.

Certain liens may have been placed on the vehicle, such as tax liens and attachment liens. These liens entitle their *lienholders* to be paid before anyone else if the car is sold—except for the legal owner, who is always paid first.

When a motor vehicle is levied on, the levying officer must send a Notice of Levy to all legal owners (if different than the judgment debtor) and to all lienholders. This notice gives the others an opportunity to protect their interests in the vehicle.

If you discover that the vehicle was very recently transferred, you may be able to seize the car from the new registered or legal owner—but only if the debtor did this to hide her assets from you. To do this you will need the help of an attorney.

a. If Debtor Isn't the Legal Owner

Often, the debtor is the registered owner of a vehicle but a bank or financing company is the legal owner. In this situation, it is extremely unlikely that you will get anything in a forced sale. The vehicle will sell for less than it's value and the legal owner must be paid before you. In addition, the debtor may be entitled to an exemption. To get a rough estimate of your chances of collecting any money, start by figuring out the low value of the car by checking the *Kelley Blue Book*. (See Section A2, above.) If you are going after a boat or plane, you can get the same type of information from dealers. If you are unable to obtain access to a used vehicles price guide, check advertised prices in the newspaper and use the lowest sales price listed for the year and type of vehicle. Now take two-thirds of the amount you came up with using either method—this represents what you can actually expect the car to go for in a forced sale.

Next, subtract the amount the debtor owes on the vehicle. You can get this information from the legal owner or from the debtor in a Debtor's Examination. (See Chapter 6.) If you have difficulty getting this information, you probably should give up right here.

If there's anything left over, subtract $1,900—the judgment debtor's personal exemption in the vehicle—and another $1,000 to cover the cost of a vehicle levy. If there is still money left over and no other liens have been placed on the vehicle, you may be one of the rare creditors who gets something from a vehicle seizure.

If there's no money to be had, you still might want to pursue this levy if you think beginning the process will force the judgment debtor into settlement, or if you want to purchase the car for yourself at a forced sale. Otherwise, don't bother.

b. If Judgment Debtor Is the Legal Owner

If the judgment debtor is the legal owner, the vehicle is paid off. Figure out the low value, take two-thirds of the amount, subtract any other liens, subtract the $1,900 exemption and $1,000 levy costs and see what's left over. If it's a positive number, you may be able to get some cash from a forced sale. Otherwise, forget it—unless you want the car for yourself or are willing to spend $1,000 in hopes of inducing a settlement.

If the legal owner is a business owned by the debtor as a sole proprietor, ask the levying officer how to proceed. Similarly, if the vehicle is jointly owned, ask the levying officer what additional documentation he needs to levy on the vehicle.

3. Provide Levying Officer With Instructions

To find the levying officer for a county, call the sheriff's office and ask if it levies on civil money judgments. If not, find out who does. Then call and find out the deposit amount required for a vehicle levy, whether the levying officer has his own instruction form, whether the vehicle must be worth a certain minimum amount and how many copies of the Writ are required.

For a car, you will need the license plate number, make and year. The vehicle identification number (VIN) helps provide positive identification, in case the license plates have been put on a different car, but it isn't required. Include the car's color and known identifying factors, such as a dent in the right rear fender, two-tone or convertible.

You also want to provide as much detail as you can about where and when the levying officer is likely to find the car. An officer can't go into a private garage unless the owner invites him in. But a vehicle on the street or in a public place is fair game. Most people park within a four block radius of their home. If you know when the debtor is likely to be home, say so in your instructions. If the debtor takes his car to work and parks it in a public parking lot, advise the officer accordingly, and give him the times when the debtor is at work.

For boats, planes, motorcycles and RVs, give the same type of identifying information, including the manufacturer, license number, color and type of vehicle or craft.

If someone other than the debtor is the legal owner or a lienholder, you must provide the levying officer with her name and address so she can be served with a Notice of Levy. The levy will be ineffective if you don't provide this information.

If the levying officer does not provide a form, use the below sample as a guide. A blank Instructions to Levying Officer form letter is in the Appendix.

Sample Letter of Instructions

May 23, 20___

Re: *Moeesha Johnson v. Jacob Cousins*

To the Sheriff, County of Mendocino:

Enclosed please find an original and ___ copies of a Writ of Execution and a check in the amount of $_____.

Please proceed to levy on (seize, store and sell) the following vehicle belonging to Jacob Cousins:

    1999 Saab 900 Turbo
    Silver with black interior
    KGOF bumper sticker
    License Number 1111ZZZZ
    Vehicle ID No. DUUUUUUUUUH999

The vehicle is almost always parked in the street in front of Jacob Cousins's place of business between the hours of 9:00 a.m. and 5:00 p.m., located at:

    Highlighter Haven
    666 Coastal Highway
    Gualala, CA

Please keep me up updated as to the status of this levy. I would like to attend the sale, so let me know when that will be.

Sincerely,

Moeesha Johnson

Moeesha Johnson

If you think the officer may have trouble finding the vehicle or the debtor may hide it, consider using a registered process server. They get paid for getting the vehicle and tend to be very creative when faced with difficulties. A private process server is likely to spend time trying to figure out where the debtor may have hidden the car and go a little further to locate it. (Information about private process servers is in Chapter 21.)

If it becomes clear that the debtor is keeping his car on property that a levying officer is not permitted to enter, your only alternative is to seek a court Seizure Order permitting an officer to enter this property. (See Chapter 19.)

4. If Debtor or Third Party Objects

After the debtor is notified of your levy, he can file a Claim of Exemption. He doesn't have to if the levy is on his only motor vehicle—he is automatically entitled to a $1,900 exemption. If he owns more than one motor vehicle, he must file a Claim of Exemption to receive the $1,900 motor vehicle or $5,000 tool of the trade exemption. The tool of the trade exemption is likely to be denied if the debtor has two cars, unless one is totally unfit for his business purposes—for example, he has a VW beetle as a second car, but needs to haul pipe for his plumbing business.

If the debtor files a Claim of Exemption, follow the procedure outlined in Chapter 15 to oppose it. There is little you can do to contest the $1,900 exemption, but that's not the case if he claims a $5,000 tool of the trade exemption and his other car is reasonably adequate for use in the business.

Third-party owners can object to the sale. If a third-party owner files a claim, and you don't oppose it by posting a deposit equal to the approximate worth of the car, the car will be released back to the debtor. As a general rule, you should oppose a third-party claim only if you are convinced you can prevail legally. You'll probably need a lawyer.

5. Attend the Sale If You Want

After you send your papers and fees to the levying officer, he will follow your instructions and proceed to seize and sell the vehicle. He may contact you to get further fee deposits, to let you know the outcome of the levy or to tell you about any problems with the levy.

Sales of vehicles and the distribution of the proceeds are governed by Code of Civil Procedure §§ 701.510-701.830. If you are contemplating buying the vehicle yourself, read these statutes to get an idea of what is involved (see Chapter 23 for more on legal research) and ask the levying officer about the specific procedures used in that county.

You and the debtor will be given notice of the time and place of the sale. The sale is conducted like an auction, with the vehicle sold to the highest bidder. As mentioned, the price normally obtained for vehicles in these auctions is far below their value. Attend if there's any chance you could use the vehicle. You may be better off buying it yourself than letting it go for an amount that most likely will get you little or nothing in satisfaction of your judgment.

If you buy the vehicle, the levying officer will pay you out of the money you spend on the vehicle. You might also use your judgment as credit in the bidding process (ask the levying officer about this) and have to put up cash only if you bid higher than the unsatisfied amount of your judgment.

6. Get Your Money

If you did not attend the sale and the levying officer has collected the proceeds of the levy, she will disburse them to you. Don't expect your money right away—delay is common. While you can call the levying officer to make sure your case hasn't fallen through the cracks, be patient. Levying officers often transmit collected funds in lump sums, rather than distributing them as they are collected.

Make sure you keep track of all money collected, as well as any costs incurred by you. We discuss how to do this in Chapter 16. ■

Chapter 13

Seizing Tangible Personal Property

Collection Factors			
	High	Moderate	Low
Potential cost to you	✓		
Potential for producing cash			✓
Potential for settlement			✓
Potential time and trouble	✓		
Potential for debtor bankruptcy			✓

➡ **Information on levying specific types of property.** Not all personal property is covered in this chapter. You might also want to look at Chapter 10 (money held by third parties on behalf of the debtor), Chapter 11 (personal property owned by a business) or Chapter 12 (motor vehicles).

*I*tems of tangible personal property are physical objects of value, such as stock certificates, bonds, cameras, stamps, coins, computers, expensive musical instruments, video equipment, stereos, jewelry, tools, recreational equipment, weapons, luxury clothing (such as a mink coat), art and precious metals. In theory, you may be able to satisfy your judgment by seizing personal property that the debtor owns and has in his possession.

But it's often in theory only. Prying personal property loose from a debtor is difficult and often not worthwhile. You face several possible obstacles, most fundamentally that the amount you'll realize from a forced sale is rarely worth the effort and expense, unless you seize items with a ready market value, such as securities, precious metals and pianos.

But if you can identify a possible source to satisfy your judgment and have tried other methods of collection without success, keep reading.

A. Limitations on Personal Property Levies

As mentioned, collecting from personal property is rarely successful. But if you are going to pursue this possibility, here are some of the problems you might face.

1. Locating Assets to Pursue

To begin, you must find out if the debtor has tangible personal property that might make this procedure worthwhile. If you don't know, you'll have to do some investigating. Here are a few suggestions:

- schedule a debtor's examination and serve a Subpena Duces Tecum (Chapter 6, Sections C and D)
- review the Judgment Debtor's Statement of Assets (Chapter 6, Section A)
- examine court records (Chapter 6, Section B), or
- hire a data search firm, asset tracing firm or investigators (Chapter 23).

Once you learn what the debtor owns, you must evaluate whether it's worth pursuing. Consider two factors:

Value at forced sale. Most personal property brings in a small fraction of its fair market value at a sale by a levying officer. For example, a dining room table that might bring $1,000 in an antique store could fetch only $250–$300 in a forced sale. The only exceptions are assets that can easily be liquidated, such as gold, gemstones, coin collections, pianos and securities (stocks, bonds, etc.).

Cost of storage and sale. The levying officer must store seized assets to give the debtor a chance to file a claim of exemption and to give notice of the sale. If a sale does occur, the cost of conducting it is substantial. In short, the costs associated with levies on personal property are significant. When these costs are deducted from the artificially low proceeds, there may be little or nothing left over to put toward the judgment.

2. Property May Be Claimed as Exempt

Debtors are allowed to keep certain items of property, called exemptions. Exemption laws attempt to strike a balance between the creditor's right to collect and the debtor's right to avoid sinking to the level of the many homeless people who haunt American cities.

Exemptions apply to property owned by individuals, not businesses. They take one of two forms: property that is fully exempt and therefore cannot be sold at all, and property that is partially exempt, so that if it is sold, the debtor is entitled to a specific amount of the proceeds before you can put the money toward your judgment. For a debtor to claim certain property as exempt, she must file a Claim of Exemption. (See Chapter 15.)

Below we list some of the exemptions for tangible personal property. Cash exemptions are covered in Chapter 8, wage exemptions in Chapter 9 and motor vehicle exemptions in Chapter 12.

Household furnishings and personal effects: The debtor is entitled to exempt all household furnishings and personal effects located at her principal residence and reasonably necessary for personal use by her or her dependents (Code of Civil Procedure § 704.020). There is no dollar limitation. A court could determine that a debtor is entitled to keep a certain item. If the court decides that a particular item is too valuable, it can allow the item to be sold and require that the debtor receive a reasonable amount from the sale to buy a replacement item. If the debtor doesn't purchase the replacement item within 90 days of the sale, the proceeds (which the court retains) are turned over to you.

Jewelry, heirlooms and works of art: The debtor is entitled to exempt up to $5,000 worth of jewelry, heirlooms and works of art (Code of Civil Procedure § 704.040). It makes little sense to seize these types of assets unless the sale will bring in considerably more than $5,000. Even then, the debtor may claim that some items of jewelry or heirlooms are personal effects, which are exempt without regard to value if they are ordinarily and reasonably necessary.

Health aids: The debtor is entitled to exempt all health aids necessary to help him work or live comfortably, such as a wheelchair (Code of Civil Procedure § 704.050).

Building materials: The debtor is entitled to exempt up to $2,000 in building supplies if they were purchased to repair her home (Code of Civil Procedure § 704.030).

Tools of the trade: The debtor is entitled to exempt up to $5,000 of tools of his trade. A tool of the trade is anything the debtor or a spouse uses to carry out a business activity, including:

- business-related equipment, such as musical instruments or cooking implements
- materials, such as paper, cloth, wood and hardware
- uniforms
- office furnishings
- books and manuals
- one commercial motor vehicle (see Chapter 12, Section A), and
- one fishing boat or other vessel used in the business.

Computer equipment needed to do desktop publishing, word processing or research also probably fits within the tools of the trade exemption. If the debtor and her spouse are in the same trade, business or profession which is also their livelihood, they are each entitled to a $5,000 tools-of-the-trade exemption, for a total exemption of $10,000 (Code of Civil Procedure § 704.060).

3. Property May Secure a Third-Party Debt

You can't, as a practical matter, reach property that is subject to a perfected security interest or to liens that have priority over yours. Chapter 4 explains liens and lien priorities.

What's a Perfected Security Interest?

A security interest in property is created when the purchaser of the property borrows money for the purchase and gives the lender title to the property until the loan is paid off. This arrangement is common in purchases of expensive equipment, jewelry and household furniture.

For the lender to assert her rights to the property as title owner, she must "perfect" her title by registering it with the California Secretary of State. Once a security interest is perfected, the security interest owner can prevent others (including you as a judgment creditor) from seizing the property until the loan has been paid and the security interest released.

We recommend that you check to see whether property is subject to a security interest before instructing a levying officer to seize and sell it. You can find out by checking with the Secretary of State, who keeps a record of all perfected security interests. We discuss this in Chapter 4, Section B2. Or, you can pay a data search firm to do it for you. (See Chapter 23, Section C.)

What happens if you levy on property that is subject to a third-party security interest? If the third party learns of the proposed sale before it happens, he can file a third-party claim of ownership to stop the sale. If he learns of the sale after it has occurred, he can file a claim to get paid what the debtor owes him out of the proceeds of the sale. If you have spent the proceeds, he can sue you for the value of the property or try to

have property seized, in which case the purchaser would come after you. And you could be liable for any costs the third party spent in his efforts to collect.

4. Property May Be Subject to an Examination Lien

If another judgment creditor has served the debtor with notice of a debtor's examination, all her personal property is automatically subject to a one-year examination lien. (See Chapter 4, Section C.) If you attempt to levy on property subject to such a lien, the fruits of your effort may end up in the lienholder's basket.

If you think that other creditors have judgments against the debtor, check the court records for each county in which a creditor may have conducted a debtor's examination. (See Chapter 4, Section C.) If you locate a judgment against the debtor, examine the file for a Proof of Service for an Application and Order for Appearance and Examination. If you find one that was served within the past year, all the judgment debtor's personal property is subject to that lien until one year from the date of service. In such a situation, you can either proceed with your levy and hope that the other lienholder won't find out about it or you can wait until the lien expires to go after the assets.

Checking for Other Creditors. Records from other court cases may give you an idea of which previous attempts to collect have worked and which have not. These records can steer you away from an asset that a previous creditor couldn't reach because it was exempt or because it subject to a perfected security interest held by a third party.

You might also find out about other creditors' collection attempts from the levying officer where the debtor or her assets are located. It makes sense to find out if there are other active creditors, because levying officers must levy on writs in the order received.

5. Property May Be Owned With Spouse

In general, you can seize a married debtor's separate property and the couple's community property, but you usually cannot go after the separate property of a non-debtor spouse. (See Chapter 1, Section D.)

Without a complete history of a how an item of property was obtained—for example, by one spouse before the marriage, by the couple during the marriage or by one spouse during the marriage through inheritance—you have no idea which partner owns the property or if it's owned by both. So how should you proceed? Go after the property and force the debtor or her spouse to prove that the property is the separate property of the non-debtor spouse.

B. How to Levy on Personal Property

Before you can levy on personal property, you must obtain a Writ of Execution directed to the county where the property is located—that is, where the debtor lives. (See Chapter 7.) Then follow these steps.

1. Obtain Seizure Order for Assets in Debtor's Home

For property located inside the debtor's house or another private location, such as the back yard, you'll need a court order permitting the levying officer to enter. To obtain such a Seizure Order, you must tell the judge what you expect to find. (See Chapter 19.) The judge will not allow the levying officer to go on a fishing expedition in search of any and all property that's not nailed down.

Even if the levying officer is willing attempt a levy without a court order—and knows to stop if the debtor refuses to allow him inside—we recommend that you get the court order first. If the debtor refuses to let the officer in, the debtor will have time to move her property while you're busy getting the Seizure Order.

2. Provide Levying Officer With Instructions

To find the levying officer for a county, call the sheriff's office and ask if it levies on civil money judgments. If not, find out who does. Then call and find out the deposit amount required for a personal property levy (you may have to put down a few hundred dollars), whether the levying officer has her own instruction form and how many copies of the Writ are required.

If the levying officer does not provide a form, use the sample below as a guide. A blank Instructions to Levying Officer form letter is in the Appendix.

Sample Letter of Instructions

May 30, 20____

Re: Gary Dekka v. Daniel Acorn

To the Sheriff, County of Solano:

Enclosed please find an original and ____ copies of a Writ of Execution, a certified copy of a Seizure Order and a check in the amount of $_____.

Please proceed to levy on (seize, store and sell) the following tangible personal property of Daniel Acorn, located in his home at 349 Mission Street, Vallejo, California:

a. Original signed lithograph set by artist DeChing

b. Camera equipment

c. Mink coat (kept in hall closet)

d. Antique bedroom set (in guest bedroom)

e. Coin collection (kept in Daniel Acorn's study)

f. Steinway baby grand piano.

Please keep me updated as to the status of this levy. I would like to attend the sale, so let me know when it will be. Thank you.

Sincerely,

Gary Dekka

Gary Dekka

After receiving your instructions, the levying officer fills out a Notice of Levy, which he serves personally on the judgment debtor. The Notice of Levy identifies the property to be levied on and the amount necessary to satisfy the judgment.

3. If Debtor or Third Party Objects

When the debtor receives a Notice of Levy, she has ten days to object. To do so, she must file a Claim of Exemption explaining why she believes that certain items identified in the Notice of Levy are exempt. She must also cite the section of the Code of Civil Procedure that permits the exemption.

If the debtor files a Claim of Exemption, the levying officer will serve you with a copy of it and a Notice of Claim of Exemption. Unless you oppose the Claim of Exemption, the debtor's property will be returned to her. Instructions for opposing a Claim of Exemption are in Chapter 15.

A third party who learns about the levy may object on any of the following grounds:

- the debtor is storing the property for him
- the debtor has the property on consignment
- the debtor borrowed the property from him
- the debtor has already sold or signed over the property to him, or
- the debtor pledged the property as security for a loan.

If a third party files a claim, the procedure for opposing it is similar to opposing a debtor's Claim of Exemption. If the amount of your judgment justifies getting legal help to pursue this, then by all means do so. Usually, however, you are better off dropping the matter.

4. Attend Sale If You Want

The levying officer posts a notice of sale and serves the notice on the debtor either personally or by mail. The notice states the date, time and place of the sale and describes the property. The notice must be posted in three public places in the city or judicial district where the property is to be sold.

The property is sold at an auction to the highest bidder (Code of Civil Procedure § 701.570(b),(d)). If you want the property yourself, you can use the judgment as a credit against your bid (Code of Civil Procedure § 701.590(b)), but you'll need cash or a certified check to pay for a bid higher than the amount of your judgment. Call the levying officer and find out more about the auction and your options as a judgment creditor.

The levying officer distributes the sale proceeds as required by law. Your share of these proceeds depends on the total fees due the levying officer (Code of Civil Procedure § 687.050), applicable exemptions, the claims of third-party owners who must be paid and the priorities of any other creditors with claims.

5. Get Your Money

If you did not attend the sale and the levying officer has collected the proceeds of the levy, she will disburse them to you. Don't expect your money right away—delay is common. While you can call the levying officer to make sure your case hasn't fallen through the cracks, be patient. Levying officers often transmit collected funds in lump sums, rather than distributing them as they are collected.

Make sure you keep track of all money collected, as well as any costs incurred by you. We discuss how to do this in Chapter 16. ■

Chapter 14

Seizing Real Estate

Collection Factors			
	High	**Moderate**	**Low**
Potential cost to you			✓
Potential for producing cash		✓	
Potential for settlement	✓		
Potential time and trouble	✓		
Potential for debtor bankruptcy			✓

*I*n Chapter 4, we explained liens—what they are and how to obtain them. As soon as you get your judgment, you should record a lien in any county in which the debtor owns or is likely to own real estate.

Collecting on a real estate lien is usually a passive act—most people wait until the debtor (owner of the real estate) refinances or sells the property, then the lien is paid out of escrow.

You can also take a more active approach, by forcing the sale of the debtor's real estate in order to get paid out of the proceeds, but few judgment debtors undertake this procedure. Seizing real estate is expensive, time-consuming and cumbersome, and usually requires a lawyer's help.

This chapter does not take you step by step through the process. It does give you a broad overview of what's involved, however, as well as guidance to get you started. If you decide to force the sale of the property, you will need to hire a lawyer. By initiating the process, however, you may get the debtor's attention—and get her to pay your judgment before you have to do anything drastic.

A. Limitations on Real Estate Levies

In addition to the expense, time and burden of the process, you may face several other obstacles in seizing real estate.

- The debtor probably owes a first mortgage and possible a second or third. These debts must be paid out of the sale before you get anything.
- If the real estate is the debtor's home, exemption laws entitle her to keep between $50,000 to $125,000 of the proceeds of the sale, before you get a penny.
- The property may be subject to liens ahead of your lien, such as tax liens, mechanics' liens or other judgment liens. These creditors will be paid before you.
- In a forced sale, real estate usually sells for less than its market value. Partly because of the scavenging nature of the process, forced sales often bring in less than what the property would fetch if sold conventionally.
- If the real estate is someone else's dwelling —for example, the debtor rents out the property—you must obtain a special order of sale, which is a fairly complex court proceeding.
- The cost of selling real estate eats up a chunk of the eventual proceeds.

B. Finding Debtor's Real Estate

If you don't know what real estate the debtor owns, the methods outlined in Chapter 6 may help you find out. In addition, you may be able to use the following sources to get that information.

1. County Tax Assessor's Records

Each county tax assessor's office has records of the owner of every piece of real estate in the county. You can look up the debtor—check under the spouse's name and any business names as well. The records won't tell you whether the debtor owns the property alone or with someone else, but it's easy to find that out by looking at the deed (Section B2, below).

You can also use the records to discover the name of the owner of a certain piece of property, if you have the property's address. If the debtor rents, you can find out the name of his landlord, who may give you useful information.

The tax assessor's records also include the address where the assessor mails the owner's tax bills. If it's different from the property address, it may help you serve the debtor with court papers—and lead you to another piece of property to satisfy your judgment.

Some assessors' offices give out information by phone. If not, you can visit or write the office. If you write, you can use our sample letter below. There should be no fee for this information, but enclose a self-addressed, stamped envelope with your request.

Sample Letter to Assessor

July 24, 20___

Assessor's Office, County of Los Angeles

Dear Assessor:

Please provide me with the following information:

1. Regarding the property located at 33902 Winding Road, Los Angeles, California 90000: the names and addresses of the current owners of record, the Assessor's Parcel Number and the date the property was acquired.

2. Whether or not Paige Ido owns any property in Los Angeles. If so, please indicate, for each property, the date the property was acquired, the property address and Assessor's Parcel Number.

Enclosed is a self-addressed, stamped envelope for the return of this information. Thank you for your assistance.

Sincerely,

Frank Slay

Frank Slay

2. County Recorder's Office

The County Recorder's Office is where the deed and other security interests are recorded. When you obtained your real estate lien (Chapter 4), you recorded it at the county recorder's office. These are public records that you'll have to search in person. Here's what you'll find.

- The names of all the owners of the property. If the debtor owns the property with someone else, your judgment lien might attach only to the debtor's share. But if the debtor and a spouse own the home as community property or in joint tenancy, you will probably be entitled to reach both spouses' shares. (See Chapter 1, Section D4.)
- Whether the debtor owes money to a bank, mortgage lender, the seller or anyone else who provided the funding to purchase the property.
- Other creditors and lienholders who have an interest in the property—lenders with a second or third mortgage or home equity loan, other judgment creditors, taxing authorities and the like.
- Any filed Declaration of Homestead, which might provide the debtor with a substantial exemption, even if she is not currently living in the house. (See Section C2.)

Deeds are usually indexed by the name of the owners. The indexes are generally alphabetical, and cover a certain number of years. So you may need to check several printouts or microfiche cards to locate all property listings for a debtor for a given 20-year period. When you visit the County Recorder's Office, ask for help finding the information you need.

3. Title Companies

Another way to find out where the judgment debtor owns property is to contact a title company. Title companies provide a large range of services to buyers and sellers of real estate, such as title searches, title insurance and escrow transactions.

Many title companies have an alphabetical listing of property owners. While some title companies have access to the entire list, including listings in every county, many have listings only for their area. This means you may have to check with title companies in several counties if you suspect the debtor has property in more than one place.

Title companies may have more detailed information—often called a property profile—on a particular piece of property. Besides listing the owner of record, a profile may include additional information of use to you, such as:

- the year the deed was recorded
- the owner's mailing address
- the assessed value of the property
- the estimated total value of the property
- the value of any existing mortgage
- the amount of taxes assessed, whether taxes have been paid and to whom the tax bill was sent, and
- a copy of the last deed and latest open deed of trust.

Title companies vary in their willingness to give out information. Some let you come in and look through their records. Others give out some information over the phone if you give them an address or the name of a property owner. Still others don't give any information to the public. Check with title companies in your area; you can find them listed in the Yellow Pages. When you call, ask to speak to customer service or an escrow officer.

4. Data Search Firms

For under $50, you can usually find a data search firm to conduct a statewide search for real estate owned by the judgment debtor. In many instances, it is worth your while to have one of these companies do your search rather than do it yourself. We discuss data search firms in Chapter 23, Section C.

C. Forcing a Sale of Property

As mentioned, forcing the sale of real estate is time-consuming and expensive, and will probably require the help of a lawyer. Here is some information to help you determine whether a forced sale appears worthwhile and, if so, how to start the process on your own.

1. Is It Economically Worthwhile?

Before levying against real estate, you want to figure out whether there is sufficient equity in the property to justify the effort. Equity is the amount of the debtor's share left over after all mortgages, liens and security interests are subtracted from the property's likely sales price. If the likely sales price is $270,000 and the debtor owes $210,000, her equity is $60,000.

2. Does a Homestead Exemption Apply?

Next, find out whether the property is covered by the California homestead exemption. The general rule is that a primary residence—be it a house, condo, boat or mobile home—qualifies for a homestead exemption, but other real estate does not (Code of Civil Procedure § 704.710(c)). If the debtor has filed a Declaration of Homestead on the property (Section B2, above), residential real estate owned by the debtor but rented out to a third party is also protected by the homestead exemption.

> EXAMPLE: Dewevai and Andrenae, a married couple, record a Declaration of Homestead on their home in Petaluma. Two years later, they decide to rent the house out to someone else and buy a new home in Santa Rosa. They decide to maintain the homestead on the Petaluma home, so they don't record a new Declaration of Homestead on the Santa Rosa home. Dewevai and Andrenae can claim the homestead exemption in the Petaluma home (the one covered by the Declaration of Homestead) but not in the Santa Rosa home.

If the property is the debtor's primary residence or is rented out with a Declaration of Homestead on file, it makes no sense to force a sale unless the sale would yield an amount above the exemption amount. In a forced sale, the homeowner (judgment debtor) receives the amount of the homestead exemption before the judgment creditor gets anything. So after you figure out the equity (Section C1, above) and subtract the cost of sale, subtract the appropriate homestead exemption amount, as follows:

- $50,000 if the debtor is unmarried
- $75,000 if the debtor is married
- $125,000 if the debtor is 65 or older or disabled, or
- $125,000 if the debtor is 55 or older, and either single and earning under $15,000 per year or married and earning under $20,000 per year.

Most judgment debtors have less equity in their homes than the amount protected by the homestead exemption. That means that it doesn't ordinarily make sense to force the sale of a home occupied by the debtor.

You could lose a lot of money. If you attempt to force a sale but no bid comes in that is sufficient to pay off the mortgages, liens, costs of sale and homestead exemption, you will not be able to recover your costs from the judgment debtor. In short, you will lose money if you unsuccessfully levy on property covered by a homestead exemption (Code of Civil Procedure § 704.840).

3. Sale Procedures

As mentioned earlier, you will probably need a lawyer's help if you really want to force the sale of the debtor's real estate. Before calling a lawyer, you might want to become familiar with the laws governing real estate levies. In a law library or on the Internet, you'll want to read California Code of Civil Procedure § 700.015 and §§ 701.540 through 701.680. If the real estate is a dwelling, you also will want to read §§ 704.710 through 704.850. (See Chapter 23 for more information on doing research.)

Here are the basic steps you'll have to take to force a sale when the property is a dwelling. If the property is not a dwelling, court hearings are not required.

Step 1: Obtain a Writ of Execution. (See Chapter 7.)

Step 2: Prepare written instructions for the levying officer. To find the levying officer for a county, call the sheriff's office and ask if it levies on civil money judgments. If not, find out who does. Then call and find out the deposit amount required for a real estate levy, whether the levying officer has his own instruction form, what documents you must provide with your levy instructions and how many copies of each document are required.

Step 3: Deliver the required papers and deposit to the levying officer.

Step 4: The levying officer serves the Writ of Execution and Notice of Levy on the judgment debtor.

Step 5: Within 30 days after Notice of Levy is served on judgment debtor, you must give the levying officer a list of all those holding a mortgage, lien or security interest on the property. (See Section B above.)

Step 6: You must file a formal motion in the county where the property is located, post notice of the motion and obtain an Order of Sale within 20 days after the Notice of Levy was served on the debtor.

Step 7: The court sets a hearing date within 45 days after the motion is filed and issues an Order to Show Cause, which requires the debtor to explain why the property shouldn't be sold.

How to Obtain an Order of Sale

Before you obtain an Order of Sale, you must get the property independently appraised, obtain a title report that reflects all mortgages, liens and other security interests and determine whether the home is subject to a homestead exemption.

Senior liens are those that were created before yours or receive priority by law, such as tax liens. Junior liens are liens created after yours. When property subject to liens is forcibly sold, senior liens are paid off first; junior liens are only paid if there is enough left over. After the forced sale, all liens are extinguished except for federal and state tax liens.

Step 8: Have the Order to Show Cause and certain other papers served on the debtor and occupants of the dwelling within 30 days of the scheduled hearing.

Step 9: If the debtor doesn't attend the hearing, she is entitled to request a second hearing.

Step 10: At the hearing, the court determines and issues an order stating the amount of any homestead exemption, the fair market value of the property and the amount of sale proceeds that must be distributed to cover all mortgages, liens and other security interests.

Step 11: The levying officer holds a sale no sooner than 120 days after the Notice of Levy was served, after giving notice to the judgment debtor, occupants of the dwelling, and all mortgage, lien and other security interest holders at least 20 days before the sale. The notice states the date, time and place of sale and the address and a description of the property. The property may be sold only if the winning bid is at least 90% of the property's fair market value. If no adequate bid is received, the court can order a new sale one year or more later.

■

Chapter 15

Opposing a Claim of Exemption

*I*f you seek to empty the debtor's bank accounts, garnish her wages, seize money or property owed her or seize her motor vehicle or other personal property, she can formally protest by filing a Claim of Exemption. You can object to the Claim of Exemption if you feel that the property is not exempt or is not necessary for the debtor's support.

There are two different procedures to object to a Claim of Exemption. One is used to garnish wages, the other to seize money (other than wages) or property.

A. Wage Garnishment

The debtor can contest your wage garnishment by filing a Claim of Exemption form with the levying officer. On the form, the debtor must state that she is contesting the wage garnishment and give her reasons. When the officer receives the Claim of Exemption, he will mail you a copy, along with a financial statement completed by the debtor and a document called Notice of Filing of Claim of Exemption (Wage Garnishment).

Only about 15% of all debtors file a Claim of Exemption to protest a wage garnishment. If your debtor decides to join this minority, however, the ball is in your court. Unless you oppose the claim, your Earnings Withholding Order (see Chapter 9) will automatically terminate or be modified to reflect any amount the debtor indicated she could pay.

1. Opposing a Claim of Exemption

You must file your notice of opposition to the Claim of Exemption with the levying officer and the court within *ten days* of when the Notice of Filing of Claim of Exemption was mailed. That date is on the form. This means you may have only a few days to respond to the Notice after you receive it.

People in the collections business quickly learn whether or not it makes sense to oppose a Claim of Exemption. They examine the financial statement for any of the following items:

- an expense that seems out of line, such as $400 for utilities
- an expense that should not be as high a priority as your judgment, for example, large payments on an expensive or second car, or
- omitted income or assets.

If you find any of these, your opposition to the debtor's Claim of Exemption may very well succeed. Similarly, if the debtor's income is well above the poverty level, the Claim of Exemption is not likely to win. On the other hand, if the debtor's financial statement appears reasonable and the debt does not fall into one of exceptions listed under the instructions for item 5 in Section 2, below, you may want to think compromise.

If you decide to oppose the debtor's Claim of Exemption, first read the "Instructions to Judgment Creditor" on the Notice of Filing of Claim of Exemption form.

Next, make five copies of the Notice of Opposition to Claim of Exemption (Wage Garnishment) and Notice of Hearing on Claim of Exemption, which are in the Appendix. Fill out these forms (see Sections A2 and A3, below) and file them with the clerk of the court and with the levying officer within ten days of the mailing date listed on the Notice. If you miss this deadline, your wage garnishment will be terminated—or modified, if the debtor asked only for a modification.

2. Completing the Notice of Opposition to Claim of Exemption

A completed sample and instructions are below; a blank copy is in the Appendix.

Caption: Follow the format of your previous court papers. Be sure to enter the levying officer's file number, which is on the Claim of Exemption you received.

Item 1: Enter your name and address.

Notice of Opposition to Claim of Exemption (Wage Garnishment)

ATTORNEY OR PARTY WITHOUT ATTORNEY *(Name and Address)*:	TELEPHONE NO.:	FOR COURT USE ONLY
Mandu Saarni 808 Winterside Court Palm Springs, CA 92260	760-555-8816	

ATTORNEY FOR *(Name)*: In Pro Per

NAME OF COURT, JUDICIAL DISTRICT OR BRANCH COURT, IF ANY:
Superior Court of California, Riverside County

PLAINTIFF: Mandu Saarni

DEFENDANT: Ponga McCoy

NOTICE OF OPPOSITION TO CLAIM OF EXEMPTION (Wage Garnishment)	LEVYING OFFICER FILE NO.: 123-45	COURT CASE NO.: 00-0101

TO THE LEVYING OFFICER:

1. Name and address of judgment creditor

   Mandu Saarni
   808 Winterside Court
   Palm Springs, CA 92260

2. Name and address of employee

   Ponga McCoy
   Ping-Pong Game Shop
   12 Crestview Terrace
   Palm Springs, CA 92260

   Social Security Number *(if known)*:

3. The Notice of Filing Claim of Exemption states it was mailed on
   (date): March 22, 20XX

4. The earnings claimed as exempt are
   a. ☐ not exempt.
   b. ☒ partially exempt. The amount *not* exempt per month is
   $ 875

5. The judgment creditor opposes the claim of exemption because
   a. ☐ the judgment was for the following common necessaries of life *(specify)*:

   b. ☒ the following expenses of the debtor are *not* necessary for the support of the debtor or the debtor's family *(specify)*:
   $1,000   toward house payments are paid by tenants
   $250   clothing excessive
   $85   laundry excessive
   $125   entertainment excessive
   c. ☐ other *(specify)*:

6. ☒ The judgment creditor will accept $ 500   per pay period for payment on account of this debt.

I declare under penalty of perjury under the laws of the State of California that the foregoing is true and correct.

Date: March 26, 20XX

Mandu Saarni	▶	*Mandu Saarni*
(TYPE OR PRINT NAME)		*(SIGNATURE OF DECLARANT)*

Form Adopted by the
Judicial Council of California
982.5(7) [Rev. July 1, 1983]

NOTICE OF OPPOSITION TO CLAIM OF EXEMPTION
(Wage Garnishment)

WEST GROUP
Official Publisher

CCP 706.128

Item 2: Enter the name and address of the debtor, and his Social Security number if you know it. It may be listed on the Employer's Return or the Claim of Exemption.

Item 3: Enter the date the Notice of Filing of Claim of Exemption was mailed. It should be in Item 1 on that form.

Item 4: Check a if you think none of the debtor's wages are exempt. Check b if you think only a portion of the wages is exempt.

Item 5: Check a, b, and/or c and elaborate as follows:

- **Item 5a:** The debtor cannot claim that her wages are exempt from collecting a judgment if the debt is for necessaries of life—shelter, food, utilities or medical care (Code of Civil Procedure § 706.051(c)(1)). For example, if you are a doctor who provided medical services to the debtor and then obtained a money judgment for your services, the debtor cannot exempt her wages from you.

- **Item 5b:** If neither 5a nor 5c apply, you want to argue that the garnishment won't prevent the debtor from adequately supporting her family. If the debtor is claiming unusual or dubious expenses, or is reserving an unreasonably high amount for living expenses, list those items here.

- **Item 5c:** The debtor cannot claim that her wages are exempt from collecting a judgment based on personal services you rendered the debtor as her employee (Code of Civil Procedure § 706.051(c)(2)). For instance, if you worked in the debtor's shop and obtained a judgment against her for back pay, she cannot exempt her wages from you. Nor can the debtor exempt her wages if your judgment is for child or spousal support (Code of Civil Procedure § 706.051(c)(3)). Other possible grounds to oppose include the debtor lying about her financial obligations or assets. If you need more room, add an attachment sheet.

Item 6: Put the amount of payment per pay period (listed on the Employer's Return) you are willing to accept.

At the end, enter the date and your name, and then sign the form.

3. Completing the Notice of Hearing on Claim of Exemption

A completed sample and instructions are below; a blank copy is in the Appendix.

Caption: Follow the format of your previous court papers. Be sure to enter the levying officer's file number.

Item 1: Enter the levying officer's name and address. Then enter the name and address of the debtor. Fill out the box for a claimant other than the judgment debtor only if you sought an Earnings Withholding Order against the spouse of the judgment debtor, a procedure that is beyond the scope of this book. Check the last box and fill in the name and address if the judgment debtor has an attorney representing her.

Item 2: Check "judgment debtor."

Item 2a: Call the court clerk for a hearing date, time and location, and enter them here. The hearing must be held within 30 days of the date you file your papers with the court. The clerk is likely to give you several alternative dates within the 30-day period.

Item 2b: Enter the address of the court.

Item 3: Check this box only if you don't intend to be at the hearing in person. We recommend that you do attend. If you can't be there, prepare a declaration on lined paper and attach it to your opposition forms. Explain why you won't be there and why you believe the Claim of Exemption should be denied—for instance, you know the debtor has other sources of income which she didn't state on her form. An example of a declaration is shown below.

Finally, enter the date and your name, and sign the form. Leave the Proof of Service on the back blank for now.

Notice of Hearing on Claim of Exemption

ATTORNEY OR PARTY WITHOUT ATTORNEY (Name and Address):	TELEPHONE NO.:	FOR COURT USE ONLY
Mandu Saarni 808 Winterside Court Palm Springs, CA 92260	760-555-8816	

ATTORNEY FOR (Name): In Pro Per

NAME OF COURT, JUDICIAL DISTRICT OR BRANCH COURT, IF ANY:
Superior Court of California, Riverside County

PLAINTIFF: Mandu Saarni

DEFENDANT: Ponga McCoy

NOTICE OF HEARING ON CLAIM OF EXEMPTION (Wage Garnishment—Enforcement of Judgment)	LEVYING OFFICER FILE NO.: 123-45	COURT CASE NO.: 00-0101

1. TO:

Name and address of levying officer	Name and address of judgment debtor
M. Levoff Riverside Sheriff 4075 Main Street Riverside, CA 922501	Ponga McCoy 63004 Abba Place Palm Desert, CA 92260

☐ Claimant, if other than judgment debtor (name and address):

☐ Judgment debtor's attorney (name and address):

2. **A hearing to determine the claim of exemption of**
   ☒ judgment debtor
   ☐ other claimant
   will be held as follows:

   a. date: April 10, 20XX   time: 10 am   ☒ dept.: 200 ☐ div.:   ☐ rm.: 200

   b. address of court: 3255 Tahquitz Canyon Way
   Palm Springs, CA 92262

3. ☐ The judgment creditor will not appear at the hearing and submits the issue on the papers filed with the court.

Date: March 26, 20XX

Mandu Saarni
....
(TYPE OR PRINT NAME)

▶ *Mandu Saarni*
(SIGNATURE OF JUDGMENT CREDITOR OR ATTORNEY)

If you do not attend the hearing, the court may determine your claim based on the Claim of Exemption, Financial Statement (when one is required), Notice of Opposition to Claim of Exemption, and other evidence that may be presented.

(Proof of service on reverse)

Form Adopted by the Judicial Council of California 982.5(8), EJ-175 [Rev. July 1, 1983]	NOTICE OF HEARING ON CLAIM OF EXEMPTION (Wage Garnishment—Enforcement of Judgment)	WEST GROUP Official Publisher	CCP 703.550, 706.105

Sample Declaration
Opposing Claim of Exemption

I, Mandu Saarni, declare as follows:

1. I obtained a judgment against Ponga McCoy from the Riverside Superior Court on September 10, 20____, in case #0000-0005.

2. The balance due on the judgment is $10,500, plus accrued interest and post-judgment costs.

3. On March 1, 20____, I sent instructions to the Riverside Sheriff for a wage garnishment of Ponga McCoy. On March 22, 20____, a Notice of Filing of Claim of Exemption was sent to me.

4. I cannot attend the Hearing on Claim of Exemption which is scheduled for April 10, 20____. I will be in Washington, D.C. for business during the second half of April.

5. In Ponga McCoy's Financial Statement, she indicates that she pays $1,500 in house payments. I am informed and believe that this is not true, but that she personally only pays $500 in house payments and receives $1,000 from two tenants each month. Ponga McCoy did not claim this $1,000 per month income in her Financial Statement.

6. Ponga McCoy claims that she needs $250 per month for clothing, $85 per month for laundry and cleaning, and $125 per month for entertainment. I believe that these expenses are excessive and unnecessary, and she should use those sums to pay off the judgment in this case.

I declare under penalty of perjury under the laws of the State of California that the foregoing is true and correct.

Dated: _____

Mandu Saarni
Mandu Saarni

4. Serve and File the Opposition Papers

You must serve the papers on the debtor and file them with the court. Your response must be served on the debtor at least 21 days before the hearing date—26 days if service is by mail (Code of Civil Procedure § 1005(b)). You can have these papers served on the judgment debtor by mail or personally. In most cases, mail is the easiest and least expensive approach, as long as it allows the debtor enough notice of the hearing date.

Either way, don't delay in serving the forms. Once they are served, you must file the forms with the court—and that filing must take place within ten days from the mailing date of the Notice of Filing of Claim of Exemption. Here's how to proceed:

1. Make at least four copies of your documents. One is for your records, another is for the levying officer, a third is for the court and a fourth is for the judgment debtor. If there is an additional claimant (such as the debtor's employer), make an extra copy.

2. Have a set served on the judgment debtor, or his attorney if he has one. Service by mail and personal service are explained in Chapter 21. Be sure whoever serves the papers completes the Proof of Service form on the back of the Notice of Hearing form.

3. Within the ten-day deadline, give or send (by overnight mail) the levying officer the original Notice of Opposition to Claim of Exemption (the one with your original signature) and a copy of the Notice of Hearing on Claim of Exemption.

4. Also within the ten-day deadline, file with the clerk of the court the original Notice of Hearing on Claim of Exemption form, a copy of the Notice of Opposition to Claim of Exemption stapled to Notice form and the original Proof of Service.

5. Attend Hearing

If you attend the hearing, review your argument the day before. On the day of the hearing, try to get to the courtroom a little early. At the entrance, there may be a bulletin board with a list of the cases to be heard that day. If your case isn't listed, check with the clerk.

Step forward when your case is called. Be prepared to answer the judge's questions. Call the judge "Your Honor" and don't interrupt the debtor, even if you disagree with what she says. The judge will give you a chance to state your disagreement. Be prepared for the judge to try to get you and the debtor to compromise. While you are entitled to remain adamant and go for it all, that attitude may lead the judge to decide for the debtor.

Understand that judges have almost complete discretion in deciding when a debtor is entitled to exempt his wages, and how much. Many judges sympathize with debtors and take their side if a creditor comes across as hard-nosed. So if the debtor offers to have less than 25% withheld, whatever the reason, it might be worthwhile to accept her offer. Judges often persuade the parties to compromise. Some judges take this opportunity to pressure the judgment debtor to agree to voluntarily pay a substantial portion of the judgment in installments. Then, the judge amends the judgment to make it an installment judgment (Code of Civil Procedure § 582.5).

If the court decides in your favor, the wage garnishment will go forward. If the judge decides that your Earnings Withholding Order should be modified or terminated, the clerk will send the judge's order to the levying officer, who will notify the employer. In either instance, you will soon receive a notice, called an Order Determining the Claim of Exemption, of what the court has decided.

If you lose the hearing on the Claim of Exemption, you can try another wage garnishment as soon as you can establish a material change of circumstance in the debtor's situation. For example, you could try again if the debtor gets a new and job or a promotion. If the debtor's situation remains the same, you can try again either 60 days after the termination of the previous garnishment order or 100 days after the previous garnishment order was first served, whichever date is later (Code of Civil Procedure § 706.105(h)).

Either you or the debtor can appeal the judge's decision on the Claim of Exemption. In the meantime, the judge's order is in effect. If you lose and appeal, the exemption is allowed while your appeal is pending. If the debtor loses, appeals and wins on appeal, any money you have collected from the garnishment will have to be returned to the debtor.

Appeals are time-consuming, and few are granted. We recommend against appealing if you lose. It is much easier to simply wait a while and try again. Similarly, the debtor is unlikely to appeal.

B. Property Seizure

The debtor can contest your property seizure by filing a Claim of Exemption form with the levying officer. On the form, the debtor must state that he is contesting the seizure because he believes the property is exempt. When the officer receives the Claim of Exemption, he will mail you a copy along with a document called Notice of Filing of Claim of Exemption.

Only about 15% of all debtors file a Claim of Exemption to protest a property seizure. If your debtor does, however, the burden is on you to oppose it. If you don't oppose the claim, your Writ of Execution will automatically terminate.

1. Opposing a Claim of Exemption

You must file your Notice of Opposition to the Claim of Exemption (Enforcement of Judgment) with the levying officer and the court within ten days after the Notice of Claim of Exemption was personally served on you, or within 15 days after the Notice of Claim of Exemption was mailed to you, if notice was sent by mail to an address in

California. This means you may have only a few days to respond to the Notice after you receive it (Code of Civil Procedure §§ 703.550, 684.120).

If you decide to oppose the debtor's Claim of Exemption, first read the "Instructions to Judgment Creditor" on the Notice of Filing of Claim of Exemption form.

Next, make five copies of the Notice of Opposition to Claim of Exemption (Enforcement of Judgment) and Notice of Hearing on Claim of Exemption, which are in the Appendix. Fill out these forms (see Sections B2 and B3, below) and file them with the clerk of the court and with the levying officer within the ten- or 15-day deadline. If you miss the deadline, your Writ will be terminated.

2. Completing the Notice of Opposition to Claim of Exemption

A completed sample and instructions are below; a blank copy is in the Appendix.

Caption: Follow the format of your previous court papers. Be sure to enter the levying officer's file number, which you can find on the Claim of Exemption you received.

Item 1: Enter your name and address.

Item 2: Enter the name and address of the debtor, and his Social Security number if you know it.

Item 3: Skip this unless someone other than the debtor made the Claim of Exemption. This might occur if you have levied on property in the debtor's possession that belongs to someone else.

Item 4: Enter the date the Notice of Filing of Claim of Exemption was mailed. You can find it in Item 1 on that form.

Item 5: Check a, b, and/or c and elaborate as follows:

- **Item 5a:** The debtor cannot claim an exemption to which she is not entitled. (See Chapter 13, Section A2, for information on exemptions.) For instance, assume the debtor is claiming that her camera equipment is

exempt as tools of the trade. You can object if she is employed full-time in another capacity and photography is only a hobby.

- **Item 5b:** The debtor cannot claim an exemption if the equity in the property is greater than the amount allowed by the exemption. For example, let's say the debtor claims his works of art as exempt for the allowable amount of $5,000. You know he has paintings in his home and office and believe they are worth much more. Obviously, it is difficult to contradict a debtor's statement as to the value of his property. Your argument is likely to prevail only if the property's value is obviously much greater than the amount claimed.
- **Item 5c:** Add any other reasons you believe the debtor's claim of exemption should be denied, such as the debtor's false statements.

Item 6: Check the first box if you need extra room to elaborate on your reasons in Item 5. Then attach a signed declaration, setting out your reasons. (We've included a sample declaration, below.) Check the second box if you can set out your facts in the space provided. Then add whatever information supports your position from Item 5.

Finally, date the form, type or print your name and sign it.

3. Completing the Notice of Hearing on Claim of Exemption

Use the instructions for Section A3, above, with the following modifications:

Item 1: Fill in any third-party claimant.

Item 2a: The hearing must be held within 20 days of the date you file your opposition papers with the court. You must have the debtor served at least 15 days before the hearing, if service is by mail, or ten days before, if service is personal.

Item 3: If you do not plan on attending the hearing, see the sample declaration below to attach to your papers.

Notice of Opposition to Claim of Exemption (Enforcement of Judgment)

ATTORNEY OR PARTY WITHOUT ATTORNEY *(Name and Address)*:	TELEPHONE NO.:	FOR COURT USE ONLY
Mandu Saarni 808 Winterside Court Palm Springs, CA 92260	760-555-8816	

ATTORNEY FOR *(Name)*: In Pro Per

NAME OF COURT:	California Superior Court
STREET ADDRESS:	County of Riverside
MAILING ADDRESS:	3255 Tahquitz Canyon Way
CITY AND ZIP CODE:	Palm Springs, CA 92262
BRANCH NAME:	Palm Springs

PLAINTIFF: Mandu Saarni

DEFENDANT: Ponga McCoy

NOTICE OF OPPOSITION TO CLAIM OF EXEMPTION (Enforcement of Judgment)	LEVYING OFFICER FILE NO.: 2872	COURT CASE NO.: 0000-0005

— *DO NOT USE THIS FORM FOR WAGE GARNISHMENTS* —

The original of this form and a Notice of Hearing on Claim of Exemption must be filed with the court.

A copy of this Notice of Opposition and the Notice of Hearing *must* be filed with the levying officer.

A copy of this Notice of Opposition and the Notice of Hearing must be served on the judgment debtor and other claimant at least 10 days *before* the hearing.

TO THE LEVYING OFFICER:

1. Name and address of judgment creditor

> Mandu Saarni
> 808 Winterside Court
> Palm Springs, CA 92260

2. Name and address of judgment debtor

> Ponga McCoy
> 63004 Abba Place
> Palm Desert, CA 92260

Social Security Number *(if known)*:

3. ☐ Name and address of claimant *(if other than judgment debtor)*

4. The notice of filing claim of exemption states it was mailed on *(date)*: September 8, 20XX

5. The item or items claimed as exempt are
   a. ☒ not exempt under the statutes relied upon in the Claim of Exemption.
   b. ☒ not exempt because the judgment debtor's equity is greater than the amount provided in the exemption.
   c. ☒ other *(specify)*: because piano belongs to Ponga, not her husband

6. The facts necessary to support item 5 are
   ☒ continued on the attachment labeled Attachment 6.
   ☐ as follows:

I declare under penalty of perjury under the laws of the State of California that the foregoing is true and correct.

Date: September 15, 20XX

Mandu Saarni
....
(TYPE OR PRINT NAME)

▶ *Mandu Saarni*
....
(SIGNATURE OF DECLARANT)

Form Approved by the
Judicial Council of California
EJ-170 [New July 1, 1983]

NOTICE OF OPPOSITION TO CLAIM OF EXEMPTION
(Enforcement of Judgment)

WEST GROUP
Official Publisher

CCP 703.550

Sample Declaration Opposing Claim of Exemption

ATTACHMENT 6

I, Mandu Saarni, declare as follows:

1. I obtained a judgment against Ponga McCoy from the Riverside Superior Court on September 10, 20____, in case #0000-0005.

2. The balance due on the judgment is $10,500, plus accrued interest and post-judgment costs.

3. On March 1, 20____, I sent instructions to the Riverside Sheriff for a levy against tangible personal property owned by and in the possession of Ponga McCoy. On March 22, 20____, a Notice of Filing of Claim of Exemption was sent to me.

4. I cannot attend the Hearing on Claim of Exemption which is scheduled for April 10, 20____. I will be in Boston for my sister's wedding from March 28 through April 26, and the claim of exemption must be heard during this time

5. Ponga McCoy states in her claim of exemption that the lithograph set by artist DeChing is worth less than $5,000 and therefore is exempt pursuant to Code of Civil Procedure § 704.040. I am informed and believe that the lithograph set is worth more than $7,000. A similar lithograph set by artist DeChing was recently sold by the 20th Street Art Gallery for the sum of $8,500. The owner of the art gallery told me over the phone that all of DeChing's lithograph sets are worth "at least $7,000 and probably much more."

6. Ponga McCoy states in her claim of exemption that the camera equipment is exempt pursuant to Code of Civil Procedure § 704.060 inasmuch as she uses it as a tool of the trade. I am informed and believe that this is not true since Ponga McCoy works for her father at Ping-Pong Game Shop.

7. Ponga McCoy states in her claim of exemption that the Steinway baby grand piano belongs solely to her husband Martin. I am informed and believe that this is not true because Ponga McCoy received it as an inheritance from her mother.

I declare under penalty of perjury under the laws of the State of California that the foregoing is true and correct.

Dated: September 19, 20XX

Mandu Saarni
Mandu Saarni

DECLARATION OF MANDU SAARNI

4. Serve and File the Opposition Papers

You must serve the papers on the debtor, then file them with the court. Your response must be served on the debtor at least 10 days before the hearing date—15 days if service is by mail. You can have these papers served on the debtor by mail or personally. In most cases, mail is the easiest and least expensive approach, as long as it allows the debtor at least 15 calendar days' notice of the hearing date.

Either way, don't delay in serving the forms. Once they are served, you must file the forms with the court—and that filing must take place within ten days of the mailing date of the Notice of Filing of Claim of Exemption. Here's how to proceed:

1. Make at least four copies of your documents. One is for your records, another is for the levying officer, a third is for the court and a fourth is for the debtor. If there is an additional claimant (such as a third party who contests your levy), make an extra copy.

2. Have a set served on the debtor, or his attorney if he has one, at the address indicated on Item 2 of the Claim of Exemption. Service by mail and personal service is explained in Chapter 21. Be sure whoever serves the papers completes the Proof of Service form on the back of the Notice of Hearing form.

3. Within the ten- or 15-day deadline, file with the clerk of the court the original Notice of Opposition to Claim of Exemption form, the original Notice of Hearing on Claim of Exemption and the original Proof of Service, which is on the back of the Notice of Hearing form.

4. Also within the ten- or 15-day deadline, give or send (by overnight mail) the levying officer a copy of the Notice of Opposition to Claim of Exemption and a copy of the Notice of Hearing on Claim of Exemption.

5. Once the levying officer receives your papers, she will file with the court the Claim of Exemption sent to her by the debtor. If you don't get these notices to the levying officer by the deadline, she will immediately return any property claimed to be exempt to the debtor or other claimant.

5. Attend Hearing

If you attend the hearing, review your argument the day before. On the day of the hearing, try to get to the courtroom a little early. At the entrance, there may be a bulletin board with a list of the cases to be heard that day. If your case isn't listed, check with the clerk.

Step forward when your case is called. Be prepared to answer the judge's questions. Call the judge "Your Honor" and don't interrupt the debtor, even if you disagree with what she says. The judge will give you a chance to state your disagreement. Be prepared for the judge to try to get you and the debtor to compromise. While you are entitled to remain adamant and go for it all, that attitude may lead the judge to decide for the debtor.

6. Wait For the Ruling

Until the court issues its decision, the levying officer will hold the property and cannot release, sell or otherwise dispose of it. You will be charged the costs of this storage, which can be very expensive but may be recoverable from the debtor. (See Chapter 16.)

You will be notified of the judge's decision at the hearing or by mail. If the court decides in your favor, the property can be sold and the proceeds applied toward satisfaction of your judgment. If the debtor wins, the levying officer must release any property found to be exempt.

A judge may order a variation on these two themes. For instance, the judge might determine property to be partially exempt but require it to be sold and replaced with a less costly item, with part of the proceeds of the sale going to the judgment creditor.

Either you or the debtor can appeal the judge's decision on the Claim of Exemption. In the meantime, the judge's order is in effect. If you lose and appeal, the exemption is allowed while your appeal is pending. If the debtor loses, appeals and wins on appeal, any property you have seized will have to be returned. Appealing is time-consuming, and few appeals are granted. We recommend against appealing. It is much easier to simply wait a while and try again. ■

Chapter 16

Collecting Post-Judgment Costs and Interest

Some court judgments are paid right away, but others take months or even years to collect. If your judgment isn't paid soon after it's awarded, you are entitled to receive interest on it until it is paid. You can also tack on most of the costs you incur in trying to collect the judgment —such as court fees and levying officers' costs.

A. Post-Judgment Costs

The law identifies specific collection costs for which you are entitled to be reimbursed—that is, these costs may be added to your judgment (Code of Civil Procedure § 685.070). On the other hand, certain collection costs are not reimbursable unless a court authorizes them.

1. Costs You Can Collect

The following collection costs may be added to your judgment:

- clerk's filing fees, such as for obtaining a Writ of Execution or Abstract of Judgment
- statutory fees charged and costs incurred by a levying officer attempting a levy under a Writ of Execution
- statutory fees charged by a process server for serving the Application and Notice of Order of Examination or Subpena Duces Tecum, if approved by the court in which the debtor's examination is conducted (Chapter 6)
- fees charged to issue and serve a bench warrant if the debtor does not appear at a debtor's examination, if approved by the court (Chapter 6)
- fees for issuing and levying an earnings withholding order (Chapter 9)
- fees for recording an Abstract of Judgment to place a lien on the debtor's real estate (Chapter 4)
- fees for filing a Notice of Judgment Lien on Business Personal Property (Chapter 4)

- notary fees incurred in the collection process
- fees connected with bringing a motion, if approved by the judge (Chapter 19), and
- attorney fees spent on collection efforts, if the judgment called for attorney fees on the basis of a contract or statute (Code of Civil Procedure § 685.040).

In general, you use a form called a Memorandum of Costs After Judgment (see Section C, below) to add costs to your judgment. But what about costs incurred by a levying officer at the moment of seizure? You can instruct the levying officer to collect the amount remaining on the judgment (as shown in the Writ of Execution) as well as his fee and costs.

EXAMPLE: You instruct the sheriff to levy on the debtor's bank account, and you pay a statutory fee and the officer's actual costs. The levy occurs the day after the debtor receives a large check, and contains enough to cover your judgment, previously incurred interest and costs approved by the court in a Memorandum of Costs, as well as the fee and costs charged by the levying officer for this levy. The officer can grab enough to cover it all.

If the levying officer doesn't collect enough even to cover your deposit, you are temporarily out of the money. You can recover it in the future, using a subsequent levy, only if you file a Memorandum of Costs with the court.

EXAMPLE: You instruct the sheriff to levy against the debtor's car and put up a $400 deposit, only to find out after the car has been seized that it is essentially worthless. The levying officer used all $400 in his efforts to seize and sell the car.

You later discover a juicy bank account that will not only satisfy your judgment, but also recover your $400. The levying officer cannot collect that $400 as part of the bank levy, because it is related to a different levy. To collect the $400, you must file a Memorandum of Costs with the court. Then you can collect it as part of the judgment.

2. Costs You Cannot Collect

Costs other than those detailed in Section 1 generally may not be added to the judgment. For example, the following costs will most likely be disallowed by the court if the debtor objects:

- fees for the time you spend enforcing the judgment
- fees for parking (including fines for parking tickets) while visiting the levying officer or court
- lunch expenses while interviewing investigators or collection professionals
- long distance telephone charges
- fees paid to process servers not approved by the court
- fax and copying charges
- postage charges
- corporate search fees, and
- mileage.

Despite this list, you are entitled to recover the "reasonable and necessary costs of enforcing a judgment" (Code of Civil Procedure § 685.040). The costs listed in Section A1 are presumed to be reasonable and necessary. For all other costs, you must file a motion with the court, give the debtor notice of the hearing on the motion and convince the judge that the cost is reasonable (Code of Civil Procedure § 685.080).

EXAMPLE: You used a registered process server for a levy on the debtor's bank account because the levying officer had a two-week backlog and you feared the funds would evaporate if you didn't act quickly. The process server's fee was $105. Fees and costs paid to a registered process server aren't listed in the statute—only fees and costs charged by a levying officer. If you can convince a judge that a registered process server was necessary and reasonable, however, the judge will award you the cost. Generally, judges award these costs when the judgment creditor demonstrates good faith.

We don't cover filing a motion for costs. In Chapter 19, however, we explain how to bring a motion for an Assignment Order. The process is very similar. If the costs warrant it, get help from an attorney.

Add reasonable costs. Many creditors claim costs in a Memorandum of Costs that are not authorized by statute. It is up to the debtor to object. We do not suggest that you add extravagant costs of collection. But if you're not sure whether a cost is authorized by the statute, and you believe that it's reasonable, try including it and see if the debtor objects.

When the Debtor Bounces a Check

If the debtor writes you a check to pay your judgment and it bounces, you will need court approval to add the bank and other fees to your cost of collections. But the court should easily approve the cost.

In addition, you can send a certified letter demanding payment on the bounced check within 30 days. Keep photocopies of the bounced checks, your demand letter to the debtor and the original signed certified receipt. If the debtor does not make the check good, you can sue in small claims court for the original amount of the bounced check plus three times the amount of the check, up to a total of $1,500 (Civil Code § 1719).

If you'd rather not get involved in a second lawsuit with the debtor, see if your county's district attorney's office has a check diversion program. To avoid criminal prosecution, the person who wrote a bad check must make the check good and comply with other rules. You cannot seek triple damages, but you'll be spared the hassle of another lawsuit.

3. Keeping Track of Costs

A form entitled Keeping Track of Costs is included in the Appendix. A completed sample is below. If you fill it out as you incur various expenses, you'll have all the information you need at your finger-tips when you prepare your Memorandum of Costs.

Be sure to keep receipts for all costs incurred—especially if you paid cash. If the judgment debtor raises any questions about the cost, you'll have proof that it's a legitimate claim.

Here's how to fill in the form:

Date Expended: Specify the date you paid each cost.

Cost Amount: Specify the amount of each cost.

Type of Cost: Specify the kind of cost. For example, it might be a filing fee for a Writ of Execution, a sheriff's deposit for a wage levy or a recording fee for an Abstract of Judgment.

Expense Record: Specify how you paid the cost. If you paid by check, insert the check number.

Date Costs Claimed: Leave this blank until you actually claim this cost on a Memorandum of Costs. At that time, fill in the date.

If you've already been reimbursed, you cannot claim the cost on a Memorandum of Costs. For example, if the sheriff repaid your Writ of Execution filing fees and deposit from the proceeds of a bank levy, you aren't entitled to collect them again. Make a note of any reimbursed costs.

B. Post-Judgment Interest

You can recover interest on the unpaid portion of your judgment and on unpaid costs that have been claimed in a Memorandum of Costs. Interest accrues from the date the judgment was first entered, even if the debtor appealed your judgment and you won on appeal. If the judgment is an installment judgment, interest accrues on each installment as it becomes due.

1. Interest Rate

Interest accrues at the rate of 10% per year (Code of Civil Procedure § 685.010). There is one exception. Interest on a judgment against the State of California or any of its agencies accrues at only 7% per year, as set forth in Article XV, Section 1 of the California Constitution (see *California Fed. Sav. & Loan Assn. v. City of Los Angeles*, 11 Cal. 4th 342 (1995)).

2. Types of Interest

For collection purposes, there are two types of interest:

- interest that accrues between the time the judgment is entered and the time the Writ of Execution is issued, and

---

Keeping Track of Costs

Date Expended	Cost Amount	Type of Cost	Expense Record	Date Costs Claimed
2/4/XX	$7.00	Writ of Execution	Cash	9/21/XX
3/15/XX	$55.00	Bank levy—Sheriff's fees	#1502	"
5/21/XX	$25.00	Process server	#1531	"
6/18/XX	$7.00	Writ of Execution	Cash	"
6/30/XX	$45.00	Wage levy—Sheriff's fees	#1561	"

- interest that accrues between the date the Writ of Execution is entered and the actual levy.

The first type of interest must be documented before the levying officer can collect it. You do this by completing a Memorandum of Costs and listing the amount on a Writ of Execution.

The levying officer can collect the second type of interest without your documenting the amount, because the Writ of Execution directs the levying officer to collect interest on the amount remaining on the judgment. A Writ of Execution lasts for 180 days, so several months' worth of interest may mount up by the time a levy is completed. If the levying officer collects enough to cover that interest, he will forward it to you.

3. Keeping Track of Interest

How much interest accrues on a judgment depends not only on the size of the judgment, but also on how long it remains unpaid. For example, a $3,000 judgment that is paid off within three months produces $75 in interest, calculated at an annual rate of 10%. A $500 judgment will produce the same amount of interest only if it remains unpaid for 18 months.

If a judgment is paid in a lump sum, computing interest is relatively easy. But it's more common for payments to dribble in, either voluntarily or through levies and wage garnishments. If you receive partial payments, you must apply the payment first to accrued interest, then apply the remainder of the payment to the judgment principal. And you must recalculate the interest every time you receive a payment. Unfortunately, there's no short-cut for doing this, although a computer spreadsheet can be a real timesaver.

We provide instructions for computing interest on a 360-day year in order to keep the calculations as easy as possible. That means that interest is based on a 12-month, 30-day per month year. If you want to be more accurate, substitute 365 days for 360.

Before getting started, make several copies of the Keeping Track of Payments form found in the Appendix. A completed sample is below.

Here is how to use the form to calculate interest:

A–Starting Date: Fill in the date your judgment was entered if you've never completed and filed a Memorandum of Costs on this judgment, or the date you last filed a Memorandum of Costs.

B–Ending Date: Fill in the date you are completing the form if you haven't received any payments on the judgment, or the date after the date in Column A that you first received a payment.

C–Number of Days: Enter the number of days in the period between the starting date (Column A) and ending date (Column B). You can assume

Keeping Track of Payments

A Starting Date	B Ending Date	C No. of Days	D Balance	E Interest Due (D x 10% x C/360)	F Payment	G Balance Reduction (F-E)	H Unpaid Interest
1/10/XX	3/28/XX	78	$6,000.00	$130.00	$621.00	$491.00	
3/29/XX	7/15/XX	106	$5,509.00	$162.21	$420.00	$257.79	
7/16/XX	8/18/XX	32	$5,251.21	$46.68	$420.00	$373.32	
8/19/XX	9/21/XX	32	$4,877.89	$43.36	$250.00	$206.64	

30 days per month. For example, if the starting date is January 10 and the ending date is March 28 of the same year, figure two months from January 10 to March 10 (60 days) plus 18 days from March 11 through March 28, for a total of 78 days.

D–Balance: Enter the original amount of your judgment if you've never completed and filed a Memorandum of Costs on this judgment, or the balance due on the date you last filed a Memorandum of Costs, less interest previously claimed.

E–Interest Due: To calculate the interest due, multiply the Balance (Column D) by 10% (or 7% if your judgment is against the state of California or one of its agencies). Then multiply the result by the Number of Days (Column C) and divide by 360.

F-Payment: Enter the payment you received on the Ending Date (Column B).

G-Payment Applicable to Principal: Subtract the Interest Due (Column E) from the Payment (Column F). Because you must apply any payments to outstanding interest first, only what's left over after you subtract the interest due can be put toward the judgment principal. If you had any unpaid interest from previous pay periods (Column H),

subtract that amount as well. That way, you will have applied the payment to all outstanding interest before you use it to reduce the principal amount.

Subtract the remainder of the payment—what's left after you subtract all outstanding interest—from your original balance to get the balance for the next pay period. Enter this amount in Column D on the next line. If the payment is less than the interest due, you'll have to fill in Column H, below.

H-Unpaid Interest: If the payment is less than the interest owed, no money will be available to pay down the Balance, so the Balance amount will stay the same and you are still entitled to any interest that wasn't paid. Subtract the Payment (Column F) from the Interest Due (Column E) and enter the result here.

When you receive another payment, repeat the process described above for the next pay period.

C. Memorandum of Costs

You must file the Memorandum of Costs After Judgment form with the court to collect post-judgment costs and interest. You don't have to file a Memorandum of Costs at any particular time, as long as you do it within two years of the date the costs were incurred (Code of Civil Procedure § 685.070b). But having your costs documented means they can be added to the judgment itself, which means that you can recover interest on them. Therefore, it makes sense to file a Memorandum of Costs whenever you incur unrecovered costs of $50 or more.

We suggest that you file a Memorandum of Costs at least once a year, unless you don't want the debtor to know that you're actively pursuing the judgment. You must have the debtor served with a copy of each Memorandum of Costs, so filing a Memorandum will definitely cost you the element of surprise.

If Service Is Not Done by Levying Officers

It used to be that the sheriff or constable served levying papers and collected funds for a judgment creditor. But in some counties, these services have been dropped due to budget cuts.

If you are in such a county, you must hire a private process server to serve wage garnishments and bank levies. But as mentioned in Section A, a private process server cannot automatically collect his fee from the levy.

There is a way around this. First, get a fee quote from the process server before he serves the papers. Then, complete a Memorandum of Costs for the fee when you file for your Writ (see "Simultaneous Writ and Memorandum of Costs," below). Technically, you're not supposed to claim costs before they're incurred. Listing them on a Memorandum of Costs keeps you from getting stuck paying the process server's fees, however, the debtor can contest them.

Don't double dip. Once you have filed a Memorandum of Costs, make sure you don't claim interest on post-judgment interest. The second time you prepare a Memorandum of Costs, subtract the interest previously claimed on a Memorandum of Costs from the total due before you start calculating. If you want to earn interest on the interest you've claimed, you must renew your judgment—an option that's available once every five years. (See Chapter 20.)

Simultaneous Writ and Memorandum of Costs

If you file a Writ of Execution at the same time as a Memorandum of Costs, you can claim up to $100 in statutory costs on the Writ for costs documented in the Memorandum of Costs. You must add the following statement: "The fees sought under this Memorandum may be disallowed by a court upon a Motion to Tax filed by the debtor notwithstanding the fees having been included in the writ of execution." (Code of Civil Procedure § 685.070(e)). If the debtor successfully contests these costs, you will not be allowed to claim them.

1. Complete the Memorandum of Costs

A blank form is in the Appendix. A completed sample is below.

Caption: Fill in your name, address and telephone number, the name and address of the court, the case name and case number.

Line 1a through h: List the costs you have incurred in each category, and the dates on which you incurred them. Use line 1h to list any additional costs (review the lists in Section A to make sure you haven't forgotten any).

Line 1i: Add up lines 1a through 1h and write the total here.

Line 2: If you have previously filed Memoranda of Costs, enter the total amount claimed as costs on those Memoranda. If this is the first time you're claiming costs, write "$0."

Line 3: Add lines 1 and 2 together, and put the total here.

Line 4: Enter the amount you have received on the judgment. This is the total of all the amounts listed in the "Payment" column of the "Keeping Track of Payments" form. If you haven't received any payments, write "$0."

Memorandum of Costs After Judgment, Acknowledgment of Credit, and Declaration of Accrued Interest

ATTORNEY OR PARTY WITHOUT ATTORNEY *(Name, state bar number, and address):*	**MC-012**
Hido Miko 17003 County Road 16 Twain, CA 94590	FOR COURT USE ONLY
TELEPHONE NO.: (530) 555-9590 FAX NO.:	
ATTORNEY FOR *(Name):* In Pro Per	
NAME OF COURT: Plumas County Superior Court STREET ADDRESS: MAILING ADDRESS: 520 Main St. CITY AND ZIP CODE: Quincy, CA 95957 BRANCH NAME:	
PLAINTIFF: Hido Miko	
DEFENDANT: Aaron Platz	
MEMORANDUM OF COSTS AFTER JUDGMENT, ACKNOWLEDGMENT OF CREDIT, AND DECLARATION OF ACCRUED INTEREST	CASE NUMBER: 0000-0006

1. I claim the following costs after judgment incurred within the last two years *(indicate if there are multiple items in any category):*

		Dates Incurred	Amount
a	Preparing and issuing abstract of judgment	6-3-20XX	$ 16
b	Recording and indexing abstract of judgment	6-4-20XX	$ 36
c	Filing notice of judgment lien on personal property	6-4-20XX	$ 10
d	Issuing writ of execution, to extent not satisfied by Code Civ. Proc., § 685.050 *(specify county):* Plumas	8-2-20XX	$ 85
e	Levying officer's fees, to extent not satisfied by Code Civ. Proc., § 685.050 or wage garnishment		$
f	Approved fee on application for order for appearance of judgment debtor, or other approved costs under Code Civ. Proc., § 708.010 et seq.		$
g	Attorney fees, if allowed by Code Civ. Proc., § 685.040		$
h	Other: *(Statute authorizing cost):*		$
i	Total of claimed costs for current memorandum of costs *(add items a-h)*		$ 147.00

2. All previously allowed postjudgment costs: . . . . $ 0

3. **Total** of all postjudgment costs *(add items 1 and 2):* . . . . **TOTAL** $ 147.00

4. **Acknowledgment of Credit.** I acknowledge total credit to date (including returns on levy process and direct payments) in the amount of: $ 1,711.00

5. **Declaration of Accrued Interest.** Interest on the judgment accruing at the legal rate from the date of entry on balances due after partial satisfactions and other credits in the amount of: $ 372.81

6. I am the [X] judgment creditor   [ ] agent for the judgment creditor   [ ] attorney for the judgment creditor.
   I have knowledge of the facts concerning the costs claimed above. To the best of my knowledge and belief, the costs claimed are correct, reasonable, and necessary, and have not been satisfied.

I declare under penalty of perjury under the laws of the State of California that the foregoing is true and correct.

Date: 8-12-20XX

Hido Miko   ▶ *Hido Miko*
_____   _____
(TYPE OR PRINT NAME)   (SIGNATURE OF DECLARANT)

NOTICE TO THE JUDGMENT DEBTOR

If this memorandum of costs is filed at the same time as an application for a writ of execution, any statutory costs, *not exceeding $100 in aggregate* and not already allowed by the court, may be included in the writ of execution. *The fees sought under this memorandum may be disallowed by the court upon a motion to tax filed by the debtor, notwithstanding the fees having been included in the writ of execution.* (Code Civ. Proc., § 685.070(e).) A motion to tax costs claimed in this memorandum must be filed within 10 days after service of the memorandum. (Code Civ. Proc., § 685.070(c).)

(Proof of service on reverse)

Form Adopted for Mandatory Use Judicial Council of California MC-012 [Rev January 1, 2000]	**MEMORANDUM OF COSTS AFTER JUDGMENT, ACKNOWLEDGMENT OF CREDIT, AND DECLARATION OF ACCRUED INTEREST**	Code of Civil Procedure, § 685.070 WEST GROUP Official Publisher

Line 5: Write down the total amount of interest that has accrued on the judgment. If you have not received any partial payments from the debtor, calculate interest by multiplying your judgment amount times 10%, then multiplying that amount by the total number of days since the judgment was granted divided by 365. For example, if you had a judgment for $2,000 that was granted a year ago, you would be entitled to claim interest of $200 (10% of $2,000 ($200) times 365/365 (1))

If you have received partial payments, add up all of the interest you entered in Column E of your Keeping Track of Payments worksheet. Then add any interest that has accrued since you received your last payment, using the formula in Section B, above. Write the total here.

Line 6: Check the box next to "judgment creditor."

Type or print your name, date and sign the bottom of the form.

2. Have Debtor Served

You must have a copy of the Memorandum of Costs served on the judgment debtor by mail to his last known address. Have the person who serves the debtor complete a Proof of Service by Mail. (You can find one on the back of the Memorandum of Costs form.)

3. File the Memorandum of Costs

After the judgment debtor is served, make two copies of the Memorandum of Costs and signed proof of service. Send the court the original and one copy of the Memorandum of Costs and signed proof of service and a self-addressed, stamped envelope. There is no filing fee. A generic cover letter is in the Appendix.

4. Give the Debtor Time to Object

The debtor has 15 days (ten days if served personally) to contest your Memorandum of Costs. If the debtor contests—which rarely happens—you can either argue against his motion in court, or forget about it and let him have his way. (See Chapter 19 for more information on motions.)

If the debtor does not contest, the Memorandum of Costs is considered final, and you are entitled to the amount claimed. If you are in the midst of a levy and want to recover the costs claimed, get a certified copy of the Memorandum of Costs from the court clerk and send it to the levying officer. He can recover the amount indicated. Or, add the costs and interest to the Writ of Execution you obtain the next time you initiate a levy. ■

Chapter 17

If the Debtor Files for Bankruptcy

Collection Factor

	High	Moderate	Low
Potential cost to you			✓
Potential for producing cash		✓	
Potential for settlement		✓	
Potential time and trouble		✓	

If the judgment debtor files for bankruptcy, you may be at the end of the collections line. As soon as the debtor files for bankruptcy, all collection activity must stop. Furthermore, funds collected shortly before the filing usually have to be turned over to the bankruptcy court. And through the bankruptcy case, a debtor may be able to wipe out your debt—and may even be able to remove any lien you recorded against her house.

But creditors also have rights in bankruptcy. The debtor may have to surrender property to be sold to pay some of her debts. Certain debts survive bankruptcy fully intact. Also, if the debtor's bankruptcy papers and any papers she gave you as a creditor contain serious inconsistencies, the court may throw out the bankruptcy case or refuse to let the debtor discharge (cancel) your debt. Finally, if the debtor lied in her bankruptcy papers, the bankruptcy court might dismiss the case outright.

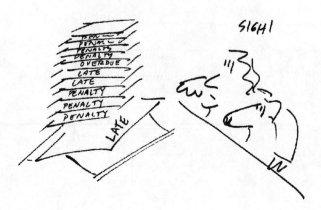

Debts That Survive Chapter 7 Bankruptcy

Several types of debts survive bankruptcy intact. Others may survive if you successfully challenge the debtor's request to have them discharged. So if you have any of the following types of debts, take heart. Your debt probably won't be wiped out by the debtor's bankruptcy case. (Note that this list applies to Chapter 7 bankruptcy, commonly filed by individuals and small businesses. If your debtor files for Chapter 13 bankruptcy, some of these debts might be wiped out.)

Debts that survive bankruptcy (see Section F5, below, for more details):

- Debts that the debtor does not list on his bankruptcy papers, as long as the creditor doesn't otherwise learn of the bankruptcy case.
- Student loans, unless repayment would cause the debtor undue hardship.
- Most federal, state and local taxes and any money borrowed to pay those taxes.
- Child and spousal support, and debts in the nature of support.
- Court-ordered fines or restitution owed to the victim of a crime.
- Court fees.
- Debts for the death of, or personal injury to, someone due to the debtor's intoxicated driving.

Debts that may be declared nondischargeable if you successfully object in court (see Section F2, below, for more details):

- Debts incurred on the basis of fraud.
- Debts from willful and malicious acts.
- Debts from embezzlement, larceny or breach of fiduciary duty.
- Debts arising from a marital settlement or divorce decree, unless discharging the debt would result in a benefit to the debtor that outweighs the detriment to the debtor's former spouse or child.

Bankruptcy Law May Change. In early 2001, the United States Congress passed legislation that makes sweeping changes to bankruptcy law. However, the Senate and House versions differ—and these differences have yet to be reconciled. Since the bill was passed, the events of September 11 occurred and the economy officially entered a recession. Also, the Senate version includes a provision limiting exemptions on homes and the President has said he would veto the bill if this provision remains. For these reasons, the bill may never become law.

To learn about the status of the bill and its provisions, check Legal Updates on Nolo's website (www.nolo.com). The websites of the American Bankruptcy Institute (www.abiworld.org) and Commercial Law League of America (www.clla.org) also have up-to-date information about the legislation.

A. Types of Bankruptcy

The different kinds of bankruptcy are named after specific chapters of the federal Bankruptcy Code.

- **Chapter 7 bankruptcy:** This is the most common form of bankruptcy filed by individuals and small businesses. A debtor asks the court to discharge (cancel) his debts. In exchange, the debtor hands over to the court any property that isn't considered exempt. The property is sold and the proceeds are distributed to creditors. If the debtor doesn't have any non-exempt assets, his creditors won't get paid anything.

- **Chapter 13 bankruptcy:** A debtor creates a plan under which she pays a portion of her debts over a three- to five-year period. The amount that the debtor must pay depends on several factors, and can vary from a few cents on the dollar to 100%. In general, the debtor holds on to all of her property and uses her income to fund the plan. If the debtor successfully completes the plan, any balances still owing on most debts are wiped out.

- **Other types of bankruptcy:** Chapter 11 bankruptcy is primarily designed to let a business restructure its debt while it continues to operate. Although individuals are permitted to file Chapter 11 bankruptcy, few do. Chapter 12 bankruptcy is designed especially for family farmers. Chapter 11 and Chapter 12 bankruptcies are beyond the scope of this book.

Steering the Debtor to Alternatives

If bankruptcy is looming large but the debtor hasn't yet filed, it is in your interest to prevent it from happening. If the debtor is looking for alternatives to bankruptcy, here are some suggestions you can pass on:

- *Money Troubles: Legal Strategies to Cope With Your Debts*, by Deanne Loonin & Robin Leonard (Nolo), helps debtors assess their situation and take the most sensible course of action. The book is available in most book stores and libraries, or you can order or download it from our website at www.nolo.com.

- Myvesta (formerly Debt Counselors of America) offers budgeting and debt management programs. Myvesta's services include a Crisis Relief Team to assist debtors who are turned away by other debt counseling agencies or who have very complex problems. Myvesta offers its services in person, over the phone or on the Internet. The debtor can contact DCA at 6 Taft Court, Suite 301, Rockville, MD 20850, by phone at 800-MYVESTA or on the internet at http://myvesta.org.

- Consumer Credit Counselor Service helps debtors avoid bankruptcy and work out a voluntary plan with their creditors to repay their debts over time. If the number isn't in the phone book, the debtor can call 800-388-2227. You can find Consumer Credit Counselor Service on the Web, at www.nfcc.org.

B. Bankruptcy and Collections

The moment a debtor files a bankruptcy petition, the court automatically issues an order called the "automatic stay." This order requires creditors and debt collectors to end all collection efforts against the debtor and his property (11 U.S.C. § 362). It remains in effect until the case is closed or the court lifts the stay for a particular creditor.

If you know of the bankruptcy filing—whether through court papers served on you or through rumors on the street—and try to collect anyway, you can be held in contempt of court and fined. So if you get even a whiff that the judgment debtor has gone bankrupt, immediately stop your collection efforts until you learn otherwise or until the court says you may proceed with collecting.

1. If You Have Started Levying

If you started levying on the debtor's wages or property before she filed for bankruptcy, immediately let the levying officer know about the bankruptcy. Give him the case name and number, and tell him to release to the bankruptcy court any funds already collected as a result of your levy. Later, you may be required to turn over funds collected during the 90 days preceding the bankruptcy filing. If you're related to the debtor or were in business with him, you may be required to turn over funds collected during the entire year directly preceding the bankruptcy filing.

2. Collecting From Codebtors

A codebtor is another person legally responsible for paying your judgment. In your situation, a codebtor is a co-defendant—that is, someone else who was named in your lawsuit and specifically found liable to pay you. If you have a judgment against just one person, you might still have a codebtor, such as:

- a cosignor or guarantor of your original debt, or
- the debtor's spouse, if the underlying debt was incurred during marriage.

After the automatic stay goes into effect, your right to collect from codebtors depends on which type of bankruptcy the debtor filed.

- **Chapter 7 bankruptcy.** You may collect from any codebtor before, during or after the bankruptcy proceeding.
- **Chapter 13 bankruptcy.** The automatic stay prevents collection activity against a codebtor while the bankruptcy case is pending. If the court approves a repayment plan in which you will receive less than 100% of your judgment, you can petition the court for relief from the stay to collect the unpaid portion from the codebtor or wait until the case is over and collect the remaining balance from the codebtor. These procedures are beyond the scope of this book.

3. Collecting in Bankruptcy

As explained below, you will be notified by the court of the type of bankruptcy the debtor has filed. If there's a chance you will be paid something through the bankruptcy case, you will be invited to file what's called a "Proof of Claim" with the bankruptcy court.

Don't give up yet. If your debtor files for bankruptcy, you may worry that you'll never collect your judgment. But not every debtor who seeks bankruptcy protection actually goes through with the procedure. Some file solely to get the protection of the automatic stay (see above), or simply to convince their creditors to quit trying to collect. If the debtor backs out before receiving a discharge, your judgment is still good and you are entitled to collect it. So remember to keep tabs on the debtor's bankruptcy case, from start to finish.

C. Examine the Bankruptcy Papers You Receive

When a debtor files for bankruptcy, she is supposed to list all of her debts and creditors. She cannot pick and choose which ones to list, even if she hopes to repay a specific creditor after her bankruptcy ends. This means that you are likely to be listed in the debtor's bankruptcy petition, unless she forgot about your debt or submits incomplete papers to the bankruptcy court.

1. Notice of Case, Meeting of Creditors and Deadlines

Assuming you are listed and notified of the bankruptcy, you will receive one of the following types of notices.

- **Chapter 7 "no asset" case.** A Chapter 7 debtor claims that all of his assets are exempt —that is, unavailable to pay his creditors. Unless you receive further instructions from the bankruptcy court, there's no reason to file a Proof of Claim requesting payment. But keep reading this chapter, as you may have other remedies.

- **Chapter 7 "asset" case.** A Chapter 7 debtor has nonexempt assets that may be used to pay his creditors. You may get paid a portion of your judgment, depending on the value of the assets and the rights of other creditors. You must file a Proof of Claim to be paid.

- **Chapter 13 case.** The debtor intends to repay a portion of his debts through a repayment plan. A copy of the plan will be enclosed with the notice or sent separately. You must file a Proof of Claim to be paid.

If you receive a bankruptcy notice but don't recognize the name of the debtor, contact the trustee. The debtor may be using a different name. For example, your judgment may be in the name of the business while the bankruptcy filing may be in the name of an individual.

If You Don't Receive Notice

If you believe the debtor has filed for bankruptcy but you don't receive any notice from the bankruptcy court, you probably weren't listed in the papers or the notice was sent to an old address. Still, act like you received the notice. Cease all collection activities. Then call the bankruptcy court for the area in which the debtor lives (check the U.S. government listing of the phone book) and ask if the debtor has filed bankruptcy. If so, get the name and phone number of the trustee handling the case. Call the trustee, state that you are a judgment creditor who did not get notice of the case and ask for notice so you can file a claim.

If you are completely unaware of a bankruptcy filing and not listed in the bankruptcy papers, your judgment might legally survive the bankruptcy. While it may be tempting to pretend you don't know about the bankruptcy if you receive no notice, debtors often can amend their papers after their cases are over to add omitted creditors and have the debts wiped out. You are better off pursuing your rights as soon as you hear that the debtor has filed.

Below are copies of notices commencing a Chapter 7 "no asset" bankruptcy, a Chapter 7 "asset" bankruptcy and a Chapter 13 bankruptcy. The fine print at the top left of each form tells you the type of case. Each notice states the name of the court and the date the debtor filed the case.

Next are boxes identifying the debtor and any attorney, the case number, and the name, address and telephone number of the trustee. As mentioned earlier, the trustee is a court-appointed official who represents the unsecured creditors in a bankruptcy case. His role is to make sure the debtor coughs up as much property (Chapter 7) or cash (Chapter 13) as possible. In most consumer bankruptcy cases, the proceedings are controlled by the trustee. Generally, the debtor can't dispose of any property without the trustee's permission.

Meeting of Creditors. This section gives you the date, time and location of the meeting of the creditors. It is usually held one to two months after the debtor files the bankruptcy papers. The debtor must appear to answer a few routine questions or to clarify any ambiguities in the papers. Despite its name, few creditors attend. You can go, however, and you should if you are curious about the process or have some questions about information in the debtor's bankruptcy papers. Most meetings last under five minutes, although you might be sitting in the room for an hour or longer waiting for the trustee to get to your debtor's case.

If you want to formally object to something in the debtor's papers, the meeting of creditors is not the place to do it. Formal objections must be brought before a bankruptcy judge. But creditors do raise objections at the meeting of creditors with the hope that the debtor will voluntarily address the creditors' concerns, rather than litigate the objection before the bankruptcy judge. (See Section F, below, for objections you can raise.)

Deadlines. In a Chapter 7 asset or Chapter 13 case, you must file a Proof of Claim with the court by the date specified in this box. If you plan to object to the discharge of a debt, a claimed exemption or the debtor's Chapter 13 plan, you must meet the deadlines specified. (See Section F about these and other objections.)

Creditors May Not Take Certain Actions. This is a notice that the automatic stay is in effect. (The automatic stay is discussed above in Section B.)

At the very bottom left is the court's address. The clerk's signature or stamp and date are at the bottom right.

The back page of each form provides explanations of the information on the front page.

2. Chapter 13 Repayment Plan

Enclosed with the Chapter 13 notice—or sent separately—will be the debtor's Chapter 13 plan.

Read it carefully. You want to figure out which category of creditor includes you. Generally, creditors fall into three categories: priority, secured and general unsecured. Priority and secured creditors usually receive 100% of what they are owed. General unsecured creditors usually receive less. Somewhere on the plan should be a number, written as a percentage, such as 33%, 54%, 72% or 100%. This indicates how much the debtor intends to repay each general unsecured creditor. So if you are a general unsecured creditor owed $8,000 and the debtor files a "54%" plan, you can hope to receive $4,320 through the debtor's bankruptcy.

The percentage is determined through a complex formula based on the debtor's disposable income each month (the amount left after basic living expenses are paid), how much the debtor owes to priority and secured creditors and the value of the debtor's nonexempt assets. (The debtor must pay his unsecured creditors at least the value of his nonexempt property.)

You are not bound by how the debtor classifies you if you feel it is wrong. For example, if the debtor lists you as a general unsecured creditor but you recorded an Abstract of Judgment in a county in which the debtor owns real estate, be sure to identify yourself as a secured creditor on the Proof of Claim. (See Section D.)

D. File Proof of Claim

If the debtor filed a Chapter 7 asset case, you must file a Proof of Claim to claim a share of the proceeds generated from the sale of the debtor's nonexempt assets. If the debtor filed a Chapter 13 bankruptcy, you must file a Proof of Claim to receive payments under the plan. The bankruptcy notice (see Section C) gives the deadline for filing the Proof of Claim. If you miss the deadline, you will probably be out of luck. There is one exception: if your debt is automatically not dischargeable, you don't have to file a Proof of Claim. Even then, however, it can never hurt.

Notice of Chapter 7 "No Asset" Bankruptcy

FORM B9A (Chapter 7 Individual or Joint Debtor No Asset Case (9/97))

UNITED STATES BANKRUPTCY COURT _____ District of _____

Notice of
Chapter 7 Bankruptcy Case, Meeting of Creditors, & Deadlines

[A chapter 7 bankruptcy case concerning the debtor(s) listed below was filed on _____ (date).]

or [A bankruptcy case concerning the debtor(s) listed below was originally filed under chapter _____ on _____ (date) and was converted to a case under chapter 7 on _____ .]

You may be a creditor of the debtor. **This notice lists important deadlines.** You may want to consult an attorney to protect your rights. All documents filed in the case may be inspected at the bankruptcy clerk's office at the address listed below. NOTE: The staff of the bankruptcy clerk's office cannot give legal advice.

See Reverse Side For Important Explanations.

Debtor(s) (name(s) and address):	Case Number:
	Social Security/Taxpayer ID Nos.:
Attorney for Debtor(s) (name and address):	Bankruptcy Trustee (name and address):
Telephone number:	Telephone number:

Meeting of Creditors:

Date:	/ /	Time:	( ) A.M.	Location:
			( ) P.M.	

Deadlines:
Papers must be *received* by the bankruptcy clerk's office by the following deadlines:

Deadline to File a Complaint Objecting to Discharge of the Debtor *or* to Determine Dischargeability of Certain Debts:
Deadline to Object to Exemptions:
Thirty (30) days after the *conclusion* of the meeting of creditors.

Creditors May Not Take Certain Actions

The filing of the bankruptcy case automatically stays certain collection and other actions against the debtor and the debtor's property. If you attempt to collect a debt or take other action in violation of the Bankruptcy Code, you may be penalized.

Please Do Not File A Proof of Claim Unless You Receive a Notice To Do So.

Address of the Bankruptcy Clerk's Office:	For the Court:
	Clerk of the Bankruptcy Court:
Telephone number:	
Hours Open:	Date:

FORM B9A (9/97)

EXPLANATIONS

Filing of Chapter 7 Bankruptcy Case	A bankruptcy case under chapter 7 of the Bankruptcy Code (title 11, United States Code) has been filed in this court by or against the debtor(s) listed on the front side, and an order for relief has been entered.
Creditors May Not Take Certain Actions	Prohibited collection actions are listed in Bankruptcy Code § 362. Common examples of prohibited actions include contacting the debtor by telephone, mail or otherwise to demand repayment; taking actions to collect money or obtain property from the debtor; repossessing the debtor's property; starting or continuing lawsuits or foreclosures; and garnishing or deducting from the debtor's wages.
Meeting of Creditors	A meeting of creditors is scheduled for the date, time and location listed on the front side. *The debtor (both spouses in a joint case) must be present at the meeting to be questioned under oath by the trustee and by creditors.* Creditors are welcome to attend, but are not required to do so. The meeting may be continued and concluded at a later date without further notice.
Do Not File a Proof of Claim at This Time	There does not appear to be any property available to the trustee to pay creditors. *You therefore should not file a proof of claim at this time.* If it later appears that assets are available to pay creditors, you will be sent another notice telling you that you may file a proof of claim, and telling you the deadline for filing your proof of claim.
Discharge of Debts	The debtor is seeking a discharge of most debts, which may include your debt. A discharge means that you may never try to collect the debt from the debtor. If you believe that the debtor is not entitled to receive a discharge under Bankruptcy Code § 727(a) *or* that a debt owed to you is not dischargeable under Bankruptcy Code § 523(a)(2), (4), (6), or (15), you must start a lawsuit by filing a complaint in the bankruptcy clerk's office by the "Deadline to File a Complaint Objecting to Discharge of the Debtor or to Determine Dischargeability of Certain Debts" listed on the front side. The bankruptcy clerk's office must receive the complaint and the required filing fee by that Deadline.
Exempt Property	The debtor is permitted by law to keep certain property as exempt. Exempt property will not be sold and distributed to creditors. The debtor must file a list of all property claimed as exempt. You may inspect that list at the bankruptcy clerk's office. If you believe that an exemption claimed by the debtor is not authorized by law, you may file an objection to that exemption. The bankruptcy clerk's office must receive the objection by the "Deadline to Object to Exemptions" listed on the front side.
Bankruptcy Clerk's Office	Any paper that you file in this bankruptcy case should be filed at the bankruptcy clerk's office at the address listed on the front side. You may inspect all papers filed, including the list of the debtor's property and debts and the list of the property claimed as exempt, at the bankruptcy clerk's office.
Legal Advice	The staff of the bankruptcy clerk's office cannot give legal advice. You may want to consult an attorney to protect your rights.
	—Refer To Other Side For Important Deadlines and Notices—

Notice of Chapter 7 "Asset" Bankruptcy

FORM B9C (Chapter 7 Individual or Joint Debtor Asset Case) (9/97)

UNITED STATES BANKRUPTCY COURT _____ District of _____

Notice of
Chapter 7 Bankruptcy Case, Meeting of Creditors, & Deadlines

[A chapter 7 bankruptcy case concerning the debtor(s) listed below was filed on _____ (date).]
or [A bankruptcy case concerning the debtor(s) listed below was originally filed under chapter _____ on _____ (date) and was converted to a case under chapter 7 on _____.]

You may be a creditor of the debtor. **This notice lists important deadlines.** You may want to consult an attorney to protect your rights. All documents filed in the case may be inspected at the bankruptcy clerk's office at the address listed below.
NOTE: The staff of the bankruptcy clerk's office cannot give legal advice.

See Reverse Side For Important Explanations.

Debtor(s) (name(s) and address):	Case Number:
	Social Security/Taxpayer ID Nos.:
Attorney for Debtor(s) (name and address):	Bankruptcy Trustee (name and address):
Telephone number:	Telephone number:

Meeting of Creditors:

Date: __/__/__   Time: ( ) A.M. ( ) P.M.   Location:

Deadlines:

Papers must be *received* by the bankruptcy clerk's office by the following deadlines:

Deadline to File a Proof of Claim:
For all creditors (except a governmental unit):   For a governmental unit:

Deadline to File a Complaint Objecting to Discharge of the Debtor or to Determine Dischargeability of Certain Debts:

Deadline to Object to Exemptions:
Thirty (30) days after the *conclusion* of the meeting of creditors.

Creditors May Not Take Certain Actions:

The filing of the bankruptcy case automatically stays certain collection and other actions against the debtor and the debtor's property.
If you attempt to collect a debt or take other action in violation of the Bankruptcy Code, you may be penalized.

Address of the Bankruptcy Clerk's Office:	For the Court:
	Clerk of the Bankruptcy Court:
Telephone number:	
Hours Open:	Date:

EXPLANATIONS   FORM B9C (9/97)

Filing of Chapter 7 Bankruptcy Case
A bankruptcy case under chapter 7 of the Bankruptcy Code (title 11, United States Code) has been filed in this court by or against the debtor(s) listed on the front side, and an order for relief has been entered.

Creditors May Not Take Certain Actions
Prohibited collection actions are listed in Bankruptcy Code § 362. Common examples of prohibited actions include contacting the debtor by telephone, mail or otherwise to demand repayment; taking actions to collect money or obtain property from the debtor; repossessing the debtor's property; starting or continuing lawsuits or foreclosures; and garnishing or deducting from the debtor's wages.

Meeting of Creditors
A meeting of creditors is scheduled for the date, time and location listed on the front side. *The debtor (both spouses in a joint case) must be present at the meeting to be questioned under oath by the trustee and by creditors.* Creditors are welcome to attend, but are not required to do so. The meeting may be continued and concluded at a later date without further notice.

Claims
A Proof of Claim is a signed statement describing a creditor's claim. If a Proof of Claim form is not included with this notice, you can obtain one at any bankruptcy clerk's office. If you do not file a Proof of Claim by the "Deadline to File a Proof of Claim" listed on the front side, you might not be paid any money on your claim against the debtor in the bankruptcy case. To be paid you must file a Proof of Claim even if your claim is listed in the schedules filed by the debtor.

Discharge of Debts
The debtor is seeking a discharge of most debts, which may include your debt. A discharge means that you may never try to collect the debt from the debtor. If you believe that the debtor is not entitled to receive a discharge under Bankruptcy Code § 727(a) or that a debt owed to you is not dischargeable under Bankruptcy Code § 523(a)(2), (4), (6), or (15), you must start a lawsuit by filing a complaint in the bankruptcy clerk's office by the "Deadline to File a Complaint Objecting to Discharge of the Debtor or to Determine Dischargeability of Certain Debts" listed on the front side. The bankruptcy clerk's office must receive the complaint and the required filing fee by that Deadline.

Exempt Property
The debtor is permitted by law to keep certain property as exempt. Exempt property will not be sold and distributed to creditors. The debtor must file a list of all property claimed as exempt. You may inspect that list at the bankruptcy clerk's office. If you believe that an exemption claimed by the debtor is not authorized by law, you may file an objection to that exemption. The bankruptcy clerk's office must receive the objection by the "Deadline to Object to Exemptions" listed on the front side.

Liquidation of the Debtor's Property and Payment of Creditors' Claims
The bankruptcy trustee listed on the front of this notice will collect and sell the debtor's property that is not exempt. If the trustee can collect enough money, creditors may be paid some or all of the debts owed to them, in the order specified by the Bankruptcy Code. To make sure you receive any share of that money, you must file a Proof of Claim, as described above.

Bankruptcy Clerk's Office
Any paper that you file in this bankruptcy case should be filed at the bankruptcy clerk's office at the address listed on the front side. You may inspect all papers filed, including the list of the debtor's property and debts and the list of the property claimed as exempt, at the bankruptcy clerk's office.

Legal Advice
The staff of the bankruptcy clerk's office cannot give legal advice. You may want to consult an attorney to protect your rights.

—Refer To Other Side For Important Deadlines and Notices—

Notice of Chapter 13 Bankruptcy

FORM B9I (9/97)

EXPLANATIONS

Filing of Chapter 13 Bankruptcy Case
A bankruptcy case under chapter 13 of the Bankruptcy Code (title 11, United States Code) has been filed in this court by the debtor(s) listed on the front side, and an order for relief has been entered. Chapter 13 allows an individual with regular income and debts below a specified amount to adjust debts pursuant to a plan. A plan is not effective unless confirmed by the bankruptcy court. You may object to confirmation of the plan and appear at the confirmation hearing. A copy or summary of the plan [is included with this notice] or [will be sent to you later], and [the confirmation hearing will be held on the date indicated on the front of this notice] or [you will be sent notice of the confirmation hearing]. The debtor will remain in possession of the debtor's property and may continue to operate the debtor's business, if any, unless the court orders otherwise.

Creditors May Not Take Certain Actions
Prohibited collection actions against the debtor and certain codebtors are listed in Bankruptcy Code § 362 and § 1301. Common examples of prohibited actions include contacting the debtor by telephone, mail or otherwise to demand repayment; taking actions to collect money or obtain property from the debtor; repossessing the debtor's property; starting or continuing lawsuits or foreclosures; and garnishing or deducting from the debtor's wages.

Meeting of Creditors
A meeting of creditors is scheduled for the date, time and location listed on the front side. *The debtor (both spouses in a joint case) must be present at the meeting to be questioned under oath by the trustee and by creditors.* Creditors are welcome to attend, but are not required to do so. The meeting may be continued and concluded at a later date without further notice.

Claims
A Proof of Claim is a signed statement describing a creditor's claim. If a Proof of Claim form is not included with this notice, you can obtain one at any bankruptcy clerk's office. If you do not file a Proof of Claim by the "Deadline to File a Proof of Claim" listed on the front side, you might not be paid any money on your claim against the debtor in the bankruptcy case. To be paid you must file a Proof of Claim even if your claim is listed in the schedules filed by the debtor.

Discharge of Debts
The debtor is seeking a discharge of most debts, which may include your debt. A discharge means that you may never try to collect the debt from the debtor.

Exempt Property
The debtor is permitted by law to keep certain property as exempt. Exempt property will not be sold and distributed to creditors, even if the debtor's case is converted to chapter 7. The debtor must file a list of all property claimed as exempt. You may inspect that list at the bankruptcy clerk's office. If you believe that an exemption claimed by the debtor is not authorized by law, you may file an objection to that exemption. The bankruptcy clerk's office must receive the objection by the "Deadline to Object to Exemptions" listed on the front side.

Bankruptcy Clerk's Office
Any paper that you file in this bankruptcy case should be filed at the bankruptcy clerk's office at the address listed on the front side. You may inspect all papers filed, including the list of the debtor's property and debts and the list of property claimed as exempt, at the bankruptcy clerk's office.

Legal Advice
The staff of the bankruptcy clerk's office cannot give legal advice. You may want to consult an attorney to protect your rights.

—Refer To Other Side For Important Deadlines and Notices—

FORM B9I (Chapter 13 Case) (9/97)

UNITED STATES BANKRUPTCY COURT _____ District of _____

Notice of
Chapter 13 Bankruptcy Case, Meeting of Creditors, & Deadlines

[The debtor(s) listed below filed a chapter 13 bankruptcy case on _____ (date).]
or [A bankruptcy case concerning the debtor(s) listed below was originally filed under chapter _____ on _____ (date) and was converted to a case under chapter 13 on _____.]

You may be a creditor of the debtor. **This notice lists important deadlines.** You may want to consult an attorney to protect your rights. All documents filed in the case may be inspected at the bankruptcy clerk's office at the address listed below.
NOTE: The staff of the bankruptcy clerk's office cannot give legal advice.

See Reverse Side For Important Explanations.

Debtor(s) (name(s) and address):	Case Number:
	Social Security/Taxpayer ID Nos.:

Attorney for Debtor(s) (name and address):	Bankruptcy Trustee (name and address):
Telephone number:	Telephone number:

Meeting of Creditors:

Date: ____ / ____ / ____   Time: ( ) A.M. ( ) P.M.   Location:

Deadlines:

Papers must be *received* by the bankruptcy clerk's office by the following deadlines:

Deadline to File a Proof of Claim:
For all creditors (except a governmental unit):   For a governmental unit:

Deadline to Object to Exemptions:
Thirty (30) days after the *conclusion* of the meeting of creditors.

Filing of Plan, Hearing on Confirmation of Plan

[The debtor has filed a plan. The plan or a summary of the plan is enclosed. The hearing on confirmation will be held:
Date: Time: Location:
or [The debtor has filed a plan. The plan or a summary of the plan and notice of confirmation hearing will be sent separately.]
or [The debtor has not filed a plan as of this date. You will be sent separate notice of the hearing on confirmation of the plan.]

Creditors May Not Take Certain Actions:

The filing of the bankruptcy case automatically stays certain collection and other actions against the debtor, debtor's property, and certain codebtors. If you attempt to collect a debt or take other action in violation of the Bankruptcy Code, you may be penalized.

Address of the Bankruptcy Clerk's Office:	For the Court:
	Clerk of the Bankruptcy Court:
Telephone number:	
Hours Open:	Date:

Even if you file a Proof of Claim, don't get too excited. In a Chapter 7 case, the assets may produce only a few cents on the dollar. Even if they generate a decent amount of money, the proceeds are distributed to creditors in a specific order—and you may get very little. Similarly, in a Chapter 13 case, priority and secured creditors must be paid in full under the plan. Many Chapter 13 plans propose paying no more than 25% to general unsecured creditors.

Still, you should complete your Proof of Claim. Getting paid something is better than getting paid nothing at all.

If the bankrupt debtor is the spouse of the judgment debtor, you should still file a Proof of Claim. Debts incurred in the course of the marriage (community debts) owed by the non-filing spouse (your judgment debtor) are wiped out in bankruptcy, and nonexempt property acquired during marriage (community property) can be taken in a bankruptcy.

1. Completing the Proof of Claim

In a Chapter 7 asset case or a Chapter 13 case, the court should have sent a Proof of Claim with the bankruptcy notice. If it didn't, use the blank in the Appendix or get a copy from the bankruptcy court. A completed sample is below.

U.S. Bankruptcy Court, Name of Debtor and Case Number: Get the information off of the debtor's bankruptcy papers.

Name of Creditor: Enter your name spelled correctly, even if it was misspelled on the notice.

Name and address where notices should be sent: Enter your name, mailing address and telephone number. Check any of the boxes at the right that apply.

Account or other number by which creditor identifies debtor. Enter the name of the court from which your judgment comes and the case number, such as "Alameda County Municipal Court Case #556-009." Check either box at the right if you are

amending or replacing a previous claim, and provide the date it was filed.

Item 1: If your judgment is based on one of the categories listed on the form, check the appropriate box. If your debt is for wages, salaries or other compensation, enter the requested information. If you don't know which category to select, check "other" and do your best to describe the basis for your judgment.

Item 2: Enter the date the debt first arose.

Item 3: Enter the date your judgment was entered in the court.

Item 4: Enter the total amount of your judgment, including costs and interest that accrued prior to the bankruptcy filing date, less any payments that have been made on the judgment, even if this amount differs from what the debtor listed in the bankruptcy papers. Check the bottom box if your claim includes post-judgment interest or costs. (See Chapter 16.)

Item 5: Check this box if you have created liens that still exist against the debtor's property. (See Chapter 4.) Then indicate whether your liens are against the debtor's real estate, motor vehicle or other property—and specify that other property. Where you are asked to enter the value of the collateral, enter the estimated value of the property to which the liens attach. If you don't know, write "don't know." In the space asking for the amount of arrearage and other charges, enter the amount you entered in Item 4.

Item 6: Priority creditors are entitled to be paid first in bankruptcy. Check the first box if your judgment is based on a priority debt. Then enter the amount of your debt entitled to priority (certain priority debts have a ceiling), and check the box describing the kind of debt you have. Your choices are as follows:

- **Wages, salaries and commissions.** If you were employed by the debtor or hired as an independent contractor, the first $4,650 owed to you and earned either within 90 days before the debtor filed for bankruptcy or within 90 days of when the debtor's business closed is a priority debt.

Proof of Claim

FORM B10 (Official Form 10) (4/01)

UNITED STATES BANKRUPTCY COURT __Southern__ DISTRICT OF __California__	PROOF OF CLAIM

Name of Debtor	Case Number
Celine Ima	0000-0007

NOTE: This form should not be used to make a claim for an administrative expense arising after the commencement of the case. A "request" for payment of an administrative expense may be filed pursuant to 11 U.S.C. § 503.

Name of Creditor (The person or other entity to whom the debtor owes money or property):

Audrey Meta

Name and address where notices should be sent:

Audrey Meta
4706 Coppermine Drive
La Jolla, CA 92000
Telephone number: 619-555-8644

☐ Check box if you are aware that anyone else has filed a proof of claim relating to your claim. Attach copy of statement giving particulars.
☐ Check box if you have never received any notices from the bankruptcy court in this case.
☐ Check box if the address differs from the address on the envelope sent to you by the court.

THIS SPACE IS FOR COURT USE ONLY

Account or other number by which creditor identifies debtor:

San Diego Country Superior Court
Case #0000-0008

Check here if this claim ☐ replaces ☐ amends a previously filed claim, dated:_____

1. Basis for Claim
☐ Goods sold
☐ Services performed
☒ Money loaned
☐ Personal injury/wrongful death
☐ Taxes
☐ Other _____

☐ Retiree benefits as defined in 11 U.S.C. § 1114(a)
☐ Wages, salaries, and compensation (fill out below)
  Your SS #: _____ _____ _____
  Unpaid compensation for services performed
  from _____ to_____
        (date)   (date)

2. Date debt was incurred: 2/6/XX

3. If court judgment, date obtained: 4/16/XX

4. Total Amount of Claim at Time Case Filed: $ __8,645.92__

If all or part of your claim is secured or entitled to priority, also complete Item 5 or 6 below.

☒ Check this box if claim includes interest or other charges in addition to the principal amount of the claim. Attach itemized statement of all interest or additional charges.

5. Secured Claim.
☒ Check this box if your claim is secured by collateral (including a right of setoff).
Brief Description of Collateral:
  ☒ Real Estate   ☐ Motor Vehicle
  ☐ Other_____

Value of Collateral: $__don't know__

Amount of arrearage and other charges at time case filed included in secured claim, if any: $ __8,645.92__

6. Unsecured Priority Claim.
☐ Check this box if you have an unsecured priority claim
Amount entitled to priority $_____
Specify the priority of the claim:
☐ Wages, salaries, or commissions (up to $4,650),* earned within 90 days before filing of the bankruptcy petition or cessation of the debtor's business, whichever is earlier - 11 U.S.C. § 507(a)(3).
☐ Contributions to an employee benefit plan - 11 U.S.C. § 507(a)(4).
☐ Up to $2,100* of deposits toward purchase, lease, or rental of property or services for personal, family, or household use - 11 U.S.C. § 507(a)(6).
☐ Alimony, maintenance, or support owed to a spouse, former spouse, or child - 11 U.S.C. § 507(a)(7).
☐ Taxes or penalties owed to governmental units - 11 U.S.C. § 507(a)(8).
☐ Other - Specify applicable paragraph of 11 U.S.C. § 507(a)(____).
Amounts are subject to adjustment on 4/1/04 and every 3 years thereafter with respect to cases commenced on or after the date of adjustment.

7. Credits: The amount of all payments on this claim has been credited and deducted for the purpose of making this proof of claim.

8. Supporting Documents: *Attach copies of supporting documents,* such as promissory notes, purchase orders, invoices, itemized statements of running accounts, contracts, court judgments, mortgages, security agreements, and evidence of perfection of lien. DO NOT SEND ORIGINAL DOCUMENTS. If the documents are not available, explain. If the documents are voluminous, attach a summary.

9. Date-Stamped Copy: To receive an acknowledgment of the filing of your claim, enclose a stamped, self-addressed envelope and copy of this proof of claim.

THIS SPACE IS FOR COURT USE ONLY

Date	Sign and print the name and title, if any, of the creditor or other person authorized to file this claim (attach copy of power of attorney, if any):
June 4, 20XX	*Audrey Meta*

Penalty for presenting fraudulent claim: Fine of up to $500,000 or imprisonment for up to 5 years, or both. 18 U.S.C. §§ 152 and 3571.

- **Contributions to employee benefit plans.** If the debtor owes contributions to an employee benefit fund that came due within 180 days before the debtor filed for bankruptcy or within 180 days of when the debtor's business closed, that debt is a priority debt.
- **Deposits toward purchase, lease or rental or property or services for personal, family or household use.** If the debtor took a deposit from you for the purpose of purchasing, leasing or renting goods or services for personal, family or household use, up to $2,100 per deposit is a priority—assuming you never received the goods or services.
- **Alimony and child support.** If your judgment is for a support obligation defined in a paternity order, separation agreement, property settlement agreement, divorce decree or other court order, or a determination of liability for support made by a governmental unit according to state law, it is a priority debt.
- **Taxes.** This won't apply to you.
- **Other.** This won't apply to you.

Item 7: This is a statement that you have deducted all money received on the judgment. Make sure the amount you listed in Item 4 includes credits for payments received.

Item 8: Attach to the Proof of Claim copies of all documents that substantiate your claim, including:

- the judgment
- the latest filed Memorandum of Costs
- your written computation of interest accrued and costs incurred after the last Memorandum of Costs was filed
- Abstract of Judgment
- Notice of Judgment Lien on Personal Property, and
- Proof of Service of Application and Order for Appearance and Examination.

Item 9: Follow the instructions.

Date and signature: Enter the date, and sign and print your name.

2. Filing Proof of Claim

Make a copy of the Proof of Claim for your records. If you attend the creditors' meeting, you can file your Proof of Claim there. If you file by mail, it must get to the court within the deadline stated in the notice. There is no need to serve the Proof of Claim on the debtor or his attorney.

3. If Debtor or Trustee Objects

The amount you list on your Proof of Claim will be deemed correct unless the debtor or the trustee objects. The most likely objections are:

- you failed to attach proper documentation in support of your claim
- the amount you claim is incorrect, or
- you improperly stated that your claim was a priority claim.

See a bankruptcy attorney if your claim is rejected for a reason you can't correct and the amount you are seeking warrants the expense.

E. After Filing the Proof of Claim

What happens after you file the Proof of Claim depends on the type of case.

1. Chapter 7 Bankruptcy

After all Proofs of Claim are filed and the meeting of the creditors takes place, the trustee sells any nonexempt property and distributes the funds to creditors. You just sit back and hope to get a check. The entire process usually takes no more than six months.

2. Chapter 13 Bankruptcy

A bankruptcy judge will accept or reject the debtor's plan at a confirmation hearing. The judge will generally accept a plan that was submitted in good faith and is feasible. The judge relies heavily on the recommendation of the trustee.

You can object to the confirmation of a debtor's plan on a number of grounds, including that the debtor's living expenses are unreasonable, that the debtor's total payments will not reach the value of his nonexempt property, that a creditor has been improperly classified as a priority or secured creditor and therefore is being paid off in full when she shouldn't be, or that the plan unfairly discriminates, meaning that the debtor is treating similarly situated creditors differently. For example, if your judgment isn't secured and the debtor proposes paying one unsecured creditor 100%—his brother, for example—while you and the other unsecured creditors receive less, the plan discriminates.

You can raise your objections informally at the meeting of the creditors. If the debtor or trustee does not adequately address your problem, you will have to file a formal motion with the court to be determined at the confirmation hearing.

Once the plan is approved, the trustee's job is to receive payments and distribute them to the creditors. It may take some time before you get paid. As mentioned, priority debts are paid first, then secured creditors. Only after those debts are paid are funds distributed to general unsecured creditors. Before you see a cent, the debtor may miss payments, modify the plan, dismiss the case or convert to a Chapter 7 bankruptcy.

If the debtor has problems making payments, it's up to the bankruptcy trustee—not you—to decide how to proceed. The trustee may give the debtor a grace period of a month or two or may allow minor adjustments in the plan. As long as the debtor appears to be acting in good faith, the trustee will try to be accommodating. If the debtor cannot complete the plan, the debtor may do any of the following:

- Ask to amend the plan to reduce the percentage paid general unsecured creditors or extend the repayment period to as much as

five years. This may reduce the total amount you receive under the plan.
- Convert to a Chapter 7 case—you will receive a notice of conversion if this happens.
- Request a discharge of debts—without converting to Chapter 7—on the basis of hardship, if the debtor's inability to pay is due to circumstances beyond his control, such as a serious illness that prevents the debtor from working. This probably means your judgment will be wiped out.
- Dismiss the Chapter 13 case. This means that you can pick up your collection activities where you left off when the bankruptcy was filed. (But note our caution in Section E3, below, in the event the debtor refiles.)

3. When the Case Is Over

In a Chapter 7 case, when the trustee has mostly completed his work, you will receive a final notice of discharge from the court. If you have been paid nothing, it means that few assets were available to be distributed to general unsecured creditors. If the debtor successfully completes a Chapter 13 case, you will receive a final notice of discharge.

After the debtor receives a discharge, the automatic stay ends. Any balance owed on your debt will be wiped out unless you have liens on the debtor's property that survived the bankruptcy, your debt automatically escapes discharge or the bankruptcy court declared your debt nondischargeable. (See Section F, below.)

If the court notifies you that the bankruptcy case has been dismissed rather than discharged, you may resume collecting—unless and until the debtor files another bankruptcy case. If that happens, a new automatic stay will take effect. Be especially wary of this in a Chapter 13 bankruptcy. One strategy used by debtors who file for Chapter 13 bankruptcy is to wait until Proofs of Claims are filed, dismiss their case and then refile, hoping the creditor won't notice it's a new case and won't refile the necessary Proof of Claim, thinking they've already done so.

F. What Else Can You Do?

In addition to filing a Proof of Claim, a number of possible avenues are open to judgment creditors in bankruptcy. Before you invest time and money pursuing your rights, however, keep in mind that the paramount purpose of bankruptcy is to give the debtor a fresh start. The debtor almost always get the benefit of the doubt and a court is generally inclined to discharge every allowable debt. Still, if you do your homework, you may be able to snatch victory from the jaws of defeat.

1. Ask Debtor to Reaffirm the Debt

Under the Bankruptcy Code, a debtor who wants to keep property that secures a debt, such as a car or house, can do so by "reaffirming" the debt—that is, agreeing to keep making payments under the original agreement. Some unsecured creditors use this section of the Bankruptcy Code to convince debtors who might have engaged in fraud or other questionable behavior to pay their debt rather than have the debt challenged in the bankruptcy court. You may be able to convince the debtor to reaffirm the debt, especially if you notice that the bankruptcy papers are inconsistent with papers the debtor gave you.

You can call the debtor and ask for reaffirmation or raise it at the creditors' meeting. If the debtor agrees, you will have to draft a reaffirmation agreement. If the debtor does not have a lawyer in her bankruptcy case, you will have to schedule a hearing to obtain the judge's approval on the agreement. And whether or not the debtor has an attorney, the reaffirmation agreement must be filed with the bankruptcy court to be valid. A sample agreement and an application for approval of the agreement and order are below.

2. Challenge the Dischargeability of Certain Debts

Certain debts can survive a Chapter 7 bankruptcy, but only if the creditor formally contests the discharge of the debt in court by filing a Complaint to Determine Dischargeability of Debt within 60 days of the date set for the first meeting of creditors. Debts that creditors can successfully preserve through the bankruptcy process are:

- Debts incurred on the basis of fraud, such as loans made in reliance on false or misleading written statements, debts based on intentional misrepresentations or debts of more than $1,075 incurred for luxuries or non-necessary items incurred within 60 days of filing for bankruptcy (11 U.S.C. § 523(a)(2)).
- Debts from willful and malicious acts, including civil judgments for damages resulting from assault and battery, theft, intentional infliction of emotional distress and other intentional torts (11 U.S.C. § 523(a)(6)).
- Debts from embezzlement, larceny or breach of fiduciary duty (11 U.S.C. § 523(a)(4)).
- Debts arising from a marital settlement or divorce decree, other than support, if the debtor has the ability to pay the debt from income or property not reasonably necessary for his support or if discharging the debt would result in a benefit to the debtor that outweighs the detriment to the debtor's former spouse or child (11 U.S.C. § 523(a)(15)).

Does it make sense for you to challenge the discharge of a debt? That depends on the amount at stake and how much it will cost you to do so. Although it is theoretically possible to handle a nondischargeability proceeding yourself, you'll probably have to hire an attorney.

Reaffirmation Agreement

1 Audrey Meta
   4706 Coppermine Drive
2 La Jolla, CA 92000
   619-555-8644
3 Creditor in Pro Per

4

5

6

7

8   UNITED STATES BANKRUPTCY COURT

9   SOUTHERN DISTRICT OF CALIFORNIA

10

11 In re:)
    Celine Ima   ) Case No. 0000-0007
12   )
) Chapter 7
13   )
)
14   )
              Debtor(s)   )
15

16

17   REAFFIRMATION AGREEMENT

18   Celine Ima, the debtor in the above-captioned bankruptcy case, and Audrey Meta hereby agree

19 that:

20   1. Celine Ima, subject to the approval of the bankruptcy court and the statutory right to rescind,

21 reaffirms her debt of $8,645.92 to Audrey Meta, secured by debtor's home, currently valued at

22 $195,000.

23   2. This debt will be paid in installments of $300 per month, at 10% simple interest, until it has

24 been paid in full.

25   3. Audrey Meta agrees to waive all previous and current defaults on this debt.

26   4. Audrey Meta further agrees that she will not act to repossess the debtor's home securing this

27 debt unless the debtor is more than thirty days in default under this agreement.

28 THIS AGREEMENT MAY BE CANCELLED BY THE DEBTOR ANY TIME BEFORE May 17, 20XX

                    REAFFIRMATION AGREEMENT   1

Reaffirmation Agreement (continued)

1   (*date 60 days after filing with the court*) OR THE DATE OF THE BANKRUPTCY DISCHARGE IF

2   THAT IS AFTER May 17,20XX, BY GIVING NOTICE TO Audrey Meta.

3   Debtor is aware that reaffirming this debt is not required by the Bankruptcy Act, by

4   nonbankruptcy law or by any agreement.

5   Debtor was not represented by an attorney during the course of negotiating this agreement.

6

7   Dated: _*March 17, 20XX*_   *Celine Ima*

8   Celine Ima

9   Dated: _*March 17, 20XX*_   *Audrey Meta*

10   Audrey Meta

11

12

13

14

15

16

17

18

19

20

21

22

23

24

25

26

27

28

Application for Approval of Reaffirmation Agreement

1 Audrey Meta
4706 Coppermine Drive
2 La Jolla, CA 92000
619-555-8644
3 Creditor in Pro Per

4

5

6

7

8 UNITED STATES BANKRUPTCY COURT

9 SOUTHERN DISTRICT OF CALIFORNIA

10

11 In re:)
Celine Ima) Case No.0000-0007
12)
) Chapter 7
13)
)
14)
)
_____)
15 Debtor(s)

16

17 APPLICATION FOR APPROVAL OF REAFFIRMATION
AGREEMENT PURSUANT TO 11 U.S.C. § 524(C)
18

19 TO THE HONORABLE _____,BANKRUPTCY JUDGE:

20 The debtor(s) in this case, Celine Ima, hereby apply for approval of their reaffirmation agreement

21 with Audrey Meta. In support of this application we hereby aver that:

22 1. Celine Ima wishes to reaffirm her debt with Audrey Meta, to the extent it is secured by

23 debtor's home.

24 2. The debtor's home is presently worth $195,000.

25 3. The reaffirmation agreement, signed by the parties and providing for the payment of

26 $8,645.92 at 10% interest, in 33 monthly installments, is attached to this application.

27

28

APPLICATION FOR APPROVAL OF REAFFIRMATION
AGREEMENT PURSUANT TO 11 U.S.C. § 524(C)

1

Application for Approval of Reaffirmation Agreement

4. The agreement does not impose a hardship on Celine Ima, because the debtor(s)' current income is $4,700 per month, and expenses are $4,000 per month.

WHEREFORE, the debtors pray that the reaffirmation of the aforesaid debt be approved.

Dated: _3/17/XX_____   _Celine Ima_____
                                          Celine Ima

ORDER APPROVING REAFFIRMATION AGREEMENT

AND NOW, this _____day of _____, 20___, the court having found that the reaffirmation agreement proposed by the debtors is in the best interest of the debtor and does not pose a hardship on the debtor or the debtor's dependents, it is hereby ordered that the reaffirmation with Audrey Meta is approved.

Dated: _____   _____
                                          U.S. Bankruptcy Judge

3. Object to Exemptions

In a Chapter 13 bankruptcy, general unsecured creditors must receive at least the value of the debtor's nonexempt property. Otherwise, exemptions have no role in a Chapter 13 case. In a Chapter 7 bankruptcy, however, exemptions are a key component. All nonexempt property may be taken by the trustee and sold to pay off the general unsecured creditors.

When the debtor files for bankruptcy, he must complete several forms called Schedules A, B and C. On Schedules A and B, he lists all of his property. On Schedule C, he lists the property he claims as exempt. Most debtors in California find a way to include all of their valuable property on Schedule C. You can visit the court and examine the schedules your debtor files.

In California, a debtor can choose between two sets of exemptions—those authorized by various provisions of section 704 of the Code of Civil Procedure (called the "System 1" exemptions) and those authorized by various provisions of section 703 of the Code of Civil Procedure (called the "System 2" exemptions). Full lists of both sets of exemptions are below.

If you examine the debtor's schedules and discover bogus exemptions or property that has been greatly undervalued to bring it within the limit of an exemption, you can object. Written objections must be made within 30 days after the Meeting of the Creditors. The court will accept any exemption claimed by a debtor if no one objects, even if the exemption has no basis in reality. Formally objecting to a claimed exemption is beyond the scope of this book. You can report your findings to the trustee, however, and hope that he'll do the job for you.

4. Make Other Objections

In every Chapter 7 bankruptcy case, a debtor must list all her property, debts, income and expenses and describe all property transactions that occurred during the year before filing. On the basis of the debtor's papers, the trustee decides whether the debtor has nonexempt assets that should be sold to repay the creditors.

That's not the only thing the trustee looks for. The trustee—and creditors—can examine the papers to see if the debtor made payments to any creditors during the 90 days preceding the bankruptcy—and during the last year to creditors who are relatives or business associates. If so, these payments are considered illegal preferences and the trustee may demand that the creditor turn the money over to the trustee to be apportioned among all of the creditors.

It might also be that the debtor has obviously unloaded (sold cheaply or given away) assets in order to hide them from creditors. This may be a basis for denying the bankruptcy altogether. Bankruptcy laws impose severe penalties on debtors who try to cheat their creditors or lie about their assets or income. Several bankruptcy courts, including the one in Los Angeles, aggressively go after debtors who try to commit fraud.

If you discover this type of questionable behavior, bring it to the attention of the trustee at once. The trustee can file a motion asking the bankruptcy court to dismiss the case. A dismissal would free you up to continue your collection efforts just as if the bankruptcy were never filed.

If you discover the questionable behavior only after the bankruptcy has ended and the debtor has received a discharge, you have up to one year after the date of the discharge to file a complaint with the bankruptcy court. You'll need a lawyer's help. If you win, the bankruptcy discharge will be nullified and you can collect the debt (11 U.S.C. §§ 727(d), 727(e), 1328(d)).

5. Enforce Liens That Survive Bankruptcy

A judgment lien that attaches to exempt property such as a house or car can usually be wiped out in bankruptcy through a process called lien

California Bankruptcy Exemptions—System 1

Asset	Exemption	Law
Homestead	Real or personal property you occupy including mobile home, boat, stock cooperative, community apartment, planned development or condo to $50,000 if single & not disabled; $75,000 for families if no other member has a homestead (if only one spouse files, may exempt one-half of amount if home held as community property and all of amount if home held as tenants in common); $125,000 if 65 or older, or physically or mentally disabled; $125,000 if 55 or older, single & earn under $15,000 or married & earn under $20,000 & creditors seek to force the sale of your home; sale proceeds received exempt for 6 months after (husband & wife may not double)	704.710, 704.720, 704.730 *In re McFall,* 112 B.R. 336 (9th Cir. B.A.P. 1990)
	May file homestead declaration	704.920
Insurance	Disability or health benefits	704.130
	Fidelity bonds	Labor 404
	Fraternal unemployment benefits	704.120
	Homeowners' insurance proceeds for 6 months after received, to homestead exemption amount	704.720(b)
	Life insurance proceeds if clause prohibits proceeds from being used to pay beneficiary's creditors	Ins. 10132, Ins. 10170, Ins. 10171
	Matured life insurance benefits needed for support	704.100(c)
	Unmatured life insurance policy loan value to $8,000 (husband & wife may double)	704.100(b)
Miscellaneous	Business or professional licenses	695.060
	Inmates' trust funds to $1,000 (husband and wife may not double)	704.090
	Property of business partnership	Corp. 16501-04
Pensions	County employees	Gov't 31452
	County firefighters	Gov't 32210
	County peace officers	Gov't 31913
	Private retirement benefits, including IRAs & Keoghs	704.115
	Public employees	Gov't 21201
	Public retirement benefits	704.110
Personal property	Appliances, furnishings, clothing & food	704.020
	Bank deposits from Social Security Administration to $2,000 ($3,000 for husband and wife)	704.080
	Building materials to repair or improve home to $2,000 (husband and wife may not double)	704.030
	Burial plot	704.200
	Funds held in escrow	Fin. 17410
	Health aids	704.050
	Homeowners' association assessments	Civil 1366(c)
	Jewelry, heirlooms & art to $5,000 total (husband and wife may not double)	704.040
	Motor vehicles to $1,900, or $1,900 in auto insurance for loss or damages (husband and wife may not double)	704.010
	Personal injury & wrongful death causes of action	704.140(a), 704.150(a)
	Personal injury & wrongful death recoveries needed for support; if receiving installments, at least 75%	704.140(b),(c),(d), 704.150(b),(c)
Public benefits	Aid to blind, aged, disabled, public assistance	704.170
	Financial aid to students	704.190
	Relocation benefits	704.180
	Unemployment benefits	704.120
	Union benefits due to labor dispute	704.120(b)(5)
	Workers' compensation	704.160

California Bankruptcy Exemptions—System 1 (continued)

Asset	Exemption	Law
Tools of trade	Tools, implements, materials, instruments, uniforms, books, furnishings & equipment to $5,000 total ($10,000 total if used by both spouses in same occupation)	704.060
	Commercial vehicle (Vehicle Code § 260) to $4,000 ($8,000 total if used by both spouses in same occupation)	704.060
Wages	Minimum 75% of wages paid within 30 days prior to filing	704.070
	Public employees vacation credits; if receiving installments, at least 75%	704.113
Wildcard	None	

California Bankruptcy Exemptions—System 2

Asset	Exemption	Law
Homestead	Real or personal property, including co-op, used as residence to $17,425; unused portion of homestead may be applied to any property	703.140 (b)(1)
Insurance	Disability benefits	703.140 (b)(10)(C)
	Life insurance proceeds needed for support of family	703.140 (b)(11)(C)
	Unmatured life insurance contract accrued avails to $9,300	703.140 (b)(8)
	Unmatured life insurance policy other than credit	703.140 (b)(7)
Miscellaneous	Alimony, child support needed for support	703.140 (b)(10)(D)
Pensions	ERISA-qualified benefits needed for support	703.140 (b)(10)(E)
Personal property	Animals, crops, appliances, furnishings, household goods, books, musical instruments & clothing to $450 per item	703.140 (b)(3)
	Burial plot to $17,425, in lieu of homestead	703.140 (b)(1)
	Health aids	703.140 (b)(9)
	Jewelry to $1,150	703.140 (b)(4)
	Motor vehicle to $2,725	703.140 (b)(2)
	Personal injury recoveries to $17,425 (not to include pain & suffering; pecuniary loss)	703.140 (b)(11)(D),(E)
	Wrongful death recoveries needed for support	703.140 (b)(11)(B)
Public benefits	Crime victims' compensation	703.140 (b)(11)(A)
	Public assistance	703.140 (b)(10)(A)
	Social Security	703.140 (b)(10)(A)
	Unemployment compensation	703.140 (b)(10)(A)
	Veterans' benefits	703.140 (b)(10)(B)
Tools of trade	Implements, books & tools of trade to $1,750	703.140 (b)(6)
Wages	None (use Federal non-bankruptcy wage exemption)	
Wildcard	$925 of any property	703.140 (b)(5)
	Unused portion of homestead or burial exemption, of any property	703.140 (b)(5)

avoidance. There are a few exceptions, however. First, if the lien existed before the debtor obtained the property, the lien cannot be wiped out. So if you got your judgment, recorded an Abstract of Judgment with the county recorder and then the debtor bought a house in that county, the debtor did not own the property before the lien was affixed and the lien cannot be eliminated.

In addition, the lien can be wiped out only if it "impairs" the exemption. If there's enough equity in the property to allow the debtor to get the full exemption and to pay off the lien, it won't be eliminated. For example, say an unmarried debtor owns a house worth $150,000; the debtor owes $125,000 to the lender, leaving $25,000 of equity. You've recorded a $10,000 judgment. But the homestead exemption for an unmarried person in California is $50,000 and the equity doesn't cover that much. Your lien can be wiped out. If the house was worth $200,000, however, and the debtor owed the lender $125,000, the debtor would have $75,000 of equity—enough to cover the exemption and your judgment. In that case, the lien would stay.

If your lien is wiped out, your debt is treated like any other unsecured debt. If your lien survives bankruptcy, the lien is your only method of collecting the judgment after your bankruptcy case ends, unless the court determines that the debt is not dischargeable. Oddly, you have to think of your debt as having two parts: 1) the debtors personal liability to pay you, and 2) your lien. The personal liability gets wiped out in bank-ruptcy, even if the lien remains. As we said in Chapter 4, this means you'll most likely be paid if the debtor sells or refinances the property.

6. Collect Nondischargeable Debts

Certain debts automatically survive the bankruptcy intact, which means you can still collect them after the bankruptcy case is over. They include:

- **Omitted debts.** Debts not listed in the bankruptcy papers are not discharged, unless the creditor had notice or actual knowledge of the bankruptcy case in time to file a Proof of Claim (11 U.S.C. § 523(a)(3)).
- **Alimony and child support.** Child and spousal support obligations, and debts that are in the nature of support, are not dischargeable (11 U.S.C. §§ 523(a)(5) and 523(a)(18)).
- **Court-ordered restitution.** A court may have ordered a convicted criminal to make restitution to you. If you convert that restitution order into a civil judgment under Penal Code § 1014(b), the debt cannot be discharged in bankruptcy (11 U.S.C. § 523(a)(17)). (Chapter 1, Section D covers converting a restitution order into a civil judgment.)
- **Debts from intoxicated driving.** Debts based on a death or personal injury resulting from the debtor's driving under the influence of alcohol or drugs are nondischargeable in bankruptcy (11 U.S.C. §§ 523(a)(9)). ■

Chapter 18

If the Debtor Dies

Collection Factor			
	High	**Moderate**	**Low**
Potential cost to you			✓
Potential for producing cash		✓	
Potential for settlement		✓	
Potential time and trouble			✓
Potential for debtor's estate to file bankruptcy			✓

*L*earning of a judgment debtor's death can be deeply sobering. No matter how zealously you have pursued your judgment, the final reality of the debtor's death will certainly make you pause. Perhaps you'll be grateful that the same fate did not befall you and simply drop the matter. Perhaps you'll think of the debtor's survivors, want to leave them in peace and abandon your claim. Or perhaps you are hoping that the deceased left assets from which you can collect your judgment.

If either of the first two scenarios describe how you feel, put down the book, hug your loved ones and celebrate what you have. If the third one is closer to how you feel, keep reading this chapter —if the debtor lived in California. If the debtor lived elsewhere, you will probably need a lawyer's help to follow the procedures of that state.

Whether you can collect from the property the debtor owned at her death depends on the value of the property and how it passes to the debtor's heirs. If the assets pass through a formal court process known as probate, you may be in luck. Probate provides an orderly procedure for you to present your claim and be paid. On the other hand, if the assets pass directly to the debtor's heirs outside of probate, there is no special collection procedure for creditors. You must track down the assets one by one—much the same as when the debtor was alive.

Note that the debtor's surviving relatives—parents, adult children and others—are not personally responsible for your debt. Your only course is to seek payment from the debtor's estate. The one possible exception is if the debt was a community debt, in which case the debtor's spouse is personally responsible for paying it.

Important Terms Used in This Chapter

Intestate succession: The rules under which property is passed to a person's heirs when he dies without a will, trust or other estate planning document, or when an estate planning document fails to pass the property for one reason or another.

Joint tenancy: A way of holding title to property that avoids probate. When one joint tenant dies, her share automatically passes to the surviving joint tenants.

Living trust: A probate-avoidance device by which a person transfers property to a trust with instructions that the trust property be transferred to a named beneficiary at the owner's death.

Non-probate property: Property that does not go through probate because the deceased, while alive, set up a mechanism to avoid probate. Examples are life insurance proceeds payable to named beneficiaries, property held in joint tenancy, property held in a living trust and pay-on-death bank account trusts.

Personal representative: A person authorized to act on behalf of a deceased's estate. If named in the will, this person is called an executor; otherwise, he is called an administrator.

Probate: The court-supervised process by which a deceased's assets are distributed and debts are paid.

Probate estate: The assets of the deceased that are distributed through probate.

There are several different ways in which you may learn of the debtor's death.

- If you are looking for the debtor or actively involved in collecting the debt, you may learn of the death from relatives, an employer or other creditors.
- If you live in the same community as the debtor, you may read of his death in an obituary in a newspaper.
- If the debtor had a will or other estate planning document and sufficient assets to pass through probate, and the personal representative knows of your debt, he must send you a document called a Notice of Administration to Creditors. The notice informs you of your right to file a Creditor's Claim against the estate. The notice must be mailed within four months of when the personal representative is named.
- If the debtor had a will or other estate planning document and sufficient assets to pass through probate, the personal representative for the estate must file a document called Petition to Administer Estate in the probate court. The court will set a date and time for a hearing. The personal representative then must publish a legal death notice in a general circulation newspaper in the city in which the debtor died, giving the date of the hearing. Collection agencies read these notices, but few others do—as a practical matter, you are unlikely to learn of the debtor's death this way.

A. Collecting Through Probate

Assets pass to heirs through probate when they are left in a will or when the deceased made no provision for how they should be passed. But not all assets pass through probate. If the debtor's assets are worth less than $100,000, they can pass to heirs without probate. Or if the debtor arranged to transfer assets through a living trust, joint tenancy property or a pay-on-death account, the assets don't go through probate. The deceased's share of community property automatically passes to a surviving spouse absent a will or other estate planning document. Section B, below, explains how to pursue assets if there's no probate proceeding.

If you learn of the debtor's death through a notice from the personal representative or you see the legal death notice in a newspaper, there will be a probate proceeding. If you learn of the death from some other source, you will need to ask around to find out if there will be a probate proceeding. First, contact the Probate Division of the Superior Court for the county in which the debtor died and ask if a probate petition has been filed in the debtor's name. If one hasn't, you can monitor the newspaper that carries legal notices for that area. You might also contact any other creditors to whom the debtor owed money and ask if they know. After a respectable amount of time (a few weeks), you can call relatives, offer your condolences and then ask politely whether there will be a probate proceeding.

Once you know that a probate proceeding has been opened, you must file a Creditor's Claim in order to request payment. In a Creditor's Claim, you assert your right to be paid out of the debtor's assets, if enough assets remain after higher priority creditors are paid. If you don't file a Creditor's Claim, you give up all right to collect your judgment.

1. When to File a Creditor's Claim

Your deadline for filing a Creditor's Claim depends on how you learned about the probate proceeding.

- If you receive a Notice of Administration to Creditors from the personal representative, you must file your claim within four months after the date the personal representative was appointed by the court or 60 days after the notice was sent to you, whichever is later (Probate Code § 9100).

- If you saw the Notice of Petition to Administer Estate in a newspaper, the deadline is four months from the hearing date stated on the Petition.
- If you learn from the court or another source, contact the probate court and find out when the personal representative was appointed. File your Creditor's Claim within four months of that date.

If you don't find out about the probate proceedings until after the deadline for filing a Creditor's Claim, see a probate attorney. If you did not receive notice of the probate proceeding, you can petition the court to file a late claim, but only if the probate court has not yet made a final order for distribution of the estate (Probate Code § 9103).

2. Complete the Creditor's Claim

To complete the Creditor's Claim, you will need the following information:
- title and address of the probate court
- probate case number, and
- name and address of the personal representative.

A blank Creditor's Claim is in the Appendix. A sample completed form and instructions are below.

Caption: Enter your name, address and phone number and indicate that you are appearing in pro per. Enter the name and address of the court handling the probate, the debtor's name and the probate case number.

Item 1: Fill in the total amount of the judgment still due. Deduct any payments you have received and add post-judgment interest and court costs. (See Chapter 16.) If you haven't filed a Memorandum of Costs within the past few months, do so and serve it on the personal representative before filing this claim.

Item 2: Enter your name and check the box that best describes your status as the creditor. If you check 2b, be sure to enter your business'

fictitious name. 2e might apply if you are the creditor's conservator or attorney-in-fact under a power of attorney.

Item 3: Enter your address.

Item 4: Check the first box if you are the creditor. Check the second box if you are acting on behalf of a creditor and state your authority.

Item 5: Leave this blank.

Item 6: Check both boxes.

Fill in the date, print or type your name and sign the form.

Page Two

Caption: Fill in the name of the debtor and the probate case number.

Facts Supporting the Creditor's Claim: Check the "See attachment" box because you'll be attaching a copy of your judgment and possibly the most recent Memorandum of Costs.

Date of Item: Fill in the date your judgment was entered.

Item and Supporting Facts: Provide a brief description of your judgment. For example: "Judgment against George Adis for failure to pay back a loan." State whether costs were claimed in Memoranda of Costs and the amount of these costs. Also describe any judicial liens that you created on the debtor's personal property or real estate. If you provide sufficient information on the liens (date, book and page, and county where recorded), you are not required to attach copies of the liens. Otherwise, provide copies of the liens.

Amount Claimed: Enter the total from Item 1 on the front of the form.

Total: Enter the same amount.

Proof of Mailing/Personal Delivery: Unlike most court documents, you can serve the Creditor's Claim yourself. Depending on whether you plan to mail or hand deliver the document, check the appropriate box before "Mailing" or "Personal delivery." Complete the rest of the Proof of Service following the guidelines in Chapter 21.

Creditor's Claim

DE-172

ATTORNEY OR PARTY WITHOUT ATTORNEY (Name, state bar number, and address):	TELEPHONE AND FAX NOS.:	FOR COURT USE ONLY
Seysu Yesh 101 North Quail Creek Lane Larkspur, CA 94900	415-555-8619	

ATTORNEY FOR (Name): In Pro Per

SUPERIOR COURT OF CALIFORNIA, COUNTY OF   MARIN

STREET ADDRESS:

MAILING ADDRESS: P.O. Box 4988

CITY AND ZIP CODE: San Rafael, CA 94913

BRANCH NAME:

ESTATE OF (Name):

   Percy McDougal

                                 DECEDENT

CREDITOR'S CLAIM	CASE NUMBER: 0000-0009

You must file this claim with the court clerk at the court address above before the LATER of (a) four months after the date letters (authority to act for the estate) were first issued to the personal representative, or (b) sixty days after the date the *Notice of Administration* was given to the creditor, if notice was given as provided in Probate Code section 9051. You must also mail or deliver a copy of this claim to the personal representative and his or her attorney. A proof of service is on the reverse.

WARNING: Your claim will in most instances be invalid if you do not properly complete this form, file it on time with the court, and mail or deliver a copy to the personal representative and his or her attorney.

1. Total amount of the claim: $ 9,400
2. Claimant (name):   Seysu Yesh
   a. [X] an individual
   b. [ ] an individual or entity doing business under the fictitious name of (specify):

   c. [ ] a partnership. The person signing has authority to sign on behalf of the partnership.
   d. [ ] a corporation. The person signing has authority to sign on behalf of the corporation.
   e. [ ] other (specify):
3. Address of claimant (specify):   101 North Quail Creek Lane
                                    Larkspur, CA 94900
4. Claimant is   [X] the creditor   [ ] a person acting on behalf of creditor (state reason):

5. [ ] Claimant is   [ ] the personal representative   [ ] the attorney for the personal representative.
6. I am authorized to make this claim which is just and due or may become due. All payments on or offsets to the claim have been credited. Facts supporting the claim are   [X] on reverse   [X] attached.

I declare under penalty of perjury under the laws of the State of California that the foregoing is true and correct.

Date: August 8, 20XX

. . Seysu .Yesh . . . .   ▶   *Seysu Yesh*
(TYPE OR PRINT NAME AND TITLE)   (SIGNATURE OF CLAIMANT)

INSTRUCTIONS TO CLAIMANT

A. On the reverse, itemize the claim and show the date the service was rendered or the debt incurred. Describe the item or service in detail, and indicate the amount claimed for each item. Do not include debts incurred after the date of death, except funeral claims.

B. If the claim is not due or contingent, or the amount is not yet ascertainable, state the facts supporting the claim.

C. If the claim is secured by a note or other written instrument, the original or a copy must be attached (state why original is unavailable.) If secured by mortgage, deed of trust, or other lien on property that is of record, it is sufficient to describe the security and refer to the date or volume and page, and county where recorded. (See Prob. Code, § 9152.)

D. Mail or take this original claim to the court clerk's office for filing. If mailed, use certified mail, with return receipt requested.

E. Mail or deliver a copy to the personal representative and his or her attorney. Complete the *Proof of Mailing or Personal Delivery* on the reverse.

F. The personal representative or his or her attorney will notify you when your claim is allowed or rejected.

G. Claims against the estate by the personal representative and the attorney for the personal representative must be filed within the claim period allowed in Probate Code section 9100. See the notice box above.

(Continued on reverse)

Form Approved by the Judicial Council of California DE-172 [Rev. January 1, 1998] Optional Form	**CREDITOR'S CLAIM** (Probate)	Probate Code, §§ 9000 et seq., 9153

Creditor's Claim (continued)

ESTATE OF *(Name):*		CASE NUMBER:
Percy McDougal	DECEDENT	0000-0009

FACTS SUPPORTING THE CREDITOR'S CLAIM
[X] **See attachment** *(if space is insufficient)*

Date of item	Item and supporting facts	Amount claimed
2/9/XX	Judgment entered in Seysu Yesh v. Percy McDougal in Marin County Superior Court, case No. 0000-0010. Judgment is based on failure to repay promissory note. No payments have been made. Post-judgment costs and interest total $611 (a copy of a Memorandum of Costs is attached). A lien was created on 3/11/XX when the Abstract of Judgment was recorded at the Marin County Recorder's office Book 472 at page 19.	$9,400
	TOTAL:	$ 9,400

PROOF OF ☐ **MAILING** ☐ **PERSONAL DELIVERY**   **TO PERSONAL REPRESENTATIVE**
(Be sure to mail or take the original to the court clerk's office for filing)

1. I am the creditor or a person acting on behalf of the creditor. At the time of mailing or delivery I was at least 18 years of age.
2. My residence or business address is *(specify):* 101 North Quail Creek Lane
   Larkspur, Ca 94900
3. I mailed or personally delivered a copy of this *Creditor's Claim* to the personal representative as follows *(check either a or b below):*

   a. [X] **Mail**. I am a resident of or employed in the county where the mailing occurred.
      (1) I enclosed a copy in an envelope AND
        (a) [X] **deposited** the sealed envelope with the United States Postal Service with the postage fully prepaid.
        (b) ☐ **placed** the envelope for collection and mailing on the date and at the place shown in items below following our ordinary business practices. I am readily familiar with this business' practice for collecting and processing correspondence for mailing. On the same day that correspondence is placed for collection and mailing, it is deposited in the ordinary course of business with the United States Postal Service in a sealed envelope with postage fully prepaid.
      (2) The envelope was addressed and mailed first-class as follows:
        (a) Name of personal representative served: Gretl Goodrich
        (b) Address on envelope: 38 Waller Rd.
           Novato, CA 94900
        (c) Date of mailing: August 8, 20XX
        (d) Place of mailing *(city and state):* Larkspur, CA

   b. ☐ **Personal delivery**. I personally delivered a copy of the claim to the personal representative as follows:
      (1) Name of personal representative served:
      (2) Address where delivered:

      (3) Date delivered:
      (4) Time delivered:

I declare under penalty of perjury under the laws of the State of California that the foregoing is true and correct.

Date: August 8, 20XX

Seysu Yesh
(TYPE OR PRINT NAME OF CLAIMANT)

▶ *Seysu Yesh*
(SIGNATURE OF CLAIMANT)

DE-172 [Rev. January 1,1998]
Optional Form

CREDITOR'S CLAIM
(Probate)

Page two

3. Send and File the Claim

Make four copies of the Creditor's Claim, including your attachments. Mail or hand deliver a copy to the personal representative. Send the original and one copy to the court to be file-stamped and returned to you in a self-addressed, stamped envelope.

4. After You Submit a Claim

After receiving your claim, the personal representative should send you an Allowance or Rejection of Claim form. If payment of your judgment is approved, you may be paid immediately or the personal representative may wait until the court issues a final order stating how estate property is to be distributed.

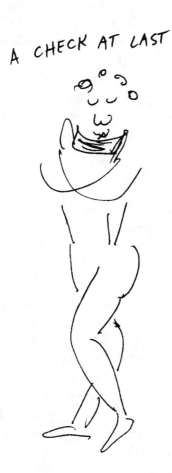

A CHECK AT LAST

How the Representative Pays Claims

The personal representative must pay off debts in the order set out below—except that debts owed the federal or state government have priority. The first five categories must be paid before the others (Probate Code § 11421).

1. Expenses of administering the estate.
2. Funeral expenses.
3. Expenses of last illness.
4. Family allowance to support the deceased's family during probate. Note also that if the debtor had filed a homestead declaration, her family members will be allowed to claim the homestead exemption if they inherit all or part of the house and are living in it at the time of the debtor's death (Code of Civil Procedure § 704.995).
5. Wages due the deceased's employees.
6. Mortgages, judgment liens and other liens. These are paid from the proceeds of the property subject to the lien; if the proceeds aren't enough, the remaining amount is classed with general debts.
7. General debts, including judgments not secured by liens.

What if the personal representative ignores or rejects your claim? You can dispute the decision formally by filing a lawsuit against the estate within three months of the date you receive a notice of rejection. If you don't ever receive a notice—that is, the personal representative just ignores your claim—you can file a lawsuit within three months of a "presumed date of rejection"—30 days after the claim was filed, or 35 days if you sent your form to the personal representative by mail.

If the personal representative disputes your claim, the court may require the estate to deposit the entire amount of the claim with the court, where it will remain until the matter is settled (Probate Code § 11463).

Before you run to court, contact the personal representative by phone or letter. The personal representative might explain the reason for the rejection or dispute. For example, if she claims the judgment has been paid, you will have the chance to show that it hasn't. Or you might be able to reach a compromise that settles the debt.

If your claim is ignored or rejected because the estate has no money, you can check the court file to learn how funds are being disbursed. There may truly be no assets to pay you with, in which case you are out of luck.

If there appear to be funds or assets from which your claim can be paid, consider suing the personal representative for payment from the estate. If the amount in question is a relatively small sum—say up to $5,000—you can probably handle it yourself in Small Claims court. There are special notice requirements for suing an estate, so check with the Small Claims advisor, a probate lawyer or a paralegal. If the amount is large enough for a regular court action, see a lawyer.

If Probate Is Opened But Assets Pass Outside of Probate

Many people pass some of their assets through probate avoidance devices such as a living trust or pay-on-death bank account, but leave enough property in their will to require a probate proceedings. Property that passes through a trust is liable for the payment of the deceased's creditors, if the property passing through probate is insufficient for that purpose (Probate Code § 19001). If the probate proceeding won't produce enough in assets to pay off your judgment, try collecting from assets passed outside of probate. See Section B, just below, for some suggestions on how to approach this task.

B. Collecting Outside of Probate

If the debtor left insufficient assets to require probate, or left insufficient funds to pay your judgment through probate but did leave property in a trust, the only way to get paid is to find assets that formerly belonged to the debtor but are now in the hands of heirs. You can attempt to levy on that property as if the debtor was alive. One possible source is a surviving spouse. Because California is a community property state, you can go after the surviving spouse's share of any community property owned prior to the debtor's death as well as property inherited by the spouse.

It may be possible for you to open a probate proceeding on behalf of a deceased debtor. Whether or not this makes sense will depend on your case. A consultation with a probate lawyer can help you decide.

It can be difficult to trace the debtor's assets once they are passed on—there is seldom a public record of what happened to the debtor's property. Real estate and business assets are the exception. So where do you turn? If the debtor was single but had children, you can reasonably expect that the children inherited most of the property. If the debtor was unmarried but had a companion, look to that person. To locate assets owned by heirs, you will have to use the procedures outlined in Chapter 6 or hire an asset-tracing firm (Chapter 23, Section C).

If you created liens on the debtor's property, you will have an easier time collecting. Liens remain on property that passes to heirs. If the heir wants to sell the property, the liens will have to be paid off in order for the property to sell with clear title. Inherited property is often sold soon after it is received, so you may be paid.

There is one important exception to this rule: liens on property held in joint tenancy property are extinguished when the joint tenant-debtor dies. This is based on the legal principle that joint tenancy property isn't technically inherited; a joint tenant's interest (including the lien) simply ends when he dies. ■

Chapter 19

Help From a Judge:
Filing Motions to Force Collections

Collection Factor			
	High	Moderate	Low
Potential cost to you		✓	
Potential for producing cash		✓	
Potential for settlement		✓	
Potential time and trouble	✓		
Potential for debtor's bankruptcy			✓

There are situations in which the collection methods outlined in this book won't get you your judgment. For example, the debtor may own valuable property that you can't levy on because it's in the debtor's private residence or the debtor is concealing it. Or, the debtor may receive periodic payments from a nonexempt source, which makes a levy impractical because it collects only what is due at the time the levy is made.

In these situations, you may be able to reach the elusive assets if you obtain a court order from a judge. You can file a motion requesting one of the following kinds of orders.

- **Seizure order:** Allows a levying officer to levy on personal property in a private home.
- **Turnover order:** Requires the debtor to turn over specified property to the levying officer.
- **Assignment order:** Requires the debtor to assign the right to receive certain payments to you.

You have two choices in filing your motion—you can give the debtor several days' advance notice or not. When you don't give the debtor several days' advance notice, your motion is called an *ex parte motion.* You simply prepare the paperwork and argue your motion before the judge at an informal hearing, often in the judge's office. If you do give the debtor notice, your motion is called a *noticed motion.* You prepare the necessary paperwork, schedule a formal hearing for a date and give the debtor 15-21 days' notice.

Ex parte motions are allowed if you convince the court that giving notice to the debtor would defeat the purpose for the order. (See California Rules of Court, Rule 379.) For instance, if you seek an order permitting a levy on property in the debtor's home, the debtor is likely to remove the property if you give advance notice.

On ex parte motions, a court will almost always require at least a little informal advance notice before the hearing, without requiring a fully noticed hearing. Typically, you'll have to phone the debtor at least 24 hours before the hearing. In extreme cases, the judge will dispense with even this type of notice.

A. Typical Ex Parte Motions

A motion for a Seizure Order or Turnover Order is typically brought ex parte, unless the judge or a local court rule requires a noticed motion. If the local rules don't address this issue, ask the court clerk if your motion can be brought ex parte. If the answer isn't clear, proceed ex parte. If the court requires a noticed motion, you'll have to start over.

1. Motion for Seizure Order

A levying officer cannot forcibly enter a debtor's private residence to seize assets unless the officer has a Writ of Execution and Seizure Order from the court. A judge will not grant a Seizure Order unless you convince her that all of the following are true:

- the debtor has property that you need to seize to collect all or part of your judgment
- you have "probable cause" for believing that the assets are on the premises in question, and
- you have no reasonable alternative method to collect your judgment.

2. Motion for Turnover Order

A Turnover Order requires the debtor to give the levying officer tangible personal property or certificates of title to personal property, such as a motor vehicle or stock certificates. You must first obtain a Writ of Execution. (See Chapter 7.) A Turnover Order may be useful in these situations:

- you know the judgment debtor has specific items of property, but you are having trouble locating them for a levy
- property belonging to the judgment debtor can't be reached by an ordinary levy and you don't want to, or can't, obtain a Seizure Order, or
- you need specific evidence, which the debtor possesses, of debts owed to the debtor by third parties, , and you'd rather proceed this way than through a subpena and debtor's examination (see Chapter 6).

Difference Between Seizure Order and Turnover Order

A Seizure Order authorizes the levying officer to enter a private place to levy on assets. A Turnover Order requires the debtor to deliver specifically named property to the levying officer. You use a Seizure Order if you want to levy on an item that can't easily be concealed —a piano, for instance—and a Turnover Order for items that are easy to hide, such as jewelry or documents.

3. Preparing a Motion for a Seizure Order or Turnover Order

If your judgment is from small claims court, check with the small claims court advisor or clerk for the specific forms you need and procedures to follow to file your motion. Most likely, filing a motion in small claims court means simplified paperwork. On the other hand, if your judgment is from regular civil court, you'll have to prepare several documents.

a. Consult Court Rules

California's Rules of Court establish the general procedures for filing and serving motions in every court. In addition, your court may have adopted local rules of procedure. You must read—and follow—both.

To find out if your court has adopted local rules, contact the court clerk where you obtained your judgment. Ask if the court has adopted local rules for filing motions. If yes, ask the court clerk for a copy of the local rules. If the court doesn't have the local rules, visit your county law library.

The specific rules you need to know—whether contained in Rules of Court or your local rules— cover the following topics:

- the days and times your motion may be heard
- the location of the hearing
- how to schedule a noticed hearing or request an ex parte hearing, and
- how many copies of the documents you must file.

b. Prepare Documents

If you think you can't deal with one more piece of paperwork, filing a motion is going to tax your patience. Even the simplest motion papers, called pleadings, must be typed on 8½" x 11" numbered paper, called pleading paper.

To prepare your papers, find the blank sheet of pleading paper in the Appendix. Make several copies. On one sheet, type your name, address and phone number, followed by the words "Appearing in Pro Per," single-spaced in the upper left corner.

Then go down to line 8. In the center of the page, type the name of the court in capital letters.

Type the caption (your name vs. the debtor's name), the case number (your judgment case number), the documents included, and the date, time and location of the hearing.

The documents included are the same no matter which motion you file; the content however, is different.

- **Notice of Motion (if applicable) and Motion:** This gives the court and debtor (if applicable) written notice of your request and the date, time and location of the hearing. The notice is required for noticed motions only.

- **Declaration:** Your declaration is a statement of the facts that gives the court a basis to grant your motion. In most situations, only your statement will be necessary. If you are relying on somebody else's observations, however, you must submit that person's statement as well—for example, if you are seeking a Seizure Order and the debtor's ex-roommate has information about property in the debtor's home, ask the ex-roommate to state what she knows in a signed declaration.

- **Memorandum of Points and Authorities:** This is a short statement of citations to the legal authority entitling you to your requested order.

- **Proposed Court Order:** This gives the judge a place to sign if he grants your motion.

Below are sample documents. You must prepare three separate documents. The first contains a Notice of Motion and a Memorandum of Points and Authorities. The second document is the Declaration, and the third is the Proposed Order. If you submit additional declarations (from witnesses other than yourself), those should be separate documents as well.

Be sure to modify these samples to fit your situation. Do not copy instructions word-for-word into your document. As you type, be sure to number the pages of each document at the bottom. You also have to include a "footer" at the bottom of each page, which identifies the document (for example, "Notice of Motion and Motion for Seizure Order" or "Declaration of Robin Laskey in Support of Motion for Seizure Order"). The sample notices contain language asking the court to dispense with the advance notice requirement. If the judge rejects this no-notice option, you'll have to re-schedule your hearing with the judge and provide notice. If you'd rather not risk the delay, leave the language out and provide the debtor with notice of the hearing.

When you're done preparing your documents, make at least three copies. Staple each set in the upper left-hand corner. You will also have to two-hole punch the top of the set you file with the court.

Motion for a Seizure Order

Ira Droffik
123 North Street
San Bernardino, CA 92400
909-555-3376

Appearing In Pro Per

SUPERIOR COURT OF CALIFORNIA

COUNTY OF SAN BERNARDINO

Ira Droffik,

Plaintiff,

vs.

Justine Mayo,

Defendant.

NO. 0000-00011

EX PARTE MOTION FOR SEIZURE ORDER AND MEMORANDUM OF POINTS AND AUTHORITIES

Date: May 26, 20XX
Time: 3:00 P.M.
Dept: A

MOTION FOR SEIZURE ORDER

Plaintiff, the judgment creditor, moves the court for an order authorizing a levy on the personal property of Justine Mayo, which is located inside her private home.

The specific items of personal property which will be subject to the levy are:

1) 1 Nikon FE camera, lens, and equipment valued at approximately $4,000; and

2) Six paintings by the artist Arnold Williams valued at approximately $12,000.

The motion is made on the grounds that 1) the judgment creditor has a judgment against the judgment debtor with a balance due, including costs and accrued interest, of $17,000; 2) the property sought in the levy is valued well above the exemptions for this type of property; 3) the property is located in the judgment debtor's private home; and 4) there are no reasonable alternatives available for collecting the judgment.

This motion is based on the Declaration of Ira Droffik, the Memorandum of Points and Authorities, and the complete files and records of this action.

MEMORANDUM OF POINTS & AUTHORITIES

This is a motion for an order permitting a levy on assets located on the judgment debtor's private property. Under the provisions of Code of Civil Procedure Section 699.030, the court may issue an order authorizing the levying officer to levy on property located in a private place of the judgment debtor if, according to the best knowledge, information and belief of the judgment creditor, the application describes with particularity both the property sought to be levied upon and the place where it is to be found.

The judgment creditor has provided these descriptions in his Declaration, and the reasons why the order is required for him to collect his judgment. Accordingly, the judgment creditor requests that his motion be granted.

Ex Parte Note: *If you are seeking an ex parte order without oral notice, as we recommend, use the following model paragraph.*

Under C.C.P. Section 699.030, the order sought in this motion can be obtained either ex parte upon 24 hours' notice to the judgment debtor or upon proof that the such notice would be self-defeating. The judgment creditor's Declaration supplies this proof, and the judgment creditor therefore requests that the 24-hour rule be dispensed with.

Dated: May 26, 20XX   Respectfully Submitted,

Ira Droffik
Judgment Creditor

/////

/////

Declaration in Support of Motion for a Seizure Order

Ira Droffik
123 North Street
San Bernardino, CA 92400
909-555-3376

Appearing In Pro Per

SUPERIOR COURT OF CALIFORNIA

COUNTY OF SAN BERNARDINO

Ira Droffik,

    Plaintiff,

vs.

Justine Mayo,

    Defendant.

NO. 0000-00011

DECLARATION IN SUPPORT OF PLAINTIFF'S EX PARTE MOTION FOR SEIZURE

Date: May 26, 20XX
Time: 3:00 P.M.
Dept: A

DECLARATION

I, Ira Droffik, declare as follows:

1. I obtained a judgment against Justine Mayo from the San Bernardino Superior Court on June 11, 20XX, in the within-referenced action.

2. The balance due on the judgment is $17,000, plus post-judgment costs and accrued interest.

3. On April 16, 20XX, I conducted a debtor's examination with Justine Mayo. In the course of this examination, Justine Mayo stated under oath that she possesses: 1) a Nikon FE camera, lens, and equipment valued at approximately $4,000, and 2) six paintings by the artist Arnold Williams, valued at approximately $12,000. She said the camera is normally kept in her office located in her home, and that the paintings are on the walls of her living room and entry hall.

4. I also determined from the debtor's examination that these are the only non-exempt items of value which Justine Mayo currently possesses. Her home has several major liens on it and her business has been liquidated. Her bank account contains funds that are mostly exempt under the wage garnishment law.

5. Justine Mayo has been unwilling to make voluntary payments on this debt, despite my suggestions that she do so.

Comment: *As mentioned earlier, if you are bringing your motion ex parte you must either include in your Declaration a statement that you gave the judgment debtor 24 hours' notice of the hearing (the first phrase set out below), or a statement explaining why giving this notice would defeat the purpose of the motion (the second phrase set out below). After you decide which approach you want to use, select and adapt the appropriate phrase to your situation.*

6. At 3:00 P.M. on May 25, 200X, I spoke to the judgment debtor at her office at 909-555-8888 and informed her that this ex parte motion would be heard by the above-captioned court at 3:00 P.M. on May 26, 200X.

OR

6. I did not provide the judgment debtor with oral notice of this hearing because I believe that to give such notice would defeat the purpose of this motion. The judgment debtor has previously taken evasive actions when I have attempted to collect this judgment. I am concerned that if she were given 24 hours' notice of this hearing, she would use that time to transfer the assets to another location, thereby avoiding the levy.

I declare under penalty of perjury under the laws of the State of California that the foregoing is true and correct.

Comment: *This last sentence is mandatory on declarations. If you don't have this language, you must have your statement witnessed and signed by a notary public.*

Dated: May 26, 20XX

Ira Droffik

Seizure Order

Ira Droffik
123 North Street
San Bernardino, CA 92400
909-555-3376

Appearing In Pro Per

SUPERIOR COURT OF CALIFORNIA

COUNTY OF SAN BERNARDINO

Ira Droffik,

Plaintiff,

vs.

Justine Mayo,

Defendant.

NO. 0000-00011

ORDER

Date: May 26, 20XX
Time: 3:00 P.M.
Dept: A

ORDER

The motion of Ira Droffik was heard by this court ex parte on the date and at the time set forth above. The judgment creditor appeared in pro per. The judgment debtor did not receive notice and did not appear. The court finds that oral notice to the judgment debtor would have defeated the purpose of the motion and that this matter was therefore properly heard without oral notice.

Comment: *If you plan on giving 24 hours' oral notice, the last two sentences of the preceding paragraph should be replaced with the following sentence:* The judgment debtor did/did not appear after being given 24 hours' oral notice of the ex parte proceeding.

The court having considered the motion and good cause appearing,

IT IS ORDERED that a levy is authorized to be made on the following property located in the home of judgment debtor Justine Mayo:

1) a Nikon FE camera, lens, and related equipment; and

ORDER

1

2) six paintings by the artist Arnold Williams.

IT IS FURTHER ORDERED that a copy of this order shall be personally served upon the judgment debtor and:

NOTICE IS HEREBY GIVEN THAT FAILURE BY THE JUDGMENT DEBTOR TO COMPLY WITH THIS ORDER MAY SUBJECT THE JUDGMENT DEBTOR TO BEING HELD IN CONTEMPT OF COURT.

Dated: _____

Signed: _____
_____
Judge of the Superior Court

ORDER

2

Motion for a Turnover

Ira Droffik
123 North Street
San Bernardino, CA 92400
909-555-3376

Appearing In Pro Per

SUPERIOR COURT OF CALIFORNIA

COUNTY OF SAN BERNARDINO

Ira Droffik,	)	NO. 0000-00011
Plaintiff,	)	EX PARTE MOTION FOR TURNOVER ORDER AND MEMORANDUM OF POINTS AND AUTHORITIES
vs.	)	
Justine Mayo,	)	Date: May 26, 20XX
Defendant.	)	Time: 3:00 P.M.
	)	Dept: A

MOTION FOR TURNOVER ORDER

Plaintiff, the judgment creditor, moves the court ex parte for an order requiring the judgment debtor to turn over to the levying officer the following described property:

1. Certificates evidencing ownership of stock in Apple Computer Corporation;
2. One Apple laser printer; and
3. Certificate of title to one 1999 Ferrari Testarossa.

This motion is made on the grounds that 1) the judgment creditor has a judgment against the judgment debtor with a balance due of $17,000, plus post-judgment costs and accrued interest; 2) the property sought to be turned over is not exempt or is valued well above the exemptions for this type of property; and 3) the property is either located in the judgment debtor's private home or has been concealed from the levying officer so that a levy could not be made.

This motion is based on the Declaration of Ira Droffik, the Memorandum of Points and Authorities, and the complete files and records of this action.

EX PARTE MOTION FOR TURNOVER ORDER AND
MEMORANDUM OF POINTS AND AUTHORITIES

1

MEMORANDUM OF POINTS AND AUTHORITIES

The judgment creditor is seeking a Turnover Order. Under the provisions of Code of Civil Procedure Section 699.040, upon a showing of need, the court may issue an order, after a Writ of Execution has issued, requiring the judgment debtor to turn over to the levying officer property, title to property and evidence of debt owed by third parties.

In the Declaration, the judgment creditor has shown that a Writ of Execution has been issued and has stated why he needs the order to collect the described property. Accordingly, the judgment creditor requests that his motion be granted.

Ex Parte Note: *If you are seeking an ex parte order without oral notice, as we recommend, use the following model paragraph. If you are providing oral notice, don't use it.*

Under C.C.P. Section 699.040, the order sought in this motion can be obtained ex parte either upon 24 hours' notice to the judgment debtor, or upon proof that such notice would be self-defeating. The judgment creditor's Declaration supplies this proof and the judgment creditor therefore requests that the 24-hour rule be dispensed with.

Respectfully Submitted,

Dated: May 26, 20XX

_____
Ira Droffik
Judgment Creditor

EX PARTE MOTION FOR TURNOVER ORDER AND
MEMORANDUM OF POINTS AND AUTHORITIES

2

Declaration in Support of Motion for a Turnover Order

Ira Droffik
123 North Street
San Bernardino, CA 92400
909-555-3376

Appearing In Pro Per

SUPERIOR COURT OF CALIFORNIA

COUNTY OF SAN BERNARDINO

Ira Droffik,

    Plaintiff,

vs.

Justine Mayo,

    Defendant.

NO. 0000-00011

DECLARATION IN SUPPORT OF PLAINTIFF'S EX PARTE MOTION FOR TURNOVER ORDER

Date: May 26, 20XX
Time: 3:00 P.M.
Dept: A

DECLARATION

I, Ira Droffik, declare as follows:

1. I obtained a judgment against Justine Mayo from the San Bernardino Superior Court on January 10, 20XX, in case # 0000-0011.

2. The balance due on the judgment is $17,000, plus post-judgment costs and accrued interest.

3. On April 16, 20XX, I conducted a debtor's examination of Justine Mayo. In the course of this examination, Justine Mayo stated under oath that she owns stock in Apple Computer Corporation, that she owns an Apple laser printer, and that she owns and drives a Ferrari Testarossa.

4. I obtained a Writ of Execution directed to the County of San Bernardino from the San Bernardino Superior Court on April 28, 20XX.

DECLARATION IN SUPPORT OF PLAINTIFF'S EX PARTE MOTION FOR TURNOVER ORDER

1

5. I transmitted the original issued Writ of Execution and instructions to the levying officer for San Bernardino County to levy on the stock, Laser printer and Ferrari. The levying officer reported back that the stock and LaserWriter are located in the judgment debtor's home, and that while he had seen the judgment debtor driving a Ferrari, he was unable to find it at the judgment debtor's house.

Comment: *When bringing an ex parte motion you must either include in your Declaration a statement that you gave the judgment debtor 24 hours' notice of the hearing (the first phrase set out below), or a statement explaining why giving this notice would defeat the purpose of the motion (the second phrase set out below). Select and adapt the appropriate phrase to your situation.*

6. At 3:00 P.M. on May 25, 20XX, I spoke to the judgment debtor at her office at 909-555-8888 and informed her that this ex parte motion would be heard by the above-captioned court at 3:00 P.M. on May 26, 20XX.

OR

6. I did not provide the judgment debtor with oral notice of this hearing because I believe that to give such notice would defeat the purpose of this motion. The judgment debtor has previously taken evasive actions when I have attempted to collect this judgment. I am concerned that if she were given 24 hours' notice of this hearing, she would use that time to transfer the assets or items sought under this Turnover Order to another location or otherwise conceal them.

I declare under penalty of perjury under the laws of the State of California that the foregoing is true and correct.

Comment: *This last sentence is mandatory on declarations. If you don't have this language, you must have your statement witnessed and signed by a notary public.*

Dated: May 26, 20XX

                    Ira Droffik

DECLARATION IN SUPPORT OF PLAINTIFF'S EX PARTE MOTION FOR TURNOVER ORDER

Motion for a Turnover Order

Ira Drofik
123 North Street
San Bernardino, CA 92400
909-555-3376

Appearing In Pro Per

SUPERIOR COURT OF CALIFORNIA

COUNTY OF SAN BERNARDINO

Ira Drofik,

Plaintiff,

vs.

Justine Mayo,

Defendant.

NO. 0000-00011

ORDER

Date: May 26, 20XX
Time: 3:00 P.M.
Dept: A

ORDER

The motion of Ira Drofik was heard by this court ex parte on the date and at the time set forth above. The judgment creditor appeared in pro per. The judgment debtor did not receive notice and did not appear. The court finds that oral notice to the judgment debtor would have defeated the purpose of the motion and that this matter was therefore properly heard without oral notice.

Comment: *If you plan on giving 24 hours' oral notice, the last two sentences of the preceding paragraph should be replaced with the following sentence:* The judgment debtor did/did not appear after being given 24 hours' oral notice of the ex parte proceeding.

The court having considered the motion and good cause appearing,

IT IS ORDERED that the following property be turned over by the judgment debtor Justine Mayo to the levying officer for San Bernardino County:

1. Certificates of title to stock in the Apple Computer Corporation;

ORDER

1

2. One Apple laser printer; and

3. One Ferrari Testarossa

IT IS FURTHER ORDERED that a copy of this order shall be personally served upon the judgment debtor and:

NOTICE IS HEREBY GIVEN THAT FAILURE BY THE JUDGMENT DEBTOR TO COMPLY WITH THIS ORDER MAY SUBJECT THE JUDGMENT DEBTOR TO BEING HELD IN CON-TEMPT OF COURT.

Dated: _____

Signed: _____
　　　　　　Judge of the Superior Court

ORDER

2

B. Motion for Assignment Order

If the debtor receives regular payments that you can't readily garnish or levy, it may be possible to have all or a portion of them paid directly to you. You do this through an Assignment Order—an order from the court requiring the judgment debtor to assign to you her right to receive some or all of the payments. The assignment puts you in the shoes of the debtor for the purposes of receiving the payments until your judgment is satisfied. Then the right to receive the payments reverts to the debtor.

Typical sources of income subject to assignment include:

- rents from tenants
- sales commissions
- royalties from a patent, copyright or other type of license
- payments due on account (called accounts receivable), and
- installment payments on promissory notes.

EXAMPLE: Justine is an author who receives royalties of approximately $3,000 from one of her publishers each quarter. Ira obtains a judgment against Justine for $15,000. He requests a court order requiring Justine to assign him the right to receive these royalties until the judgment is satisfied. If the royalties were Justine's sole or primary source of income, the judge would probably order considerably less than 100% assigned.

1. Payments Not Subject to an Assignment Order

Several types of income are legally nonassignable or exempt from execution—meaning that you cannot use an Assignment Order to have the payments directed to you. These income sources include:

- Social Security
- Supplemental Security Income (SSI)

- Medicare and Medicaid payments (if the debtor is a medical provider)
- public assistance benefits (welfare)
- worker's compensation
- unemployment insurance
- IRAs or Keogh plans
- most payments from pension or retirement plans, and
- payments from an irrevocable trust.

2. Grounds for Granting an Assignment Order

The court will consider several issues when deciding whether or not to grant an Assignment Order:

- **The reasonable needs of the debtor and his family.** The court will not order an assignment that will strip the debtor of income necessary to meet a basic standard of living.
- **How long the payments are likely to continue.** If the payments to the debtor won't last much more than a few months, the court is not likely to order the payments assigned to you.
- **The balance remaining compared to the payments sought to be assigned.** If little is left on the judgment—only one or two assigned payments will cover the balance—the court may not order the assignment, especially if a levy could do the job. But if your entire judgment is outstanding and many payments will be needed to pay it off, the court is more likely to order the assignment.

3. Preparing a Motion for Assignment Order

Follow the material in Section A3, above, on finding out the applicable rules. In addition, follow the general information in the same section on preparing court papers. There is one difference, however.

Normally, the debtor must sign the Assignment Order before it can take effect. You may be able to get around this by changing the language of the Order slightly. You want to avoid having to have the debtor sign the Order because the debtor may not do so, and your only recourse then is to hire a lawyer to bring a motion for contempt against the debtor.

The statute doesn't authorize this change, but many judges accept it anyway. If you want to chance it, do the following:

- Eliminate the following, as shown in the sample Order:

  I hereby make the assignments required by this Court Order.

  _____
  Judgment Debtor

- Replace it with the following:

  The judgment debtor Justine Mayo's right to receive the following payments shall be and hereby is assigned to the judgment creditor Ira Droffik until the judgment is satisfied or this order is amended.

  Dated: _____

C. After You Prepare the Papers

Once you have completed your papers, you must file them with the court.

1. Serve (If Applicable) and File Papers With Court

If you are scheduling a noticed motion, you must have one set of your papers served on the debtor before you file them with the court. Most judgment creditors have the debtor served by mail at his last known address. Service by mail must take place at least 26 days before the hearing date. (Code of Civil Procedure § 1005.)

After the papers are served, have the person who did the serving complete and sign a Proof of Service. (Instructions for serving documents and preparing Proofs of Service are in Chapter 21.) Attach the signed Proof of Service to your motion papers.

At least a week before the hearing date, visit the court or send in your documents. Take the original and the remaining copies of the papers and your checkbook. If you mail the papers, find out the fee in advance, enclose a letter requesting a hearing date if you don't already have one, enclose a self-addressed, stamped envelope and ask that a file-stamped copy of your documents be returned to you.

2. Provide Informal Notice (If Applicable)

The judgment debtor is entitled to short advance notice of an ex parte hearing unless you convince the judge that even 24-hours' notice would defeat the purpose of your motion. To give notice, call the debtor, inform her of your motion, its date, time and location, and find out if the debtor plans on attending or opposing your motion. (You don't need to do this if you've filed a noticed motion.)

3. Review Objections or Claim of Exemption

If the debtor objects to your motion, she must file and serve a Claim of Exemption at least three days before the hearing (Code of Civil Procedure § 708.550). The debtor may claim that the property you seek to seize or the payments you want assigned are exempt, or that a portion is of the payments are needed to support the debtor and her family. Review the documents carefully. To win your motion, you will have to counter the debtor's arguments at the hearing.

Motion for Assignment Order

Ira Droffik
123 North Street
San Bernardino, CA 92400
909-555-3376

Appearing In Pro Per

SUPERIOR COURT OF CALIFORNIA

COUNTY OF SAN BERNARDINO

Ira Droffik,	NO. 0000-00011
Plaintiff,	NOTICE OF MOTION AND MOTION FOR ASSIGNMENT ORDER AND MEMORANDUM OF POINTS AND AUTHORITIES
vs.	
Justine Mayo,	Date: May 26, 20XX Time: 3:00 P.M. Dept: A
Defendant.	

NOTICE OF MOTION AND MOTION FOR ASSIGNMENT ORDER

TO THE JUDGMENT DEBTOR(S) AND TO ANY ATTORNEY(S) OF RECORD FOR

THE JUDGMENT DEBTOR(S):

NOTICE IS HEREBY GIVEN that on May 26, 20XX, at 3:00 p.m. in Department A of the court located at 351 North Arrowhead Ave., San Bernardino, California, Ira Droffik, judgment creditor, will move the court for an order instructing Justine Mayo, judgment debtor, to assign to her the judgment debtor's interest in, and all rights to payment under, the following assets to the extent necessary to satisfy the judgment:

a) copyright royalties from Lilac Press on a quarterly basis;

b) rents from her tenant Paul Simonson, on a monthly basis in the amount of $500; and

c) monthly installment payments of $400 on a promissory note executed by Katherine Piper on July 6, 20XX.

ASSIGNMENT ORDER AND MEMORANDUM
OF POINTS AND AUTHORITIES

1

This motion is made on the grounds that:

a) the judgment creditor has a judgment against the judgment debtor;

b) the balance due on this judgment is $17,000, plus post-judgment costs and accrued interest; and

c) the judgment debtor has an assignable right to the payments described above.

This motion will be based on this Notice of Motion and Motion, the Declaration of Ira Droffik, the Memorandum of Points and Authorities and the records and file of this action.

MEMORANDUM OF POINTS & AUTHORITIES

The judgment creditor's motion for an Assignment Order seeks an assignment of three categories of payments due the judgment debtor, as described in the Declaration of Ira Droffik.

Under Code of Civil Procedure Section 708.510, the court is authorized to order all or part of a judgment debtor's right to payments due, or to become due, assigned to the judgment creditor. This assignment may be ordered to the extent necessary to satisfy the money judgment. Accordingly, Ira Droffik, judgment creditor, requests that the court issue an Assignment Order, and that the assignment made under this order continue until the judgment specified in Ira Droffik's Declaration, plus post-judgment costs and accrued interest, is fully satisfied.

Dated: May 26, 20XX　　　　Respectfully Submitted,

Ira Droffik
Judgment Creditor

ASSIGNMENT ORDER AND MEMORANDUM
OF POINTS AND AUTHORITIES

2

Declaration in Support of Motion for Assignment Order

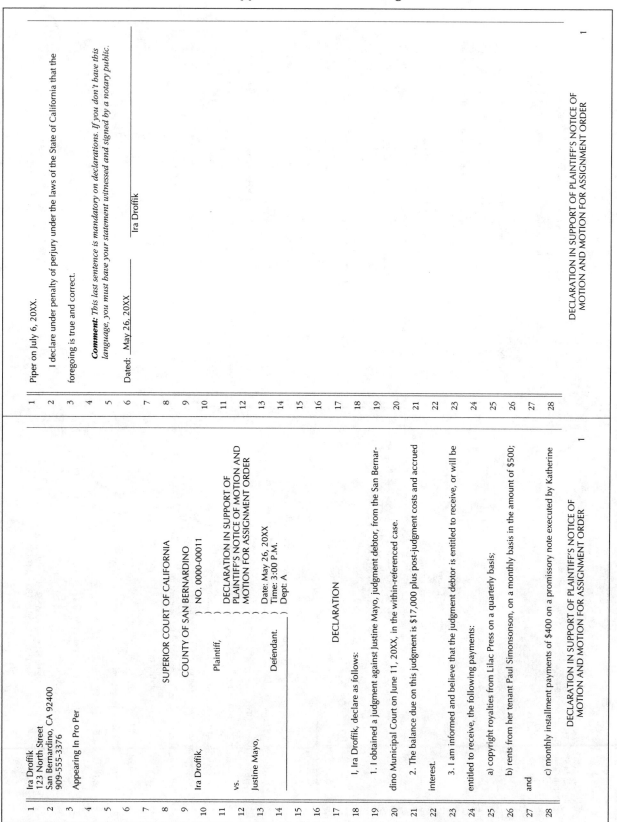

Ira Droffik
123 North Street
San Bernardino, CA 92400
909-555-3376

Appearing In Pro Per

SUPERIOR COURT OF CALIFORNIA

COUNTY OF SAN BERNARDINO

Ira Droffik,

      Plaintiff,   )   NO. 0000-00011
)   DECLARATION IN SUPPORT OF
vs.   )   PLAINTIFF'S NOTICE OF MOTION AND
)   MOTION FOR ASSIGNMENT ORDER
Justine Mayo,

      Defendant.)   Date: May 26, 20XX
)   Time: 3:00 P.M.
)   Dept: A

DECLARATION

I, Ira Droffik, declare as follows:

1. I obtained a judgment against Justine Mayo, judgment debtor, from the San Bernardino Municipal Court on June 11, 20XX, in the within-referenced case.

2. The balance due on this judgment is $17,000 plus post-judgment costs and accrued interest.

3. I am informed and believe that the judgment debtor is entitled to receive, or will be entitled to receive, the following payments:

a) copyright royalties from Lilac Press on a quarterly basis;

b) rents from her tenant Paul Simonsonson, on a monthly basis in the amount of $500; and

c) monthly installment payments of $400 on a promissory note executed by Katherine

DECLARATION IN SUPPORT OF PLAINTIFF'S NOTICE OF
MOTION AND MOTION FOR ASSIGNMENT ORDER

1

Piper on July 6, 20XX.

I declare under penalty of perjury under the laws of the State of California that the

foregoing is true and correct.

Comment: *This last sentence is mandatory on declarations. If you don't have this language, you must have your statement witnessed and signed by a notary public.*

Dated: May 26, 20XX

          Ira Droffik

DECLARATION IN SUPPORT OF PLAINTIFF'S NOTICE OF
MOTION AND MOTION FOR ASSIGNMENT ORDER

1

Assignment Order

Ira Droffik
123 North Street
San Bernardino, CA 92400
909-555-3376

Appearing In Pro Per

SUPERIOR COURT OF CALIFORNIA

COUNTY OF SAN BERNARDINO

Ira Droffik,

Plaintiff,   NO. 0000-00011

vs.   ASSIGNMENT ORDER

Justine Mayo,

Defendant.

Date: May 26, 20XX
Time: 3:00 P.M.
Dept: A

ASSIGNMENT ORDER

The motion of Ira Droffik came on regularly for hearing before this court on _____. Ira Droffik, judgment creditor, and Justine Mayo, judgment debtor, both appeared in pro per. The court having considered the motion and good cause appearing;

IT IS ORDERED THAT:

1. The judgment debtor, Justine Mayo, shall assign to Ira Droffik, the judgment creditor, the judgment debtor's right to receive the following payments until the judgment is fully satisfied or this Order is amended:

a) 100% of the copyright royalties owed to the judgment debtor by Lilac Press on a quarterly basis.

b) 50% of the rents due the judgment debtor from her tenant Paul Simonson, on a monthly basis in the amount of $250.

ASSIGNMENT ORDER   1

This motion is made on the grounds that:

a) the judgment creditor has a judgment against the judgment debtor;

b) the balance due on this judgment is $17,000, plus post-judgment costs and accrued interest; and

c) the judgment debtor has an assignable right to the payments described above.

This motion will be based on this Notice of Motion and Motion, the Declaration of Ira Droffik, the Memorandum of Points and Authorities and the records and file of this action.

MEMORANDUM OF POINTS & AUTHORITIES

The judgment creditor's motion for an Assignment Order seeks an assignment of three categories of payments due the judgment debtor, as described in the Declaration of Ira Droffik.

Under Code of Civil Procedure Section 708.510, the court is authorized to order all or part of a judgment debtor's right to payments due, or to become due, assigned to the judgment creditor. This assignment may be ordered to the extent necessary to satisfy the money judgment. Accordingly, Ira Droffik, judgment creditor, requests that the court issue an Assignment Order, and that the assignment made under this order continue until the judgment specified in Ira Droffik's Declaration, plus post-judgment costs and accrued interest, is fully satisfied.

Dated: May 26, 20XX

Respectfully Submitted,

Ira Droffik
Judgment Creditor

ASSIGNMENT ORDER AND MEMORANDUM OF POINTS AND AUTHORITIES   2

4. Attend the Hearing

The day before the hearing, review your motion papers. On the day of the hearing, go a little early. Go right to the designated room or courtroom. Before you go in, check outside for a bulletin board listing the cases to be heard. If your case isn't listed, check with the courtroom clerk.

Bring copies of all your documents, including the unsigned Order and any unfiled Proofs of Service. Let the clerk or bailiff know you are present.

When your case is called, step forward. Always address the judge as "Your Honor." Some judges prefer to ask questions, but others will ask you to begin. Explain your request in your own words.

> **EXAMPLE:** Good morning, Your Honor. I am the judgment creditor in this case and I am seeking an order assigning to me certain payments due the judgment debtor from third parties. Specifically, the judgment debtor receives monthly payments from Katherine Piper on a promissory note, monthly rent from Paul Simonson and quarterly royalty payments from Lilac Press. The judgment debtor owes $17,000 on the judgment, plus costs and interest. If the assignments are ordered as I request, the judgment will be satisfied in approximately 15 months. Otherwise, I will have to repeatedly levy on these payments.

If the debtor has filed a Claim of Exemption or otherwise responded to your motion, he has an opportunity to speak after you. You then have a chance to reply. Your reply to a Claim of Exemption must be either that the payments or property are not exempt or that the payments are not needed to support the judgment debtor or her family. (Chapter 15 covers how to oppose a Claim of Exemption.)

Once the court hears your motion, the judge must make a ruling. She may grant your request in full or part, deny it or take the matter under submission, which means she will mail out her decision in a few days. If you lose, nothing happens and you may proceed with other collection efforts. While it is possible to appeal the judge's decision, it's almost never worth the time and expense. Regardless of the outcome, you can claim costs incurred, such as filing fees and service of process fees. (See Chapter 16.)

If the judge grants your motion, she will sign your proposed Order, possibly with changes. Once the Order is signed, conform your copies by printing the judge's name below the signature line, and copying all other information and markings that the judge put on the original order.

5. Serve Order

Once you receive a signed order from the court and conform your copies, you must have a copy personally served on the judgment debtor for it to be valid, unless the judge orders otherwise. In addition, you must have any affected third parties served with a notice of the order. For example, you should have one copy of your Assignment Order mailed to each source of payments being assigned. (See Chapter 21 for instructions on personal service and service by mail.)

Sample Assignment Order Notice

To Lilac Press:

NOTICE IS HEREBY GIVEN that under the terms of an Assignment Order dated July 31, 20___, a copy of which is attached to this notice, Justine Mayo's right to receive royalty payments from you has been assigned to Ira Droffik, 123 North St., San Bernardino, California 92400 to the extent necessary to satisfy the judgment that Ira Droffik obtained against Justine Mayo.

The amount necessary to satisfy this judgment is now $17,000 plus costs and accrued interest. Interest accrues on the unpaid balance of this judgment at the rate of 10% per year.

If you make any payments to Justine Mayo after you receive this notice, you will not satisfy the obligation that has been assigned and will still be liable for full payment to the judgment creditor, Ira Droffik.

_____ _____
Date   Ira Droffik

After you prepare your notices, have the orders served on the affected parties and have the original Proofs of Service filed with the court. (See Chapter 21.) Any third party must comply with the order. If the third party does not, send a letter reminding him of his obligation under the order. If he still doesn't comply, and there is enough at stake to justify pursuing the matter, consult an attorney. (See Chapter 23.)

6. Change of Circumstances

If circumstances change after an Assignment Order is made, either party can bring a noticed motion to amend or set aside the order (Code of Civil Procedure § 708.560). For example, the debtor might argue that he now needs the assigned payments to support a new child or you might argue that the debtor can afford to assign a greater portion of the payments because he received a raise in pay. This rule doesn't apply to Seizure Orders or Turnover Orders because they are not ongoing. Changed circumstances don't affect these orders one way or the other. ∎

Chapter 20

Renewing Your Judgment and Liens

A judgment (and any real estate liens associated with that judgment) issued by a California state or federal court lasts for ten years. With any luck, you will be able to collect your judgment within that ten-year period.

If you don't, however, you can renew your judgment along with any judgment liens you created on the debtor's real estate. The judgment and liens can be renewed for successive ten-year periods.

There is one exception: Judgments for child or spousal support do not need to be renewed. They are enforceable until paid in full.

A. Renewing a Judgment

If your judgment isn't fully satisfied and it's been close to ten years since your judgment was entered, you need to act quickly. That is because you must renew a judgment *before* it expires. If you try to renew a judgment even one day after it expires, you are out of luck. You may be able to file another lawsuit to obtain a judgment on your judgment, but there are limitations to doing this and you will need a lawyer's help.

When you renew a judgment, all interest and costs you've claimed in Memoranda of Costs (see Chapter 16) become part of the new judgment. In effect, this entitles you to receive compound interest on your judgment, because you'll be allowed to earn interest on accrued interest.

1. Get Current Renewal Forms

The first step is to make sure that you have the most current version of the forms. Call the court clerk. If either form in the Appendix is out of date, see Chapter 23, Section A3, for information on how to get a current form.

2. Prepare the Application

The Application for and Renewal of Judgment is the form you use to request an extension of your judgment. A sample completed form and instructions follow.

Caption: Follow the format of your other court papers. Check the box that says "judgment creditor." Leave the "case number" box empty.

Item 1: Enter your name exactly as it appears on the original judgment and your address.

Item 2: Enter the judgment debtor's name exactly as it appears on the original judgment and last known address.

Item 3a: Enter the case number of the original judgment.

Item 3b: Enter the date the original judgment was entered.

Item 3c: If you've created real estate liens by recording an Abstract of Judgment in any county, indicate here the date and county in which you recorded the Abstract, as well as the recorded Abstract's instrument number. If you haven't recorded an Abstract, leave this section blank.

Item 4: Check this box and enter the dates if you've previously renewed your judgment.

Item 5: Check this box.

Item 5a: Enter the total amount of the original judgment.

Item 5b: Enter the total post-judgment costs you have claimed in Memoranda of Costs. (See Chapter 16.)

Item 5c: Enter the total of Items 5a and 5b.

Item 5d: Enter the total credits made on the judgment—voluntary payments and money recovered through levies.

Item 5e: Subtract Item 5d from item 5c and enter the difference.

Item 5f: Enter the total post-judgment interest you have claimed in Memoranda of Costs. (See Chapter 16.)

Item 5g: Enter the fee for filing the renewal application. Check with the court clerk.

Item 5h: Enter the total of Items 5e, 5f and 5g. This is the amount of your renewed judgment.

Application for and Renewal of Judgment

EJ-190

ATTORNEY OR PARTY WITHOUT ATTORNEY *(Name and Address):* TEL NO.:

[ ] Recording requested by and return to:

805-555-7104

Sidney Chan
310 Oceanfront Court
Oxnard, CA 93000

[ ] ATTORNEY FOR [X] JUDGMENT CREDITOR [ ] ASSIGNEE OF RECORD

NAME OF COURT: Ventura County Superior Court
STREET ADDRESS: 800 South Victoria Ave.
MAILING ADDRESS:
CITY AND ZIP CODE: Ventura, CA 93009
BRANCH NAME:

FOR RECORDER'S USE ONLY
CASE NUMBER:

PLAINTIFF: Sidney Chan

DEFENDANT: Monique DuBois

FOR COURT USE ONLY

APPLICATION FOR AND RENEWAL OF JUDGMENT

[X] Judgment creditor
[ ] Assignee of record
applies for renewal of the judgment as follows:

1. Applicant *(name and address):*

Sidney Chan
310 Oceanfront Court
Oxnard, CA 93000

2. Judgment debtor *(name and last known address):*

Monique Dubois
17 Western Sky Way
Montalvo, CA 93000

3. Original judgment

a. Case number *(specify):* 0000-0013

b. Entered on *(date):* 3/23/XX

c. Recorded:
   (1) Date: 4/24/XX
   (2) County: Ventura
   (3) Instrument No.: 0014-0014

4. [ ] Judgment previously renewed *(specify each case number and date):*

5. [X] Renewal of money judgment
   a. Total judgment .... $ 4,300.00
   b. Costs after judgment .... $ 374.00
   c. Subtotal *(add a and b)* .... $ 4,674.00
   d. Credits after judgment .... $ 807.00
   e. Subtotal *(subtract d from c)* .... $ 3,867.00
   f. Interest after judgment .... $ 4,017.11
   g. Fee for filing renewal application .... $ 7.00
   h. **Total renewed judgment** *(add e, f, and g)* . $ 7,891.11

   i. [ ] The amounts called for in items a – h are different for each debtor.
   These amounts are stated for each debtor on Attachment 5.

Page 1 of 2

Form Approved for Optional Use
Judicial Council of California
EJ-190 [Rev. January 1, 2002]
APPLICATION FOR AND RENEWAL OF JUDGMENT
Code of Civil Procedure, § 683.140

Application for and Renewal of Judgment (continued)

SHORT TITLE: Sidney Chan v. Monique Dubois	CASE NUMBER:

6. ☐ Renewal of judgment for ☐ possession.
☐ sale.

a. ☐ If judgment was not previously renewed, terms of judgment as entered:

b. ☐ If judgment was previously renewed, terms of judgment as last renewed:

c. ☐ Terms of judgment remaining unsatisfied:

I declare under penalty of perjury under the laws of the State of California that the foregoing is true and correct.

Date: February 4, 20XX

Sidney Chan
(TYPE OR PRINT NAME)

▶ *Sidney Chan*
(SIGNATURE OF DECLARANT)

EJ-190 [Rev. January 1, 2002]   **APPLICATION FOR AND RENEWAL OF JUDGMENT**   Page 2 of 2

Item 5i: Leave this box blank unless your judgment is against different debtors, and each owes you different amounts. In this case, include a separate page, labeled Attachment 5, listing each debtor and the amount owed.

Page two

Short Title: Enter the name of the plaintiff and defendant. Leave the case number blank.

Item 6: Skip this entire item. This book covers only money judgments.

At the bottom, date the form, enter your name and sign.

3. Prepare Notice of Renewal of Judgment

The Notice of Renewal of Judgment is used to notify the debtor that you are renewing the judgment. A sample completed form and instructions follow.

To judgment debtor (name): Enter the name of the judgment debtor exactly as it appears on the original judgment.

Leave the rest of the form blank.

4. File Papers With Court

Give or send the clerk of the court the original and two copies of the Application for and Renewal of Judgment and the Notice of Renewal of Judgment

The filing fee is currently $14 to renew a judgment from small claims court and $23 to renew a superior court judgment. The clerk issues a Notice of Renewal of Judgment, which will serve as your renewed judgment, and file-stamp your copies. If you send the documents, include a letter of explanation and a self-addressed stamped envelope.

Don't miss the deadline! If you're facing the ten-year renewal deadline, take your papers to the court for filing. Don't rely on the mail—if you made any errors filling in the forms and the court doesn't accept them, you may be out of luck.

5. Have Debtor Served

After you renew your judgment, you must have a copy of the Application for and Renewal of Judgment and the Notice of Renewal of Judgment served personally or by first-class mail on the debtor before you can initiate collection activities (Code of Civil Procedure § 683.160(a)). (Chapter 21 covers service.)

Once the judgment debtor has been served with the renewal papers, prepare a Proof of Service (See Chapter 21.) Have the process server sign the Proof of Service and then file it with the court.

The judgment is actually renewed once the clerk issues the Notice of Renewal of Judgment. You don't need to serve the debtor to renew the judgment, but you must serve him before you can resume collecting.

After the debtor is served, he has 30 days to file a motion asking the court to vacate or modify the renewal. If the debtor makes such a motion, he must serve you personally or by mail, and schedule a court hearing on the motion. It is very unlikely that a debtor will object to renewal—he has few grounds to do so. If he does, however, see Chapter 19 on noticed motion procedures.

B. Renewing Liens

In Chapter 4, we explained how to record real estate, business asset and personal property liens against the debtor. As with judgments, liens expire after a certain period of time. Some liens may be renewed; others may be re-recorded.

1. Real Estate Lien

Liens on a debtor's real estate expire when the underlying judgment expires. This means that you must renew your liens before the judgment expires. Logically, before the ten years are up, you can renew your judgment and then renew your liens.

Notice of Renewal of Judgment

ATTORNEY OR PARTY WITHOUT ATTORNEY *(Name and Address):* **TELEPHONE NO.:**	**FOR COURT USE ONLY**

Sidney Chan
310 Oceanfront Court
Oxnard, CA 93000

TELEPHONE NO.: 905-555-7104

ATTORNEY FOR *(Name):*   In Pro Per

NAME OF COURT:	Superior Court
STREET ADDRESS:	County of Ventura
MAILING ADDRESS:	800 South Victoria Ave.
CITY AND ZIP CODE:	Ventura, CA 93009
BRANCH NAME:	
PLAINTIFF:	Sidney Chan
DEFENDANT:	Monique DuBois

NOTICE OF RENEWAL OF JUDGMENT	**CASE NUMBER:** 0000-0013

TO JUDGMENT DEBTOR *(name):*   Monique DuBois

1. **This renewal extends** the period of enforceability of the judgment until 10 years from the date the application for renewal was filed.

2. **If you object** to this renewal, you may make a motion to vacate or modify the renewal with this court.

3. You must make this motion within **30 days** after service of this notice on you.

4. A copy of the *Application for and Renewal of Judgment* is attached *(Cal. Rules of Court, rule 986).*

Date: _____   Clerk, by _____, Deputy

[SEAL]

See CCP 683.160 for information on method of service

Form Approved by the
Judicial Council of California
EJ-195 [Rev. July 1, 1989]

NOTICE OF RENEWAL OF JUDGMENT

WEST GROUP
Official Publisher

CCP 683.160

To be safe, renew your judgment several months before the expiration of the ten-year period, so you have time to renew the liens.

EXAMPLE: Sidney obtains a $5,000 judgment against Monique, which is entered on July 1, 1991. He records an Abstract of Judgment to establish a lien against Monique's cabin in Tahoe. On April 1, 2001, Sidney renews the judgment for another ten years. He also renews the lien. If Monique continues to avoid payment, Sidney can renew the judment and lien again. If, however, Sidney forgets about or gives up on the judgment and lien and fails to renew them by April 1, 2011, they will be dead.

As soon as you renew your judgment, you can renew your real estate liens following these steps:

1. Obtain a certified copy of your Application for and Renewal of Judgment from the court. You must pay a small fee.
2. Record the certified Application with each county where you have recorded an Abstract of Judgment. (See Chapter 4, Section A2, for information on recording documents.)

2. Business Asset Lien

If you have not collected your judgment within five years of creating a business asset lien, your lien will expire. You can obtain another one. (See Chapter 4, Section B.)

3. Personal Property Lien

As explained in Chapters 4 and 6, it is possible to create a short-term lien against a judgment debtor's personal property when you schedule a debtor's examination. It remains in effect for a year. You can renew the lien by serving the debtor with a new Application and Order for Appearance and Examination. ■

Chapter 21

Serving Papers on a Judgment Debtor

7hroughout this book we discuss procedures that require the debtor, and
occasionally third parties, to be served
with legal papers. Service requirements—how,
when and by whom documents must be delivered
—must be followed to the letter. A person affected
by a court action is constitutionally entitled to be
properly notified of the action so that she can
have her say.

There are three basic ways to serve legal papers:
- personal service
- substituted personal service, and
- service by mail.

Documents can often be served in more than one
way—that is, you will have a choice. To find out
the specific types of service available for a particular procedure, check the chapter covering that
procedure. Always keep photocopies of documents
served. Keep the originals to file with the court.

It is important that you allow yourself enough
time (as explained with each procedure) to have
the debtor or another party served with papers.
Collection procedures can easily get sidetracked if
service is done incorrectly.

After proper service is made, the court must be
notified, in writing, of how and when it was
accomplished. This is done in a document called
a Proof of Service, which is filed with the court.

A. Who Can Serve Papers

Legally, only a nonparty to the case—meaning
someone other than you, other plaintiffs and the
debtor—may serve court papers. The person must
be 18 or older and, if service is by mail, a resident
or an employee in the county in which the papers
are mailed.

1. Friend or Relative

A spouse, adult child, other relative, employee,
friend or neighbor can serve papers as long as
she is not a party to your case.

It's fine to use a nonprofessional process
server when service is through the mail (Section
D, below). When documents are deposited in the
U.S. mail, the law presumes that they were
received.

If, however, you need to use personal service
(Section B, below), you may want to use a
professional process server—sheriff or registered
process server. Then, if the debtor claims he
didn't receive the papers or that service was done
incorrectly, having a neutral process server testify
about the service is more persuasive than having
a friend or relative testify. In addition, professional
process servers know how to find and serve
evasive debtors.

2. Law Enforcement Officers

To have a law enforcement officer serve papers,
call the sheriff's office in the county where the
debtor is to be served. Ask whether the sheriff
serves legal papers. If not, find out who does. In
some counties, law enforcement officers don't
serve papers due to budget problems.

When you find the right law enforcement
officer, find out the fee for serving the papers—
usually less than $30 per person and per document.
Then, either complete an instruction form provided
by the law enforcement officer or draft your own

instructions, giving information such as the best hours to find the party being served at home or work and a general physical description. Law enforcement officers serve papers only during regular business hours. Finally, take or send the fee, instructions and papers to be served to the levying officer. (You can usually request that the debtor pay the law enforcement officer's process serving fees; see Chapter 16.)

3. Registered Process Server

A registered process server is someone who makes a living serving legal papers. While a law enforcement office usually serves legal papers, it's one of many responsibilities handled by that office. Registered process servers, on the other hand, specialize in it.

Registered process servers are usually faster than law enforcement officers and more resourceful at serving evasive people. They work nights and weekends—not just Monday through Friday, 9 to 5. They usually cost more, but the extra expense may be justified if your collection strategy demands quick service. Here are some situations when you might want to use a registered process server:

- the judgment debtor is hard to find
- you need service fast—for example, the debtor is leaving the state and you want to conduct a debtor's examination before he leaves
- you want to start a levy ahead of someone else
- the levying officer won't handle a particular levy, or
- the debtor can't be served during normal business hours.

Some registered process servers charge a flat fee for a given geographical area; others charge for each attempted delivery. Shop around. If you know an attorney, ask her to recommend a good process-serving firm or check the Yellow Pages for process servers in the area where the party is

to be served. (You can request that the debtor pay the process server's reasonable fees; see Chapter 16.)

If you use a registered process server for a levy, you may have to prepare extra papers, such as a Notice of Levy. Ask the process server about those requirements.

B. Personal Service

Personal service of legal papers means that the process server—your friend, the sheriff or a registered process server—hands copies of the papers to an individual or a representative of a business.

1. Personal Service on an Individual

Personal service on an individual is required for a few of the procedures described in this book. More often, however, you have a choice of using personal service or another kind. If you have a choice, understand that personal service is more expensive than other types of service. But it's the most effective, too. If you have a hearing scheduled and think the debtor won't show, claiming she never received the papers, use personal service. Your process server can come to court and testify that the debtor actually received the papers.

A professional process server—a law enforcement officer or registered process server—knows the technical rules for making personal service. If you use a relative or friend (which we usually don't recommend), you must provide careful instructions.

No matter who you will use to do the serving, the process server needs as detailed a description of the person to be served as possible—for example, "he's 47, has gray hair, is about 5'10" with a medium build, and looks a little like a bookish accountant." Provide a photograph if you have one.

Personal service can be done anywhere—home, work, grocery store—you name it. But serving a debtor or third party anywhere but his home is tricky and should not be tried by anyone who is not a professional process server. In other words, if your friend or relative will do the serving, direct her only to serve the papers at the debtor or third-party's home.

Have your process server go to the house at a time she expects the person to be served to be there—not during the day in the middle of the week if the person works regular hours. Be sure your process server doesn't disturb the person very early or very late in the day. The best times are just before he leaves for work, just after he comes back or during the day on the weekend.

Personal service is not made if the process server simply leaves the papers on the porch, at the door or in the mailbox. The server must hand the papers to the debtor or third party. This means that the server must see the person and talk to him. A typical approach is to knock on the door. If a person matching the person's description opens it, the server asks, "Are you Fred Anderson?" If the response is "yes," the process server hands him the papers and says "You are being served" or "These are for you." If someone else answers the door, the process server asks for Fred Anderson and hands the papers to him when he appears.

If the person is home but not answering the door, the process server must do something to make him answer the door and identify himself. Your server can use whatever ruse she wants to get the person to open the door. For example, she can park her car in the person's driveway, knock on the door, and then say, "Is that your car in the driveway?" The debtor or third party will come out to see the car and the server can say: "Are you Fred Michaels?" (using a wrong name). The person, confused about the strange car, will usually correct the server ("No, I'm Fred Anderson") and the server can hand him the papers.

Whatever technique your server uses, she must be sure she is serving the right person. If the person being served does not respond to a direct question about his identity, the server will have to be creative. She can call the person's name and when the person reacts, say "You are Fred Anderson, aren't you?" and then give him the papers if the response is affirmative. Or she might bring flowers or a gift-wrapped box—with the papers inside, of course.

Once the process server ascertains that the person is the debtor or third party to be served and is close enough to make the service, the process server can complete personal service even if the person refuses to take the papers, gets angry or runs away. The server can place the papers on the ground as close as possible to his feet, saying "This is for you," or "You are being served," and then leave.

Once the process server hands over the papers or puts them on the ground, she should leave. She should not engage in conversation. Under no circumstance should she pick up the papers if she left them at the person's feet. If she does, service will be considered invalid and have to be done again.

If the server makes several—often three—unsuccessful attempts at personal service, she can try substituted personal service. (See Section C, below.)

2. Personal Service on a Corporation

If the debtor or third party is a corporation, personal service must be made either on an officer of the corporation such as a president, vice-president, secretary or treasurer, or on the person who has been designated as agent for service of process. Call the corporation and ask who the officers are and in which office they are located.

If you can't get the information this way—either because the business won't give you the information or the business is a large corporation doing business in California—go to the website of the Secretary of State, at www.ss.ca.gov. Click on "California Business Portal," then go to the Corporate Records page. You can look up the agent for service of process online, or follow the instructions to learn who the corporation's officers are.

Once you have the name and location of an officer or the agent for service of process, have your process server simply hand deliver the papers. She shouldn't meet with any resistance.

If the corporation's officers work in a local office, you have the option of using substituted personal service. (See Section C, below.) You don't have to try personal service first. If you cannot serve an agent or corporate officer, you may be able to serve the California Secretary of State instead. That procedure is beyond the scope of this book.

3. Personal Service on a Partnership

To serve a partnership, your process server must personally serve one of the partners. (See Section B1, above.) If you cannot serve one of the partners, you may be able to serve a limited partnership or foreign general partnership by serving the Secretary of State. That procedure is beyond the scope of this book.

C. Substituted Personal Service

If the process server attempts personal service with reasonable diligence, but never finds the debtor or third party at home, she can leave the papers with an adult at the person's home with instructions to give the papers to the debtor or third party. In addition, she must mail a second copy of the papers to the debtor or third party at the address where the papers were left. The papers may be left with a competent member of the household who is at least 18 years old (Code of Civil Procedure § 415.20(b)). This method is called substituted personal service.

Some courts specify how many and when personal service attempts must be made before substituted personal service is allowed. A professional process server will know this information.

If you are using a friend or relative, check the local rules or ask the court clerk.

Posting-and-Mailing Service

In rare instances, a server can post copies of the papers on the party's front door and mail him a second set of copies at that address. We don't cover this procedure, which is sometimes allowed when real property is being sold.

D. Service by Mail

Often, the debtor or third party can be served by mail. Someone other than yourself who is over 18 and not a party to the case must do the mailing. It costs no more than the first-class postage.

Here's how to serve papers through the mail:

1. Gather together the papers to be served.
2. Complete a Proof of Service by mail form (see Section E, below)—except for the signature.
3. Make copies of the papers to be served and copies of the unsigned Proof of Service, keeping one set for yourself.
4. Put one copy of the papers, including one copy of the unsigned Proof of Service, in an envelope addressed to the person to be served. Use the person's residence address or office address stated on any document the person filed in your court case. If the person has an attorney, send it to the attorney.
5. Affix sufficient postage on the envelope for first-class mail.
6. Have the process server put the envelope into a mailbox. If the process server mails the papers from a business, she may deposit them in the business's mail, as long as it will be taken for collection that day.

7. Have the server sign the Proof of Service, then give it to you so you can copy it and file it with the court. (See Section E, below.)

When service is done by mail, the person being served is usually entitled to an extra five to ten days to respond—assuming he has been served with papers requiring a response. For example, if you are required to give the judgment debtor 15 days' notice of a hearing, and you serve the judgment debtor with notice through the mail, the hearing must be scheduled at least 20 days in the future—25 days if the debtor does not live in California (Code of Civil Procedure § 1013).

Certified mail is not necessary unless a statute specifically requires certified mail. Otherwise, certified mail may be to a disadvantage. When you mail something first class, the party to whom it is addressed is presumed to receive it. But when you send something certified mail, the party is not presumed to have received it unless he signs for it. Certified mail is often signed for by other people in the house or isn't picked up at the post office.

E. Proof of Service Form

After papers are served, the process server must fill out and file with the court a document called a Proof of Service, which states when and how service was made.

Throughout the book we tell you when a Proof of Service must be filed. If you are notifying the debtor of a court hearing (except on an ex parte motion; see Chapter 19), the Proof of Service must be filed before the hearing. How long in advance varies by court and procedure, but five business days is common.

Some documents have an official Proof of Service form on the back; if so, use that form. If not, you can use our generic form, which covers personal service, substitute personal service and service by mail. The content of the forms is pretty much the same. Below are samples for personal service and for service by mail. A blank copy is in the Appendix. Make plenty of copies before you begin.

Sample Proof of Service #1

ATTORNEY OR PARTY WITHOUT ATTORNEY *(Name and Address)*:	TELEPHONE NO.:	FOR COURT USE ONLY
Sally Johnson 1127 Maxie Loop Visalia, CA 93220	303-555-9311	

ATTORNEY FOR *(Name)*:   In Pro Per

NAME OF COURT:	Superior Court
STREET ADDRESS:	Tulare County
MAILING ADDRESS:	County Civic Center
CITY AND ZIP CODE:	Visalia, CA 93291
BRANCH NAME:	

PLAINTIFF/JUDGMENT CREDITOR: Sally Johnson

DEFENDANT/JUDGMENT DEBTOR: Rhonda Skeen

PROOF OF SERVICE	CASE NUMBER: 0000-00014

1. At the time of service I was at least 18 years of age and not a party to this action, and **I served copies** of the *(specify documents)*:

   Application Order for Appearance and Examination

2. a. Party served *(specify name of party as shown on the documents served)*:

   Rhonda Skeen

   b. Person served: [X] party in item 2a   [ ] other *(specify name and title or relationship to the party named in item 2a)*:

   c. Address: 122 Rightmire Ave., Lindsay, CA 93200

3. I served the party named in item 2
   a. [ ]   **by personally delivering** the copies   (1) on *(date)*:   (2) at *(time)*:
   b. [ ]   **by leaving** the copies with or in the presence of *(name and title or relationship to person indicated in item 2b)*:

        (1) [ ]   **(business)** a person at least 18 years of age apparently in charge at the office or usual place of business of the person served. I informed him or her of the general nature of the papers.
        (2) [ ]   **(home)** a competent member of the household (at least 18 years of age) at the dwelling house or usual place of abode of the person served. I informed him or her of the general nature of the papers.
        (3) on *(date)*:   (4) at *(time)*:
        (5) [ ]   A **declaration of diligence** is attached. *(Substituted service on natural person, minor, conservatee, or candidate.)*
   c. [X]   **by mailing** the copies to the person served, addressed as shown in item 2c, by first-class mail, postage prepaid,
        (1) on *(date)*:   6/19/XX   (2) from *(city)*:   Visalia
        (3) [ ]   with two copies of the Notice and Acknowledgment of Receipt and a postage-paid return envelope addressed to m
        (4) [ ]   to an address outside California with return receipt requested.   *(Attach completed form.)* ↖
   d. [ ]   **by causing** copies to be mailed. A declaration of mailing is attached.
   e. [ ]   **other** *(specify other manner of service and authorizing code section)*:

4. **Person serving** *(name, address, and telephone No.)*:
   Emma Frend
   100 Whalebone Street
   Visalia, CA 93200
   303-555-8319

   a. **Fee** for service: $ 0
   b. [ ] Not a registered California process server.
   c. [ ] Exempt from registration under B&P § 22350(b).
   d. [ ] Registered California process server.
        (1) [ ] Employee or independent contractor.
        (2) Registration No.:
        (3) County:

5. [X] **I declare** under penalty of perjury under the laws of the State of California that the foregoing is true and correct.
6. [ ] **I am a California sheriff, marshal, or constable and** I certify that the foregoing is true and correct.

6/19/XX

▶ *Emma Frend*
         (SIGNATURE)

Sample Proof of Service #2

ATTORNEY OR PARTY WITHOUT ATTORNEY (Name and Address):	TELEPHONE NO.:	FOR COURT USE ONLY
Sally Johnson 1127 Maxie Loop Visalia, CA 93220	303-555-9311	

ATTORNEY FOR (Name):   In Pro Per

NAME OF COURT:	Superior Court
STREET ADDRESS:	Tulare County
MAILING ADDRESS:	County Civic Center
CITY AND ZIP CODE:	Visalia, CA 93291
BRANCH NAME:	

PLAINTIFF/JUDGMENT CREDITOR: Sally Johnson

DEFENDANT/JUDGMENT DEBTOR: Rhonda Skeen

PROOF OF SERVICE	CASE NUMBER: 0000-00014

1. At the time of service I was at least 18 years of age and not a party to this action, and **I served copies** of the (specify documents):

   Application Order for Appearance and Examination

2. a. Party served (specify name of party as shown on the documents served):

   Rhonda Skeen

   b. Person served: [X] party in item 2a   ☐ other (specify name and title or relationship to the party named in item 2a):

   c. Address: 122 Rightmire Ave., Lindsay, CA 93200

3. I served the party named in item 2
   a. [X]   **by personally delivering** the copies   (1) on (date):   6/19/XX   (2) at (time):   1:30 pm
   b. ☐   **by leaving** the copies with or in the presence of (name and title or relationship to person indicated in item 2b):

       (1) ☐   **(business)** a person at least 18 years of age apparently in charge at the office or usual place of business of the person served. I informed him or her of the general nature of the papers.
       (2) ☐   **(home)** a competent member of the household (at least 18 years of age) at the dwelling house or usual place of abode of the person served. I informed him or her of the general nature of the papers.
       (3) on (date):   (4) at (time):
       (5) ☐   A **declaration of diligence** is attached. (Substituted service on natural person, minor, conservatee, or candidate.)
   c. ☐   **by mailing** the copies to the person served, addressed as shown in item 2c, by first-class mail, postage prepaid,
       (1) on (date):   (2) from (city):
       (3) ☐   with two copies of the Notice and Acknowledgment of Receipt and a postage-paid return envelope addressed to m
       (4) ☐   to an address outside California with return receipt requested.   (Attach completed form.) ↖
   d. ☐   **by** causing copies to be mailed. A declaration of mailing is attached.
   e. ☐   **other** (specify other manner of service and authorizing code section):

4. **Person serving** (name, address, and telephone No.):

   Emma Frend
100 Whalebone Street
Visalia, CA 93200
303-555-8319

   a. **Fee** for service: $ 0
   b. ☐ Not a registered California process server.
   c. ☐ Exempt from registration under B&P § 22350(b).
   d. ☐ Registered California process server.
       (1) ☐ Employee or independent contractor.
       (2) Registration No.:
       (3) County:

5. [X]   **I declare** under penalty of perjury under the laws of the State of California that the foregoing is true and correct.
6. ☐   **I am a California sheriff, marshal, or constable and** I certify that the foregoing is true and correct.

    6/19/XX   ▶   *Emma Frend*
                                               (SIGNATURE)

Chapter 22

After the Judgment Is Paid

ongratulations. Let's hope you are reading this chapter because your collection efforts have reached a happy end. Either you've collected your judgment in full or you've accepted less as payment in full.

But before you get carried away celebrating, you must complete a bit more paperwork. The task is simple, but essential; if you don't do this promptly, you could end up owing the debtor money.

Here are the steps you need to take when your judgment is paid.

1. Complete an Acknowledgment of Satisfaction of Judgment form.

2. Have a copy of the form served on the debtor.

3. File the form with the court to show that the judgment has been paid—(technically, "satisfied.")

4. Release any liens you created on the debtor's real estate or personal business property, or give the debtor the opportunity to do so himself.

If your judgment was from small claims court and the debtor paid the small claims court directly, the court clerk is responsible for filing a Satisfaction of Judgment. You must release any liens you've created, however—or give the debtor an opportunity to do so himself.

A. Why File an Acknowledgment?

The debtor has the right to demand that you file an Acknowledgment of Satisfaction of Judgment within 15 days after your judgment is satisfied—14 days for small claims judgments. In addition, the debtor can serve you with a written demand to file an Acknowledgment for partial satisfaction of the judgment if you have collected some payments on the judgment. Again, you must comply with the 15-day deadline (Code of Civil Procedure § 724.050). A debtor might want a partial Acknowledgment filed, for example, if she is selling or refinancing real estate and needs proof of how much she has paid on the judgment.

If you don't file the Acknowledgment, the debtor can take you to court. You may be liable for any damages the debtor sustains because you failed to file the Acknowledgment, plus reasonable attorneys' fees and court costs. On top of all that, you may be ordered to pay the debtor $100 in damages (Code of Civil Procedure § 724.050(e)). Although this scenario is unlikely to happen, why chance it?

What harm can a debtor suffer if you don't promptly file an Acknowledgment? If the judgment shows up on the debtor's credit report, the debtor might be denied credit or prevented from buying real estate or renting an apartment. If you have recorded a lien, she might not be able to sell her property.

> **EXAMPLE:** Joe and Fred had a business dispute. Joe got a judgment against Fred for $10,000, which Fred paid over a ten-month period. Joe never filed a Satisfaction of Judgment, although Fred asked him to twice. Fred filed a small claims action of $2,500 against Joe, claiming his bad credit report lost him two profitable jobs. Joe ended up owing Fred $1,400.

B. Complete Acknowledgment Form

You have to complete the Acknowledgment of Satisfaction of Judgment form after your judgment is paid. A sample copy and instructions are below; a blank copy is in the Appendix.

Caption: Follow the format of your previous court papers for the first three sections and the case number.

Acknowledgment of Satisfaction of Judgment:

- Check the first box if the judgment is fully satisfied. This means you are willing to end the matter with regard to the debtors you name. It doesn't necessarily mean that you received full payment.

- Check the second box if the judgment is partially satisfied. This means that only part of the judgment has been paid and you intend to collect (or to try to collect) the rest.
- Check the third box if the debtor has been paying you on an installment judgment and all installments have been paid.

Item 1a: Check this box if the judgment is fully satisfied, as defined above.

Item 1a(1): Check this box if the judgment, costs and interest were paid in full.

Item 1a(2): Check this box if you have settled for less than the total amount but consider the judgment fully satisfied.

Item 1b: Check this box if the judgment is only partially satisfied, as defined above. Then enter the amount you have received to date.

Item 1c: Check this box if all installments have been paid on an installment judgment. Enter the date the last installment was paid.

Item 2: Enter your full name and address as it appears on the judgment.

Item 3: Leave this blank unless you were assigned the right to collect this judgment.

Item 4: Enter the full name of the judgment debtor exactly as it appears on the judgment, and enter the debtor's address. If more than one judgment debtor is liable for your judgment, name only the debtors being released.

Item 5a: Enter the date the judgment was entered.

Item 5a(1): Check this box and enter the book volume number and page number if you have this information. Otherwise, leave it blank.

Item 5b: Check this box if you renewed the judgment, then enter the date of renewal.

Item 5b(1): If you renewed the judgment, check this box and enter the book volume number and page number if you have this information.

Item 6: Check this box if you have recorded any Abstracts of Judgment or certified copies of the judgment—that is, if you recorded any liens

on the debtor's property. Then specify what you recorded by checking the appropriate box. Enter the county or counties where you recorded the forms, the dates of recording and the book and page numbers. You can find this information on the documents you recorded or at the recorder's office.

Item 7: Check this box if you created a judgment lien against the debtor's business personal property by filing a Notice of Judgment Lien with the Secretary of State; then enter the file number you were given.

Do not sign or date the Acknowledgment of Satisfaction of Judgment yet; you must do so in front of a notary public.

C. Have Your Signature Notarized

Find a notary public. Real estate offices and title companies are good places to call, or you can look in the yellow pages. Take your original Acknowledgment of Satisfaction of Judgment form and ask that your signature be notarized. The notary will ask you to provide some identification, such as your driver's license. After you sign, the notary will fill out a short form for you to attach

Acknowledgment of Satisfaction of Judgment

ATTORNEY OR PARTY WITHOUT ATTORNEY *(Name and Address)*:	TELEPHONE NO.: **707-555-9011**

ATTORNEY OR PARTY WITHOUT ATTORNEY *(Name and Address)*:

    Susan Monroe
    17006 4th Street
    Arcata, CA 95500

TELEPHONE NO.: 707-555-9011

FOR RECORDER'S OR SECRETARY OF STATE'S USE ONLY

ATTORNEY FOR *(Name)*: **In Pro Per**

NAME OF COURT: Superior Court of California
STREET ADDRESS: County of Humboldt
MAILING ADDRESS: 825 Fifth Street
CITY AND ZIP CODE: Eureka, CA 95501
BRANCH NAME:

PLAINTIFF: Susan Monroe

DEFENDANT: Shakey Wallace

ACKNOWLEDGMENT OF SATISFACTION OF JUDGMENT
[X] FULL   [ ] PARTIAL   [ ] MATURED INSTALLMENT

CASE NUMBER: 0000-00014

FOR COURT USE ONLY

1. Satisfaction of the judgment is acknowledged as follows *(see footnote* before completing)*:
   a. [X] Full satisfaction
      (1) [X] Judgment is satisfied in full.
      (2) [ ] The judgment creditor has accepted payment or performance other than that specified in the judgment in full satisfaction of the judgment.
   b. [ ] Partial satisfaction
      The amount received in partial satisfaction of the judgment is
      $
   c. [ ] Matured installment
      All matured installments under the installment judgment have been satisfied as of *(date)*:

2. Full name and address of judgment creditor: Susan Monroe
    17006 4th Street
    Arcata, CA 95500

3. Full name and address of assignee of record, if any:

4. Full name and address of judgment debtor being fully or partially released: Shakey Wallace
    711 Circle Circle
    Blue Lake, CA 95000

5. a. Judgment entered on *(date)*: 9/12/XX
      [ ] (1) in judgment book volume no.:   (2) page no.:
   b. [ ] Renewal entered on *(date)*:
      [ ] (1) in judgment book volume no.:   (2) page no.:

6. [X] An [X] abstract of judgment [ ] certified copy of the judgment has been recorded as follows *(complete all information for each county where recorded)*:

COUNTY	DATE OF RECORDING	BOOK NUMBER	PAGE NUMBER
Humboldt	10/20/XX	17	304

7. [ ] A notice of judgment lien has been filed in the office of the Secretary of State as file number *(specify)*:

NOTICE TO JUDGMENT DEBTOR: If this is an acknowledgment of full satisfaction of judgment, it will have to be recorded in each county shown in item 6 above, if any, in order to release the judgment lien, and will have to be filed in the office of the Secretary of State to terminate any judgment lien on personal property.

Date: 11/14/XX

▶ *Susan Monroe*
(SIGNATURE OF JUDGMENT CREDITOR OR ASSIGNEE OF CREDITOR OR ATTORNEY)

*The names of the judgment creditor and judgment debtor must be stated as shown in any Abstract of Judgment which was recorded and is being released by this satisfaction. **A separate notary acknowledgment must be attached for each signature.**

Form Approved by the
Judicial Council of California
EJ-100 [Rev. July 1, 1983] (Cor. 7/84)

ACKNOWLEDGMENT OF SATISFACTION OF JUDGMENT

WEST GROUP
Official Publisher

CCP 724.060, 724.120, 724.250

to the Acknowledgment of Satisfaction of Judgment. The notary will enter your name, her signature and her official seal. She will charge a fee for her service, usually about $10.

D. Serve and File Acknowledgment

The debtor may be served either personally or by mail with a copy of the Acknowledgment. (See Chapter 21 for information on serving papers.) If you have the debtor served by mail, you must file a copy of the form with the court. If you have the debtor served personally, he is responsible for filing a copy with the court. Even if he is responsible for filing a copy, do it yourself if you have filed any liens. Keep a file-stamped copy of the form for your records.

E. Release Any Liens

Once you have officially informed the court that the judgment has been satisfied, you must take steps to release any liens you have created against the debtor's property. The procedures and costs are about the same as recording the lien. (See Chapter 4.) If you have recorded several liens, this can add up—and it's not money you can recover. But you must still remove the liens or give the debtor the paperwork she needs to remove them herself. You had the right to collect and the debtor has the right to have liens removed.

1. Real Estate Liens

If you recorded an Abstract of Judgment with any county recorder, you have two choices. You must either record a certified copy of the Acknowledgment with that county recorder or send a certified copy of the Acknowledgment to the debtor, along with a letter telling her that she will have to record the document in order to release the lien

(see sample letter, below). Once the Acknowledgment is filed with the county recorder, the judgment lien is released.

Sample Letter to Debtor to Release Lien

September 26, 20XX

Tom Johnson
250 Oak Street
Greenbrae, CA 94904

Dear Tom,

I have enclosed a certified, notarized copy of the Acknowledgment of Satisfaction of Judgment. I filed this document with the Marin County Superior Court on September 24, 20XX. The document informs the court that you have paid the judgment in full.

As you know, I recorded a real estate lien against your property in Marin County. In order to release this lien, you need to record the enclosed Acknowledgment with the recorder's office in Marin County. Unless and until you record this Acknowledgment, the county's property records will continue to show that you have a lien against your property.

Sincerely,

Gabriela Martinez
Gabriela Martinez

2. Business Personal Property Liens

If you created a judgment lien on any business personal property belonging to the debtor, you'll need to file a form called Notice of Judgment Lien Release or Subordination. A sample completed form is below. You can find a blank copy of the form in the Appendix. Instructions are printed on the back of the form, but two items require further explanation.

NOTICE OFJUDGMENT LIEN RELEASE OR SUBORDINATION
FOLLOW INSTRUCTIONS CAREFULLY (front and back of form)

A. NAME & PHONE OF FILER CONTACT (optional)

Susan Monroe   707-555-9011

B. SEND ACKNOWLEDGMENT TO: (NAME AND ADDRESS)

[

Susan Monroe
17006 4th Street
Arcata, CA 95500

[

THIS SPACE FOR FILING OFFICE USE ONLY

C. SECRETARY OF STATE FILE NO. (ON NOTICE OF JUDGMENT LIEN)	D. DATE OF FILING (ON NOTICE OF JUDGMENT LIEN)
0000-0015	April 3, 20XX

1. JUDGMENT DEBTOR'S EXACT LEGAL NAME – Insert only one name, either 1a or 1b. Do not abbreviate or combine names.
1a. ORGANIZATION'S NAME

1b. INDIVIDUAL'S LAST NAME	FIRST NAME	MIDDLE NAME	SUFFIX
Wallace	Shakey		
1c. MAILING ADDRESS	CITY	STATE POSTAL CODE	COUNTRY
711 Circle Circle	Blue Lake	CA 95000	USA

2. ADDITIONAL JUDGMENT DEBTOR'S EXACT LEGAL NAME – Enter one name, either 2a or 2b. Do not abbreviate or combine names.
2 a. ORGANIZATION'S NAME

2b. INDIVIDUAL'S LAST NAME	FIRST NAME	MIDDLE NAME	SUFFIX
2\c. MAILING ADDRESS	CITY	STATE POSTAL CODE	COUNTRY

3. JUDGMENT CREDITOR'S EXACT NAME– Do not abbreviate or combine names.
3a. ORGANIZATION'S NAME

3b. INDIVIDUAL'S LAST NAME	FIRST NAME	MIDDLE	SUFFIX
Monroe	Susan		
3c. MAILING ADDRESS	CITY	STATE POSTAL CODE	COUNTRY
17006 4th Street	Arcata	CA 95500	USA

4. RELEASE OF JUDGMENT LIEN ON PERSONAL PROPERTY

[X]   THE JUDGMENT LIEN ON THE PERSONAL PROPERTY DESCRIBED IN ITEM 6 BELOW IS HEREBY RELEASED.

5. SUBORDINATION OF JUDGMENT LIEN ON PERSONAL PROPERTY

[ ]   THE NOTICE OF JUDGMENT LIEN ON THE PERSONAL PROPERTY SUBJECT TO LIEN IS HEREBY SUBORDINATED AS DESCRIBED IN ITEM 6 BELOW (SEE CODE OF CIVIL PROCEDURE, SECTION 697.650(B)).

6. DESCRIPTION OF PERSONAL PROPERTY

All property subject to judgment lien #0000-0015

7.

Susan Wallace   11-3-XX

SIGNATURE OF JUDGMENT CREDITOR (SEE INSTRUCTION NO. 7   DATE

FOR _____

JUDGMENT LIEN (FORM JL3) Rev 6/01
Approved CA Secretary of State

Item 5: Leave this box blank.

Item 6: In this space, write "All property subject to judgment lien #_____." In the blank, insert the number the Secretary of State assigned to your judgment lien.

Once you have completed the form, send the original and one copy to the Secretary of State's office at P.O. Box 942835, Sacramento, CA 94235-0001, along with a $10 filing fee. Also, serve a copy of the Release on the debtor. ■

Chapter 23

Help Beyond the Book

7he point of this book is to give you the tools to collect a judgment on your own. But no book on this subject can be complete. Some methods of collecting are beyond the scope of this book. Some judgments aren't covered by this book. At some point, you may need information we don't provide.

This chapter gives you information on where to go for more help: the law library, the Internet, collections attorneys and other collections professionals, such as asset tracing firms, data search companies and collection agencies.

A. Legal Research

If you need more legal information than this book provides, and you can't get the answer from the levying officer or clerk, consider visiting a law library or doing some research online.

1. Using a Law Library

Every California county has a law library open to the public without charge. Most law librarians are willing and even happy to help, as long as you don't ask them to give you legal advice or interpret what you find in the books.

How To Find and Understand the Law

If you decide to do some legal research, get a copy of *Legal Research: How to Find and Understand the Law*, by Stephen Elias and Susan Levinkind (Nolo). This hands-on guide to the law library will answer most of the questions likely to arise in the course of your research. The library will probably have a copy.

If you want a guided tour through the basics of legal research, ask the librarian if the library carries a copy of *Legal Research Made Easy: A Roadmap Through the Law Library Maze*, a video by Nolo Press and Legal Star Communications.

Several resources have background information on the law governing judgment collection. Your library may carry any or all of these.

- *California Practice Guide: Enforcing Judgments and Debts* (Rutter Group), describes the basic procedures used in collecting judgments and provides forms and legal references.
- *California Forms of Pleading and Practice* (Mathew Bender) provides step-by-step guidance for many court procedures. Unfortunately, these volumes do not comprehensively include judgment enforcement procedures.
- *California Jurisprudence, Third Series* (Cal. Jur. 3d), "Enforcement of Judgments" article discusses the Enforcement of Judgments Act.

Background resources, including this book, provide citations to relevant statutes and court interpretations of these laws. Reading these statutes and court interpretations, called cases, may be a crucial step in doing legal research.

In California, statutes passed by the California legislature—called the Enforcement of Judgments Act—govern virtually every phase of the collections processes we describe in this book. You can find the Enforcement of Judgments Act at § 680.010 to § 724.260 of the California Code of Civil Procedure.

Reading these statutes may leave you less than fully enlightened. They tend to be difficult to understand and sometimes ambiguous. It often helps to read the case summaries that follow a statute, and then the cases themselves. Ask the librarian for help in finding the cases.

2. Using the Internet

Many legal resources are available online through the Internet. There are a number of ways to use the Internet to search for material, but by far the most important and common tool for doing research on the Internet is the World Wide Web.

A wide variety of sources intended for both lawyers and the general public have been posted on the Internet by publishers, law schools and firms. If you are on the Web, for example, a good way to find these sources is to visit any of the following Web sites, each of which provides links to legal information by specific subject.

- www.nolo.com: Nolo's online site includes a vast amount of legal information for consumers. This includes sets of FAQs (frequently asked questions) on a wide variety of legal topics and articles on legal issues. You can also use Nolo's site to find cases and statutes—just click on "Legal Research" at the bottom of the page, then follow the instructions.
- www.findlaw.com: An easy-to-use site that points to legal resources on the Web.

- www.law.cornell.edu/index.html: This site, another law pointer, is maintained by Cornell Law School.
- www.law.indiana.edu/v-lib: A third useful pointer is maintained by Indiana University's School of Law at Bloomington.

If you want to read California statutes, visit www.leginfo.ca.gov, the official site for California legislative information. This site contains the current codes, Assembly and Senate bills, information on accessing California Legislative Information on the Internet, frequently asked questions and links to other Websites.

3. Obtaining Judicial Council Forms

This book contains several California Judicial Council forms. To make sure our forms are the most current or to obtain additional forms, check any of the following:

- court clerk
- *California Forms of Pleading and Practice* (at a law library)
- *West's California Judicial Council Forms* (at a law library), or
- www.courtinfo.ca.gov/forms—the Website of the Judicial Council.

B. Collections Lawyers

If collecting your judgment starts to get complicated—for example, the debtor has assets that are hard to reach—and the stakes are high enough ($5,000 or more), consider handing your case over to a lawyer who specializes in collecting judgments. You may be able to recover your attorney's fees from the debtor (Code of Civil Procedure § 685.040).

There are two ways to work with an attorney collecting your judgment. The first is to turn over the judgment to her. You pay the attorney's bills and wait for her to collect the judgment and hand the money over to you.

The second, which will let you keep more of what you collect, is for you get help from the attorney but do most of the work yourself. You pay the attorney by the hour for her advice.

1. Will a Lawyer Take Your Case?

If your judgment is for less than $5,000, it probably isn't cost-effective to give your case to an attorney. And an attorney probably won't take even a case worth substantially more if she thinks collection will be difficult. The attorney will make that assessment based on whether the debtor is an individual or a business and what assets might be available. The attorney will also consider whether the debtor is a settled member of the community, has a job or owns real estate or other valuable non-exempt assets. Usually, if the debtor is a going business or settled in the community, the attorney will be more optimistic about collecting.

If the attorney agrees to collect your judgment, she will ask you to assign it to her. This means, in essence, that the attorney will now own the judgment. You will be paid your share if and when the attorney collects all or part of it.

2. What Lawyers Charge

For consultations, collection attorneys' going rates are normally $125 to $200 an hour. Some lawyers charge up to $250 per hour. There is seldom reason to pay a high-end fee. Shop around, both for an experienced lawyer and a reasonable fee.

If you want an attorney to take over your collection efforts, you agree to pay a contingency fee—that is, a set percentage of what is collected. For collecting from individual debtors, an attorney usually will want a contingency fee of 33% to 50%, depending on the size of the judgment. The smaller the judgment amount, the bigger percentage you can expect to pay. For business debtors, the percentage is generally lower—because the attorney is more likely to be able to collect.

The nice thing about a contingency fee is that you don't pay if the lawyer doesn't collect—although you might have to pay the attorney's costs. The down side is that lawyers usually refuse to take collection cases unless they see from the outset that collection is likely to be profitable and relatively easy. The lawyer may put in little time and effort, but earn a lot. That only makes sense if the procedure the lawyer will use is beyond your means. In most cases, you can probably use this book and keep the lawyer's cut in your own pocket.

If you hire an attorney under a contingency fee agreement, you are entitled to a written contract setting out the terms of the agreement. If you hire an attorney on an hourly fee basis and the attorney expects to bill more than $1,000, you are also entitled to a written contract. Always request a written contract, even if the law doesn't require it.

Regardless of the fee arrangement, you may have to pay the costs of collecting the judgment. Make sure you agree on this in advance. If you will be responsible for costs, the attorney will ask you to advance the costs or will advance the costs and have you reimburse him. Most collections involve at least $200 in costs; many, of course, cost much more. (See Chapter 16 for how costs are paid and how to keep track of them.)

Finally, make sure the attorney charges you fairly. Many collections attorneys rely heavily on paralegals. Some attorneys charge customers attorney rates for paralegal work while others charge at a lower paralegal rate.

3. How to Find a Collections Lawyer

Be sure to choose a collections lawyer rather than a general business lawyer. The collections field is a specialty unto itself. There are three advantages of using a collections attorney.

- A collections attorney is in a good position to find out information on the debtor, because he is part of a network of collection lawyers who exchange information. A lawyer who is not actively involved in collections is an outsider and may have trouble getting needed information.

- A collections lawyer is set up to handle collection cases on a systematic, efficient basis. He can zero in on the problem and select the most efficient strategies.
- An experienced collections lawyer has a valuable understanding of the normal debtor's psychology and uses it in the course of negotiations.

a. Location of the Lawyer

As a general principle, select an attorney geographically close to the court where he will be doing his work. This normally means the county in which the court that issued the judgment is located. You may want an attorney where the debtor lives, works, has a business or owns assets.

If the judgment debtor's home and assets are widely separated, you may have a difficult choice to make in choosing a lawyer. Here are some tips:

- If you are turning the judgment over to the attorney to collect, choose one close to where the debtor lives.
- If you are hiring an attorney to consult at different stages in your collection effort—for instance, you need guidance on bringing a particular motion—select an attorney near the court.
- If the assets you seek to levy on are in another state, find an attorney in that state.
- If you don't know where the debtor is or the debtor is temporarily judgment-proof and you plan to wait a year or two before trying to collect, find an attorney close to you.

b. Getting Referrals

To find a good collections attorney, check one or more of the following sources:

- **Friends or business associates:** Make sure the lawyer is a collections specialist or can suggest one.
- **Lawyers who have served you well:** If you are satisfied with a lawyer who you used for some other purpose, that lawyer may be able to steer you to a good and honest collections lawyer.
- **Lawyer lists:** You can use a lawyer list, available in libraries and on the Internet, to locate lawyers who specialize in collections.
- **Local collection agency:** Because most collection agencies refer their uncollected claims to attorneys, find out who handles their cases in your area and see if she will take your judgment.

C. Other Collections Professionals

Lawyers aren't the only professionals who can provide help in your collection efforts. Others include data search companies, asset tracing firms, private investigators, collection agencies and judgment enforcement specialists.

If your main problem is locating the debtor or her assets, try a data search firm, collection agency or investigator instead of a lawyer, because they often have good skip-tracing departments. ("Skip-tracing" means tracking down a person and finding out about his personal and business affairs.) You can find lists of these firms in the yellow pages or on the Internet.

1. Data Search Firms

Data search firms specialize in efficiently ferreting out, from government and private databases, the information you need to carry out collection activities. You may be a lot better off having one of these firms do your search than spending hours trying to do it yourself. For example, a statewide real estate search usually costs about

$50. It would take countless hours to get that information without the use of a database.

2. Investigators and Asset Tracing Firms

Probably the biggest impediment to collecting a judgment is finding out what the debtor owns and where the property is located. Sometimes, this information can be obtained cheaply through a data search; other times, it takes plain hard work by a knowledgeable person.

Private investigators are skilled in locating individuals and, sometimes, assets; asset-tracing firms are skilled in locating assets. Both charge a fair amount for their services, but if your judgment is large enough to warrant the costs, you may save yourself a lot of grief in the long run.

The best place to find references to investigators or asset tracing firms is the advertisements in newspapers or periodicals directed to California attorneys. These can be found in your county law library. You can also find investigators through the yellow pages.

3. Collection Agencies

We generally recommend against collection agencies because you often pay more to an agency than to a lawyer for much the same result. Collection agencies usually work hand-in-glove with attorneys, so they tack on an added fee. Agencies usually require a 50% commission on judgments. This percentage may include all court costs and levying fees, however, meaning you're not out anything if the agency doesn't collect. Make sure you're clear about this in advance.

Many agencies don't deal with judgments, because their best techniques—telephone appeals and letters—usually aren't effective. After all, you got a judgment because nothing else worked. In deciding whether to collect your judgment, the collection agency will assess the likelihood of success. If the debtor is employed, owns real estate or has a business, the agency will be likely to pursue your judgment. But remember, if you know about the debtor's assets, you can go after them yourself, using the instructions in this book.

4. Judgment Professionals

Unlike a collection agency, a judgment professional (also known as a judgment enforcement specialist) specializes in collecting judgments. These professionals generally take judgments on assignment—this means that you assign the judgment to the specialist, who then collects the judgment as if it were his or her own.

A judgment professional will have experience using the collection procedures described in this book, and will have access to a variety of information sources—databases, search tools and asset locating services—that are available only by subscription, and not to the general public. If you've reached a dead end in tracking down the debtor's assets, or if your case is particularly complicated, using a judgment professional might be a good idea. However, judgment professionals, like attorneys, charge a contingency fee of up to 50%. That's money you can hang onto if you are able to enforce the judgment yourself.

You can find a judgment professional in your area by logging on to the Website of the California Association of Judgment Professionals, at www.cajp.org. ■

Appendix

Tear-Out Forms

This Appendix contains most of the forms you will need to complete the procedures covered in this book.

Tips On Using Forms

- Never fill out forms without making photo-copies first. You may make a mistake, or you may need a copy of the original form later on.
- If a form has printing on both sides, make sure you copy both sides. You can make a two-sided copy or you can copy them on to single-sided copy pages and staple them together.
- Carefully follow the instructions in this book for completing the forms. Use the completed samples as guides.
- If possible, type the forms. If that is not possible, print clearly and neatly.
- Whenever you send forms to the court or levy-ing officer, keep copies for yourself. Forms can get lost in the mail, get misplaced by a clerk or end up in the twilight zone.
- If you type up your own forms on lined pleading paper, remember to include the name of the form at the bottom.

Judicial Council Forms

Many of the forms you will be using are published by the California Judicial Council for use in all California courts. At the bottom of each Judicial Council form is its title, the form number and the revision date.

The forms were current when this book was published. Judicial Council forms are subject to change, however. If you discover that a Judicial Council form we provide here is out-of-date—a court clerk rejects your documents—see Chapter 24, Section A3, for information about obtaining Judicial Council forms.

If you want to make sure the forms are up-to-date before you complete them, call the court and give them the name and number of the forms. Some courts are real sticklers about requiring the most up-to-date form; other courts are fairly lenient.

Date: _____

To: _____

           _____

           _____

           _____

Re: _____ v. _____

Court: _____

Case No. _____

Dear Clerk:

Enclosed please find:

1) Original and _____ copy/copies of the following document(s):

     _____

     _____

     _____

     _____

     _____

2) Check in the amount of $_____ (if required);

3) Self-addressed stamped envelope; and

4) Other:

     _____

     _____

     _____

     _____

Please file, issue or record these documents and return conformed copies to me.

Sincerely,

_____

Address:

_____

_____

_____

Phone:

(_____) _____ - _____

Cover Letter to Clerk

Date: _____

Instructions to Levying Officer, County of _____

Please take the action described below to collect this court judgment. Please hold the Writ for its entire 180-day duration, or until the judgment has been satisfied, unless I contact and instruct you differently.

1. **Case Information:**

   Case: _____

   Court: _____

   Case No. _____

   Levying Officer No. (*on previous papers, if you have attempted levies in this county*): _____

2. **Enclosures:**

   ☐ Original Writ of Execution and _____ copy/copies

   ☐ Check or money order in the amount of $_____

   ☐ Separate written levy instructions (*Check only if applicable.*)

3. **Levy Instructions:**

   ☐ Type of levy: _____

   ☐ Please proceed as follows: _____

   _____

   _____

   _____

   _____

   _____

   _____

   _____

   _____

Sincerely,   Your Address:

_____   _____
(your signature)
                                               _____

                                               _____

                                               _____

Your Printed Name: Your Phone Number:

_____   (_____) _____

ATTORNEY OR PARTY WITHOUT ATTORNEY (Name and Address): TEL NO.:

☐ Recording requested by and return to:

☐ ATTORNEY FOR ☐ JUDGMENT CREDITOR ☐ ASSIGNEE OF RECORD

NAME OF COURT:
STREET ADDRESS:
MAILING ADDRESS:
CITY AND ZIP CODE:
BRANCH NAME:

FOR RECORDER'S USE ONLY

PLAINTIFF:

DEFENDANT:

ABSTRACT OF JUDGMENT ☐ **Amended**

CASE NUMBER:

FOR COURT USE ONLY

1. The ☐ judgment creditor ☐ assignee of record
applies for an abstract of judgment and represents the following:
a. Judgment debtor's

Name and last known address

b. Driver's license No. and state: ☐ Unknown
c. Social security No.: ☐ Unknown
d. Summons or notice of entry of sister-state judgment was personally served or
mailed to (name and address):

e. ☐ Original abstract recorded in this county:
(1) Date:
(2) Instrument No.:

f. ☐ Information on additional judgment debtors is
shown on page two.

Date:

_____ ▶ _____
(TYPE OR PRINT NAME) (SIGNATURE OF APPLICANT OR ATTORNEY)

2. a. ☐ I certify that the following is a true and correct abstract
of the judgment entered in this action.
b. ☐ A certified copy of the judgment is attached.

3. Judgment creditor (name and address):

4. Judgment debtor (full name as it appears in judgment):

[SEAL]

5. a. Judgment entered on
(date):
b. Renewal entered on
(date):
c. Renewal entered on
(date):

This abstract issued on (date):

6. Total amount of judgment as entered or last renewed:
$

7. ☐ An ☐ execution lien ☐ attachment lien
is endorsed on the judgment as follows:
a. Amount: $
b. In favor of (name and address):

8. A stay of enforcement has
a. ☐ not been ordered by the court.
b. ☐ been ordered by the court effective until
(date):
9. ☐ This judgment is an installment judgment.

Clerk, by _____, Deputy

Form Adopted for Mandatory Use
Judicial Council of California
EJ-001 [Rev. January 1, 2002]

ABSTRACT OF JUDGMENT
(CIVIL)

Page 1 of 2
Code of Civil Procedure, §§ 488.480,
674, 700.190

PLAINTIFF:	CASE NUMBER:
DEFENDANT:	

INFORMATION ON ADDITIONAL JUDGMENT DEBTORS

10.   Name and last known address

Driver's license No. & state: ☐ Unknown
Social security No.: ☐ Unknown
Summons was personally served at or mailed to *(address)*:

11.   Name and last known address

Driver's license No. & state: ☐ Unknown
Social security No.: ☐ Unknown
Summons was personally served at or mailed to *(address)*:

12.   Name and last known address

Driver's license No. & state: ☐ Unknown
Social security No.: ☐ Unknown
Summons was personally served at or mailed to *(address)*:

13.   Name and last known address

Driver's license No. & state: ☐ Unknown
Social security No.: ☐ Unknown
Summons was personally served at or mailed to *(address)*:

14.   Name and last known address

Driver's license No. & state: ☐ Unknown
Social security No.: ☐ Unknown
Summons was personally served at or mailed to *(address)*:

15.   Name and last known address

Driver's license No. & state: ☐ Unknown
Social security No.: ☐ Unknown
Summons was personally served at or mailed to *(address)*:

16.   Name and last known address

Driver's license No. & state: ☐ Unknown
Social security No.: ☐ Unknown
Summons was personally served at or mailed to *(address)*:

17.   Name and last known address

Driver's license No. & state: ☐ Unknown
Social security No.: ☐ Unknown
Summons was personally served at or mailed to *(address)*:

18. ☐ Continued on Attachment 18.

ABSTRACT OF JUDGMENT
(CIVIL)

ATTORNEY OR PARTY WITHOUT ATTORNEY *(Name and Address)*:

☐ Recording requested by and return to:

TELEPHONE NO.:

FOR RECORDER'S USE ONLY

☐ ATTORNEY FOR ☐ JUDGMENT CREDITOR ☐ ASSIGNEE OF RECORD

SUPERIOR COURT OF CALIFORNIA, COUNTY OF

STREET ADDRESS:

MAILING ADDRESS:

CITY AND ZIP CODE:

BRANCH NAME:

PETITIONER/PLAINTIFF:

RESPONDENT/DEFENDANT:

ABSTRACT OF SUPPORT JUDGMENT

CASE NUMBER:

FOR COURT USE ONLY

1. The ☐ judgment creditor ☐ assignee of record
   applies for an abstract of a support judgment and represents the following:
   a. Judgment debtor's

      Name and last known address

   b. Driver's license No. and state: ☐ unknown
   c. Social Security number: ☐ unknown
   d. Birthdate: ☐ unknown

Date:

▶

....
(TYPE OR PRINT NAME)

_____
(SIGNATURE OF APPLICANT OR ATTORNEY)

2. I CERTIFY that the judgment entered in this action contains an order for payment of spousal, family, or child support.

3. Judgment creditor *(name)*:

   whose address appears on this form above the court's name.

4. ☐ The support is ordered to be paid to the following county officer *(name and address)*:

5. Judgment debtor *(full name as it appears in judgment)*:

6. a. A judgment was entered on *(date)*:
   b. Renewal was entered on *(date)*:
   c. Renewal was entered on *(date)*:

7. ☐ An execution lien is endorsed on the judgment as follows:
   a. Amount: $
   b. In favor of *(name and address)*:

[SEAL]

8. A stay of enforcement has
   a ☐ not been ordered by the court.
   b ☐ been ordered by the court effective until *(date)*

9. ☐ This is an installment judgment.

This abstract issued on *(date)*:

Clerk, by _____, Deputy

Form Adopted by Rule 1285.80
Judicial Council of California
1285.80 [Rev. July 1, 1989]
Mandatory Form

ABSTRACT OF SUPPORT JUDGMENT
(Family Law)

CCP 488.480, 674
697.320, 700.190

JL FILING INSTRUCTIONS

Please type or laser-print information on this form. Be sure information provided is legible. Read all instructions and follow them completely. Complete the form very carefully as mistakes may have important legal consequences. Do not insert anything in the open space in the upper right portion of this form as it is reserved for filing office use. Do not staple or otherwise mutilate the barcode in the upper left corner of the document, this will render the barcode ineffective.

To provide the requester with an acknowledgment of filing, the original and a duplicate copy of the notice must be presented for filing. This Notice of Judgment Lien must be filed according to provisions of Section 697.510 of the Code of Civil Procedure.

Section A:	To assist filing office communication with the filer, information in this section should be provided.
Section B:	Enter name and mailing address of requester in this section. This is required information.
ITEM 1a or 1b:	Enter the exact legal name of the organization or the name of the individual that is the debtor appearing on the court judgment. Use the judgment lien addendum to add additional judgment debtor names.
ITEMS 1c:	Enter the last known mailing address of the judgment debtor.
ITEM 2a or 2b:	Enter the exact legal name of the organization or the name of the individual that is the creditor appearing on the court judgment. Use the judgment lien addendum for additional judgment creditor names.
ITEMS 2c:	Enter the last known mailing address of the judgment creditor.
ITEM 3A-E:	Enter information from the court judgment.
ITEM 3F:	Enter the amount of the court judgment adjusted for interest and payments to the date of the notice.
ITEM 3G:	The date of the statement will normally be the date the notice is executed.
ITEM 4:	The signature of either the judgment creditor or the judgment creditor's attorney is required. (Section 697.550, Code of Civil Procedure)
	If the individual signing the statement signs on behalf of a law firm, which is the attorney of record, the name of the law firm should be entered BENEATH, not above, the signature. If the signature is for a judgment creditor, which is an entity, the name of the entity should be entered BENEATH, not above, the signature of the person signing for the judgment creditor.

The Judgment Lien must be submitted with a filing fee of ten dollars ($10.00) if the original document is two pages or less and twenty dollars ($20.00) if the original document is three pages or more. Please send a check made payable to the **Secretary of State**. DOCUMENTS NOT ACCOMPANIED BY THE FILING FEE WILL NOT BE PROCESSED.

When properly completed, send **payment**, and the **original** and a **duplicate copy** of the notice to:

Secretary of State
P.O. Box 942835
Sacramento, CA 94235-0001

JUDGMENT LIEN ADDENDUM INSTRUCTIONS

This form is to be used for listing additional judgment debtors and/or creditors to the NOTICE OF JUDGMENT LIEN.

Please type or laser-print information on this form. Be sure information provided is legible. Read all instructions and follow them completely. Complete the form very carefully as mistakes may have important legal consequences. **Attach this ADDENDUM to the completed NOTICE OF JUDGMENT LIEN.**

ITEM 5: Provide the name of the judgment debtor shown in Item 1 of the original NOTICE OF JUDGMENT LIEN. Provide only one name by completing either 5a or 5b, as applicable.

ITEMS 6, 7, 8: To add additional debtor names to the judgment lien record, enter the appropriate information in Item 6, 7 or 8, as needed. For each of these items, enter either an organization name or an individual name, not both.

Provide the complete mailing address for each judgment debtor.

ITEMS 9, 10: To add additional creditor names to the judgment lien record, enter the appropriate information in Item 9 or 10, as needed. For each of these items, enter either an organization name or an individual name, not both.

Provide the complete mailing address for each judgment creditor.

NOTICE OF JUDGMENT LIEN
FOLLOW INSTRUCTIONS CAREFULLY (front and back of form)

A. NAME & PHONE OF FILER'S CONTACT (optional)

B. SEND ACKNOWLEDGMENT TO: (NAME AND ADDRESS)

THIS SPACE FOR FILING OFFICE USE ONLY

1. JUDGMENT DEBTOR'S EXACT LEGAL NAME –Insert only one name, either 1a or 1b. Do not abbreviate or combine names.

1a. ORGANIZATION'S NAME

1b. INDIVIDUAL'S LAST NAME	FIRST NAME	MIDDLE NAME	SUFFIX
1c. MAILING ADDRESS	CITY	STATE	POSTAL CODE	COUNTRY

2. JUDGMENT CREDITOR'S NAME– Do not abbreviate or combine names.

2a . ORGANIZATION'S NAME

2b. INDIVIDUAL'S LAST NAME	FIRST NAME	MIDDLE	SUFFIX
2c.. MAILING ADDRESS	CITY	STATE	POSTAL CODE	COUNTRY

3. ALL PROPERTY SUBJECT TO ENFORCEMENT OF A MONEY JUDGMENT AGAINST THE JUDGMENT DEBTOR TO WHICH A JUDGMENT LIEN ON PERSONAL PROPERTY MAY ATTACH UNDER SECTION 697.530 OF THE CODE OF CIVIL PROCEDURE IS SUBJECT TO THIS JUDGMENT LIEN.

A. Title of court where judgment was entered: _____

B. Title of the action: _____

C. Number of this action: _____

D. Date judgment was entered: _____

E. Date of subsequent renewals of judgment (if any): _____

F. Amount required to satisfy judgment at date of this notice: $ _____

G. Date of this notice: _____

4. I *declare under penalty of perjury under the laws of the State of California that the foregoing is true and correct:*

_____

SIGNATURE – SEE INSTRUCTION NO. 4

Dated: _____
(If not indicated, use same as date in item 3G.)

FOR: _____

JUDGMENT LIEN ADDENDUM

FOLLOW INSTRUCTIONS CAREFULLY (FRONT AND BACK OF FORM)

5. NAME OF JUDGMENT DEBTOR: (NAME OF FIRST DEBTOR ON RELATED JUDGMENT LIEN)

5a. ORGANIZATION'S NAME			
5b. INDIVIDUAL'S LAST NAME	FIRST NAME	MIDDLE NAME	SUFFIX

6. ADDITIONAL JUDGMENT DEBTOR – insert only one name (6a or 6b):

6a. ORGANIZATION'S NAME				
6b. INDIVIDUAL'S LAST NAME	FIRST NAME		MIDDLE NAME	SUFFIX
6c. MAILING ADDRESS	CITY	STATE	POSTAL CODE	COUNTRY

7. ADDITIONAL JUDGMENT DEBTOR – insert only one name (7a or 7b):

7a. ORGANIZATION'S NAME				
7b. INDIVIDUAL'S LAST NAME	FIRST NAME	MIDDLE NAME	SUFFIX	
7c. MAILING ADDRESS	CITY	STATE	POSTAL CODE	COUNTRY

8. ADDITIONAL JUDGMENT DEBTOR – insert only one name (8a or 8b):

8a. ORGANIZATION'S NAME				
8b. INDIVIDUAL'S LAST NAME	FIRST NAME	MIDDLE NAME	SUFFIX	
8c. MAILING ADDRESS	CITY	STATE	POSTAL CODE	COUNTRY

9. ADDITIONAL JUDGMENT CREDITOR – insert only one name (9a or 9b):

9a. ORGANIZATION'S NAME				
9b. INDIVIDUAL'S LAST NAME	FIRST NAME	MIDDLE NAME	SUFFIX	
9c. MAILING ADDRESS	CITY	STATE	POSTAL CODE	COUNTRY

10. ADDITIONAL JUDGMENT CREDITOR – insert only one name (10a or 10b):

10a. ORGANIZATION'S NAME				
10b. INDIVIDUAL'S LAST NAME	FIRST NAME	MIDDLE NAME	SUFFIX	
10c. MAILING ADDRESS	CITY	STATE	POSTAL CODE	COUNTRY

TO: DEFENDANT/JUDGMENT DEBTOR:	*(do not file with the court)*

FROM: PLAINTIFF/JUDGMENT CREDITOR:

COURT NAME:

INCOME AND EXPENSE STATEMENT	CASE NUMBER:

(Attach additional sheets if you need more room)

EMPLOYMENT AND INCOME

1. What is your occupation?

2. Name and address of your business and employer:

   _____

   _____

3. How often are you paid? ☐ daily ☐ every week ☐ every two weeks ☐ twice a month ☐ monthly
   ☐ other: _____

4. Your gross pay for each pay period: $_____

5. Your take home pay for each pay period: _____ $_____

6. If your spouse earns any income, give the name and address of the business or employer, and an estimate of your spouse's monthly take-home pay: _____

7. Other income you and your spouse receive (support payments, public benefits, royalties, patents, business income, etc.):

Amount	When are payments received?	Source (name and address)
_____	_____	_____
_____	_____	_____
_____	_____	_____

8. I, my spouse, and my other dependents own the following property:

   a. Cash: $_____

   b. Checking, savings, credit union, money market, CD and other financial accounts (specify below):

Account no.	Institution name and address	Type of account	Co-owner, if any	Balance
_____	_____	_____	_____	_____
_____	_____	_____	_____	_____
_____	_____	_____	_____	_____

   c. Stocks, bonds, and other liquid assets (specify below):

Account no.	Institution name and address	Type of account	Co-owner, if any	Balance
_____	_____	_____	_____	_____
_____	_____	_____	_____	_____
_____	_____	_____	_____	_____

   d. Cars, other vehicles, boat equity (specify below):

Make and year	Legal owner's name and address, if not you	Amount owed	Value
_____	_____	_____	_____
_____	_____	_____	_____

INCOME AND EXPENSE STATEMENT

e. Real estate equity:

Address	Mortgage, trust deed holder	Amount owed	Value

f. Other personal property (jewelry, antiques, artwork, coin collections, furs, safety-deposit boxes, equipment, machinery, livestock, etc.):

Description	Address where property located	Co-owner, if any	Value

EXPENSE INFORMATION

1. Monthly expenses for me, my spouse and my other dependents

    a. Rent or house payment and maintenance $_____

    b. Food and household supplies $_____

    c. Utilities and telephone $_____

    d. Clothing $_____

    e. Medical and dental payments $_____

    f. Insurance (life, health, accident, etc.) $_____

    g. School, childcare $_____

    h. Child, spousal support (prior relationship) $_____

    i. Transportation, auto expenses (insurance, gas, repair) $_____

    j. Laundry, cleaning $_____

    k. Entertainment $_____

    l. Other (specify): $_____

2. I, my spouse and other dependents owe the following debts (include other judgments, loans, etc.):

Creditor's name	For	Monthly Payments	Balance owed	Owed by

3. The following persons depend, in whole or in part, on me or my spouse for support:

Name	Age	Relationship to me	Amount spent monthly

4. Other facts that affect my ability to pay this judgment:

_____

_____

_____

I declare under penalty under the laws of the State of California that the foregoing is true and correct.

Date: _____   Signature: _____

ATTORNEY OR PARTY WITHOUT ATTORNEY (Name, state bar number, and address):	FOR COURT USE ONLY
TELEPHONE NO.: FAX NO.:	
ATTORNEY FOR (Name):	

NAME OF COURT:
STREET ADDRESS:
MAILING ADDRESS:
CITY AND ZIP CODE:
BRANCH NAME:

PLAINTIFF:
DEFENDANT:

APPLICATION AND ORDER FOR APPEARANCE AND EXAMINATION	CASE NUMBER:

☐ **ENFORCEMENT OF JUDGMENT**   ☐ **ATTACHMENT (Third Person)**
     ☐ **Judgment Debtor**   ☐ **Third Person**

ORDER TO APPEAR FOR EXAMINATION

1. TO (name):

2. YOU ARE ORDERED TO APPEAR personally before this court, or before a referee appointed by the court, to
   a. ☐ furnish information to aid in enforcement of a money judgment against you.
   b. ☐ answer concerning property of the judgment debtor in your possession or control or concerning a debt you owe the judgment debtor.
   c. ☐ answer concerning property of the defendant in your possession or control or concerning a debt you owe the defendant that is subject to attachment.

Date: Time: Dept. or Div.:   Rm.:
Address of court ☐ shown above ☐ is:

3. This order may be served by a sheriff, marshal, registered process server, **or** the following specially appointed person (name):

Date: _____   _____
                                                     JUDGE OR REFEREE

This order must be served not less than 10 days before the date set for the examination.
IMPORTANT NOTICES ON REVERSE

APPLICATION FOR ORDER TO APPEAR FOR EXAMINATION

4. ☐ Judgment creditor   ☐ Assignee of record   ☐ Plaintiff who has a right to attach order   to appear and furnish information
   applies for an order requiring (name):
   to aid in enforcement of the money judgment or to answer concerning property or debt.

5. The person to be examined is
   a. ☐ the judgment debtor.
   b. ☐ a third person (1) who has possession or control of property belonging to the judgment debtor or the defendant or (2) who owes the judgment debtor or the defendant more than $250. An affidavit supporting this application under Code of Civil Procedure section 491.110 or 708.120 is attached.

6. The person to be examined resides or has a place of business in this county or within 150 miles of the place of examination.

7. ☐ This court is **not** the court in which the money judgment is entered or (attachment only) the court that issued the writ of attachment. An affidavit supporting an application under Code of Civil Procedure section 491.150 or 708.160 is attached.

8. ☐ The judgment debtor has been examined within the past 120 days. An affidavit showing good cause for another examination is attached.

I declare under penalty of perjury under the laws of the State of California that the foregoing is true and correct.

Date:

▶

_____   _____
(TYPE OR PRINT NAME)   (SIGNATURE OF DECLARANT)

(Continued on reverse)

Form Adopted for Mandatory Use
Judicial Council of California
AT-138, EJ-125 [Rev. July 1, 2000]

**APPLICATION AND ORDER
FOR APPEARANCE AND EXAMINATION**
(Attachment—Enforcement of Judgment)

WEST GROUP
Official Publisher

Code of Civil Procedure,
§§ 491.110, 708.110, 708.120

AT-138, EJ-125 [Rev. July 1, 2000]

APPLICATION AND ORDER
FOR APPEARANCE AND EXAMINATION
(Attachment—Enforcement of Judgment)

WEST GROUP Official Publisher

Page two

APPEARANCE OF JUDGMENT DEBTOR (ENFORCEMENT OF JUDGMENT)

NOTICE TO JUDGMENT DEBTOR If you fail to appear at the time and place specified in this order, you may be subject to arrest and punishment for contempt of court, and the court may make an order requiring you to pay the reasonable attorney fees incurred by the judgment creditor in this proceeding.

APPEARANCE OF A THIRD PERSON (ENFORCEMENT OF JUDGMENT)

(1) NOTICE TO PERSON SERVED If you fail to appear at the time and place specified in this order, you may be subject to arrest and punishment for contempt of court, and the court may make an order requiring you to pay the reasonable attorney fees incurred by the judgment creditor in this proceeding.

(2) NOTICE TO JUDGMENT DEBTOR The person in whose favor the judgment was entered in this action claims that the person to be examined pursuant to this order has possession or control of property which is yours or owes you a debt. This property or debt is as follows (*Describe the property or debt using typewritten capital letters*):

If you claim that all or any portion of this property or debt is exempt from enforcement of the money judgment, you must file your exemption claim in writing with the court and have a copy personally served on the judgment creditor not later than three days before the date set for the examination. You must appear at the time and place set for the examination to establish your claim of exemption or your exemption may be waived.

APPEARANCE OF A THIRD PERSON (ATTACHMENT)

NOTICE TO PERSON SERVED If you fail to appear at the time and place specified in this order, you may be subject to arrest and punishment for contempt of court, and the court may make an order requiring you to pay the reasonable attorney fees incurred by the plaintiff in this proceeding.

APPEARANCE OF A CORPORATION, PARTNERSHIP, ASSOCIATION, TRUST, OR OTHER ORGANIZATION

It is your duty to designate one or more of the following to appear and be examined: officers, directors, managing agents, or other persons who are familiar with your property and debts.

Questions for Debtor's Examination

1. What is your full name and your spouse's full name (if married)?

2. Have you ever used another name or nickname on any documents such as a driver's license, credit application or other important papers? If so:
   a. give name, and
   b. give location and approximate time when name was used.

3. What is your current address and length of time lived there?

4. What is your current phone number?

5. What was your previous address?

6. What was your previous phone number?

7. What is your California driver's license (or California identification card) number?

8. What is your Social Security number?

9. What is your date of birth?

10. If married, what is your spouse's maiden name?

11. Are you employed as an employee, either part-time or full-time? If so:
    a. name, address and phone number of employer,
    b. frequency of payment (weekly, bi-weekly, monthly, etc.),
    c. gross pay,
    d. take-home pay,
    e. commissions if any,
    f. how much is due you at the present time, and
    g. how long on this job?

12. Where and with whom was your previous job?

13. Do you perform labor or services for someone else as an independent contractor rather than as an employee? If so:

   a. names, addresses and phone numbers of persons or businesses for whom you perform services,
   b. nature of services performed for each such person or business,
   c. frequency of services, and
   d. method of billing (e.g., flat rate, hourly rate, job rate).

14. Do you own a business (in whole, in part, as a partner or as a corporation), or have you owned a business within the past five years? If so:
    a. describe business,
    b. name who you do business with,
    c. describe major people or businesses who owe you money (names, addresses and telephone numbers),
    d. describe any business assets such as tools, equipment, computers, furniture, fixtures, machinery, etc., wholly owned by business,
    e. identify which of these assets you still owe money on and the approximate amount owed,
    f. describe, generally, method of doing business, and
    g. provide names and addresses of partners (if the business is a partnership), and corporate officers (if the business is a corporation).

15. Do you own stock in any corporation or shares in a mutual fund? If so:
    a. name of corporation or mutual fund,
    b. form of ownership (certificates, computer account, etc.),
    c. location of certificates or account, and
    d. amount of ownership and approximate value.

16. Do you maintain a brokerage account with any stock broker? If so:
    a. name and address of broker,
    b. account number(s), and
    c. approximate amount in brokerage account.

17. Do you or your spouse have any funds in banks, savings and loans, money market accounts, certificates of deposit, escrow accounts, credit

unions, or any other financial institutions, either in your name or jointly with any other individual? If so:
  a. name of each financial institution and address of branch possessing the funds,
  b. the account number of each account,
  c. name(s) the account is under,
  d. the approximate balance in the account,
  e. date the last deposit was made,
  f. source of the funds in the account, and
  g. when you typically make deposits and with-drawals.

18. Do you or your spouse own a safe-deposit box? If so:
  a. name of bank and address of branch,
  b. name(s) of holder of safe-deposit box, and
  c. contents of box.

19. Do you own any securities (that is, any document which grants a share of ownership in exchange for a loan or investment) such as bonds, annuities, etc.? If so:
  a. describe nature of security, bond, annuity, etc.,
  b. institution or person issuing it, and
  c. approximate worth.

20. Do you own any whole life insurance policies? If so:
  a. the name of the insurance company,
  b. the name of your insurance agent,
  c. the face amount of the policy, and
  d. the cash value of the policy, if any.

21. Do you own any of the following items? If so, describe the item, the item's location, approximate value and any joint owner.
  a. office equipment,
  b. gemstones, gems or jewelry,
  c. camera equipment,
  d. computers,
  e. antiques,
  f. precious metals (gold, silver),
  g. musical instruments including pianos and organs,
  h. weapons (guns, swords, other),

  i. furs,
  j. watches,
  k. stamp or coin collections,
  l. china,
  m. original artworks,
  n. crystal,
  o. sports equipment, including exercise machines,
  p. stereo or musical equipment, and
  q. any other items of value not mentioned above.

22. Do you own, in your own name, or jointly with others, an automobile, truck, motorcycle, RV, motor home, mobile home, boat or plane? If so, provide the following information:
  a. brief description (make, model and year),
  b. approximate value,
  c. legal owner,
  d. registered owner,
  e. license number,
  f. vehicle identification number,
  g. amount owed, if any, to a legal owner, and
  h. any other lienholder you are aware of.

23. Does a person, company or institution owe you money? If so:
  a. name, address and telephone number of person or institution,
  b. amount of each debt, and
  c. how each debt arose (e.g., judgment, loan, inheritance).

24. Do you owe money to anyone else besides this current judgment creditor where you have been sued and the other person or business has received a judgment? If so:
  a. to whom (address and telephone no.),
  b. amount owed, and
  c. amount currently paid.

25. Did you ever file for bankruptcy? If so:
  a. when,
  b. where (district and branch),
  c. type of bankruptcy (Chapter 7 or Chapter 13, if you know), and
  d. case number of the bankruptcy.

26. Are you a party (e.g., defendant or plaintiff) in any current action? This could be an action brought against you for a money judgment, an action in which you are the plaintiff, or any other action (including divorce, will contest, etc.)? If so:
    a. Who are the parties in each action?
    b. Who are the attorneys in each action (names, addresses and phone numbers; include information for parties if they are appearing in pro per)?
    c. Supply a brief description of each lawsuit.
    d. What is your position in the lawsuit, and do you expect to win?

27. Does your wife or husband receive any salary, commissions or other income, as an employee or independent contractor, from an employer or business? If so:
    a. Name, address and telephone number of employer, and
    b. income and pay period

28. Any other sources of income? If so:
    a. amount of income,
    b. when income is received, and is it received on a regular basis, and
    c. brief description of source.

29. Do you own any real estate individually or jointly (single family home, vacation home, co-op/condominium, duplex, rental property, business property, mobile home park, time share, undeveloped land, agricultural land, boat/marina dock space, airplane hangar, stationary mobile home)? If so:
    a. address and county,
    b. approximate fair market value,
    c. amount owed (first mortgage, second deed of trust), and
        1. to whom, and
        2. amount and frequency of payments,
    d. when the property was obtained,
    e. what names are on the deed,
    f. has title to the property been transferred since its acquisition by you,
    g. known debts or claims that affect the title (easements, tax liens, judgment liens, etc.),

    h. approximate amount of your actual owner-ship (equity) in the property,
    i. if a declaration of homestead been filed,
    j. anyone lives on the property, and
    k. if the property is developed, what kind of building(s)?

30. Are you a landlord? If so:
    a. name and address of tenants, and
    b. amount of rent paid and interval of payment.

31. Do you rent where you are now living? If so:
    a. amount of rent paid,
    b. landlord's name, and
    c. landlord's address and phone number.

32. Are you the trustee for, or beneficiary of, any property held in trust for yourself or a third person? If so:
    a. briefly describe type of trust (e.g., living, bank account, spousal, Q-TIP),
    b. identify whether you are the trustee or beneficiary, or both, and
    c. describe what the nature of the property is that is being held in trust.

33. Do you receive benefits from any government agency (e.g., unemployment insurance, disability insurance, workers' compensation, Social Security, retirement, pension)? If so:
    a. name of agency,
    b. type of benefit,
    c. amount of benefit,
    d. frequency of benefit,
    e. the expected duration of the payments, and
    f. basis for the benefit (e.g., unemployment, industrial injury, etc.).

34. Do you receive benefits from or through a private business or entity such as an insurance company or financial institution (e.g., insurance, annuity, retirement, pension, workers' compensation benefits)? If so:
    a. name of provider,
    b. type of benefit,
    c. amount of benefit,
    d. frequency of benefit,

e. the expected duration of the payments, and

f. the basis for the benefit.

35. Do you pay alimony/child support? If so:
a. name, address and telephone number of recipient, and
b. amount and frequency of support.

36. Do you receive alimony/child support? If so:
a. name, address and telephone number of provider, and
b. amount and frequency of support.

37. Do you own any property (cash, tangible personal property items) that is currently in the possession of others? If so:
a. briefly describe the property,
b. name, address and telephone number of possessor,
c. purpose of possession, and
d. physical location of property.

38. Is there any reason why you can't pay on this judgment now or in the future? If so, briefly describe reason.

39. Do you foresee your financial position changing in the future? If so, how?

40. Identify each item of property (cash, other personal property including motor vehicles, or real estate) you have sold or given away within the past three months, and when the transaction occurred.

41. Identify each service you have received from an individual or business (e.g., medical care, legal consultation, car repair) within the past three months, and when the service was provided. Also indicate whether you have paid for that service, and in what manner (cash, check, credit card, etc.).

42. Do you hold an occupational license of any type? If so:

a. name of license,
b. agency granting the license,
c. expiration date of license, and
d. license number.

43. Do you own any mortgages or deeds of trust on any real estate? If so:
a. property involved (address, county),
b. approximate value of mortgage,
c. date of mortgage or deed of trust, and
d. persons or institutions involved.

44. Do you own, solely or jointly, any copyrights, patents, trademarks, trade names or trade secrets? If so:
a. item protected by the copyright, patent, etc.,
b. where registered (if registered) and registration number,
c. co-owners, if any,
d. royalties or other payments received under the copyright patent, etc.

45. Do you or your spouse have any personal property in pawn? If so:
a. name and address of pawnbroker, and
b. brief description of property and approximate value.

46. Have you made a will? If so:
a. describe bequests, and
b. physical location of will.

47. How much money in cash or traveller's checks do you have with you at this time? Identify specifically.

48. Any checks or money orders payable to you? If so, describe.

49. Do you or your spouse have an IRA or Keogh account? If so:
a. institution and branch where account is maintained, and
b. amount in account.

1 _____

2 _____

3 _____

4 (_____)

5 _____

6

7

8 _____ COURT OF CALIFORNIA

9 COUNTY OF _____

10

11 _____ ,) Case No. _____

   Plaintiff,)

12 vs.) ORDER FOR DELIVERY OF
) PROPERTY AFTER EXAMINATION
13 _____ ,) [CCP Section 708.205]

   Defendant.)

14   ) Examination Date: _____
) Time: _____
15 _____) Place: _____

16

17 The examination of _____

18 (judgment debtor or third person) was conducted on the date and at the time set forth above. It appearing from

19 this examination that:

20 ☐ the judgment debtor has an interest in property in the possession or under the control of

21 _____ (judgment debtor or third person); OR

22 ☐ a third person owes the judgment debtor $_____ (or property described as follows:

23 _____

24 _____),

25 and that the property described above is not exempt from enforcement of a money judgment:

26 IT IS ORDERED THAT _____

27 (judgment debtor or third person) shall ☐ immediately/ ☐ within _____ days of entry of this order

28 deliver to _____

_____

1   (judgment creditor or levying officer of _____ County at

2   the following address: _____,

3   California) the property: _____

4   _____

5   which shall be applied toward the satisfaction of the judgment entered in this action on

6   _____ (date).

7

8   DATED:

9

10

11 _____

    Judge/Commissioner of the _____ Court

12

13

14

15

16

17

18

19

20

21

22

23

24

25

26 /////////

27 /////////

28 /////////

ATTORNEY OR PARTY WITHOUT ATTORNEY *(Name and Address):*	TELEPHONE NO.:	FOR RECORDER'S USE ONLY

☐ Recording requested by and return to:

☐ ATTORNEY FOR ☐ JUDGMENT CREDITOR ☐ ASSIGNEE OF RECORD

NAME OF COURT:
STREET ADDRESS:
MAILING ADDRESS:
CITY AND ZIP CODE:
BRANCH NAME:

PLAINTIFF:

DEFENDANT:

WRIT OF

☐ **EXECUTION (Money Judgment)**
☐ **POSSESSION OF** ☐ **Personal Property**
☐ **Real Property**
☐ **SALE**

CASE NUMBER:

FOR COURT USE ONLY

1. **To the Sheriff or any Marshal or Constable of the County of:**

   You are directed to enforce the judgment described below with daily interest and your costs as provided by law.

2. **To any registered process server:** You are authorized to serve this writ only in accord with CCP 699.080 or CCP 715.040.

3. *(Name):*
   is the ☐ judgment creditor ☐ assignee of record
   whose address is shown on this form above the court's name.

4. **Judgment debtor** *(name and last known address):*

   ☐ additional judgment debtors on reverse

5. **Judgment entered** on *(date):*

6. ☐ **Judgment renewed** on *(dates):*

7. **Notice of sale** under this writ
   a. ☐ has not been requested.
   b. ☐ has been requested *(see reverse).*

8. ☐ Joint debtor information on reverse.

   [SEAL]

9. ☐ See reverse for information on real or personal property to be delivered under a writ of possession or sold under a writ of sale.

10. ☐ This writ is issued on a sister-state judgment.

11. Total judgment . . . . $

12. Costs after judgment (per filed order or memo CCP 685.090) . . . . $

13. Subtotal *(add 11 and 12)* . . . . $ _____

14. Credits . . . . $

15. Subtotal *(subtract 14 from 13)*. . . . . . $ _____

16. Interest after judgment (per filed affidavit CCP 685.050) . . . . $

17. Fee for issuance of writ . . . . $

18. **Total** *(add 15, 16, and 17)* . . . . . . $ _____

19. Levying officer:
    (a) Add daily interest from date of writ *(at the legal rate on 15)* of . . . . . $
    (b) Pay directly to court costs included in 11 and 17 (GC 6103.5, 68511.3; CCP 699.520(i)) . . . . $

20. ☐ The amounts called for in items 11-19 are different for each debtor. These amounts are stated for each debtor on Attachment 20.

Issued on *(date):*	Clerk, by _____, Deputy

— NOTICE TO PERSON SERVED: SEE REVERSE FOR IMPORTANT INFORMATION. —

(Continued on reverse)

WRIT OF EXECUTION

Form Approved by the
Judicial Council of California
EJ-130 [Rev. January 1, 1997*]

Code of Civil Procedure, §§ 699.520, 712.010, 715.010

WEST GROUP
Official Publisher

* See note on reverse.

SHORT TITLE:	CASE NUMBER:

— Items continued from the first page —

4. ☐ **Additional judgment debtor** *(name and last known address)*:

7. ☐ **Notice of sale** has been requested by *(name and address)*:

8. ☐ **Joint debtor** was declared bound by the judgment (CCP 989-994)
    a. on *(date)*:
    b. name and address of joint debtor:

    a. on *(date)*:
    b. name and address of joint debtor:

    c. ☐ additional costs against certain joint debtors *(itemize)*:

9. ☐ *(Writ of Possession or Writ of Sale)* **Judgment** was entered for the following:
    a. ☐ Possession of real property: The complaint was filed on *(date)*:   ***(Check (1) or (2))***:
        (1) ☐ The Prejudgment Claim of Right to Possession was served in compliance with CCP 415.46.
             The judgment includes all tenants, subtenants, named claimants, and other occupants of the premises.
        (2) ☐ The Prejudgment Claim of Right to Possession was NOT served in compliance with CCP 415.46.
             (a) $ was the daily rental value on the date the complaint was filed.
             (b) The court will hear objections to enforcement of the judgment under CCP 1174.3 on the following
                dates *(specify)*:
    b. ☐ Possession of personal property
        ☐ If delivery cannot be had, then for the value *(itemize in 9e)* specified in the judgment or supplemental order.
    c. ☐ Sale of personal property
    d. ☐ Sale of real property
    e. Description of property:

— NOTICE TO PERSON SERVED —

WRIT OF EXECUTION OR SALE. Your rights and duties are indicated on the accompanying Notice of Levy.
WRIT OF POSSESSION OF PERSONAL PROPERTY. If the levying officer is not able to take custody of the property, the levying officer will make a demand upon you for the property. If custody is not obtained following demand, the judgment may be enforced as a money judgment for the value of the property specified in the judgment or in a supplemental order.
WRIT OF POSSESSION OF REAL PROPERTY. If the premises are not vacated within five days after the date of service on the occupant or, if service is by posting, within five days after service on you, the levying officer will remove the occupants from the real property and place the judgment creditor in possession of the property. Except for a mobile home, personal property remaining on the premises will be sold or otherwise disposed of in accordance with CCP 1174 unless you or the owner of the property pays the judgment creditor the reasonable cost of storage and takes possession of the personal property not later than 15 days after the time the judgment creditor takes possession of the premises.
► *A Claim of Right to Possession form accompanies this writ (unless the Summons was served in compliance with CCP 415.46).*

Date Received in Office of Designated Agent

APPLICATION FOR FEDERAL EMPLOYEE COMMERCIAL GARNISHMENT

Approved by OMB
3206-0229
Approval Expires
08/31/99

INSTRUCTIONS

1. Federal law, 5 U.S.C. § 5520a, provides for the commercial garnishment of the pay of Federal employees.
2. Each garnishment order or similar legal process in the nature of garnishment must be delivered to the agency's Designated Agent. (See 5 CFR Part 582 Appendix A and 5 CFR Part 581 Appendix A for the lists of Designated Agents to receive legal process.)

3. Employing agencies will generally begin to disburse amounts withheld from employee-obligor's pay within 30 days of receipt by Designated Agent.
4. Employing agencies will **not** modify compensation schedules or pay disbursement cycles in responding to legal process.
5. 31 CFR Part 210 governs funds remitted by Electronic Funds Transfer.
6. See reverse side for Public Burden Statement.

Title and Address of Employing Agency's Designated Agent

Note: Service of legal process **may** be accomplished by certified or registered mail, return receipt requested, or by personal service only upon the agent to receive process as explained in 5 CFR 582.201, or if no agent has been designated, then upon the head of the employee-obligor's employing agency.

A. EMPLOYEE IDENTIFICATION - 5 U.S.C. § 5520a requires sufficient information to enable the employing agency to identify the employee-obligor. Please provide as much of the information in items 1 through 5 as possible.

1. Full Name of Employee-Obligor

2. Date of Birth

3. Employee/Social Security Number

4. Employing Agency, Component, and Employee's Official Duty Station/Worksite Address and ZIP Code

5. Home Address or Current Mailing Address and ZIP Code

6. For Agency Use

B. CASE INFORMATION

1. Name of Court and Case Number in Garnishment Order

2. Garnishment Amount

$

3. Legal process expiration date (if time limited)

4. Is there a dollar amount or percentage limitation under the applicable law of the jurisdiction where the order has been issued that will result in a lower amount to be garnished than would otherwise be applicable under the Consumer Credit Protection Act, 15 U.S.C. § 1673? ☐ Yes ☐ No   If Yes, provide a citation and a copy of the applicable provision:_____

5. Does the law of the jurisdiction where this legal process is issued have a "one order at a time" rule that precludes employers from garnishing more than one order at a time?
☐ Yes ☐ No

6. Does the law of the jurisdiction where this legal process is issued provide for the garnishment of interest amounts that are not reflected on the order or in item number B2?
☐ Yes ☐ No

C. AUTHORIZED PAYEE IDENTIFICATION

1. Full Name of Person Authorized to Receive Payment, as it appears on Court Order

2. Address of Authorized Payee, including ZIP Code

3. Daytime Telephone - Area Code and Number

4. Signature of Authorized Payee, Creditor, or Creditor's Representative, and Date Signed

D. ELECTRONIC FUNDS TRANSFER (if available)

If you wish to request that the funds be remitted by electronic funds transfer rather than by paper check, please complete items D1 through D5.

1. Name and Address of Authorized Payee's Financial Institution

2. Depositor (Payee) Account No. and Title

3. 9-Digit Routing Transit No. of Authorized Payee's Financial Institution (Verify with Financial Institution)

Type of Account: ☐ Checking ☐ Savings

4. Name and Title of Authorized Payee's Representative

5. Signature of Authorized Payee's Representative and Date Signed

U. S. Office of Personnel Management

Optional Form 311 (March 1997)

ATTORNEY OR PARTY WITHOUT ATTORNEY *(Name and Address)*:	TELEPHONE NO.:	LEVYING OFFICER *(Name and Address)*:
ATTORNEY FOR *(Name)*:		

NAME OF COURT, JUDICIAL DISTRICT OR BRANCH COURT, IF ANY:	
PLAINTIFF:	
DEFENDANT:	

APPLICATION FOR EARNINGS WITHHOLDING ORDER **(Wage Garnishment)**	LEVYING OFFICER FILE NO.:	COURT CASE NO.:

TO THE SHERIFF OR ANY MARSHAL OR CONSTABLE OF THE COUNTY OF
OR ANY REGISTERED PROCESS SERVER

1. The judgment creditor *(name)*:

requests issuance of an Earnings Withholding Order directing the employer to withhold the earnings of the judgment debtor (employee).

Name and address of employer

Name and address of employee

Social Security Number *(if known)*:

2. The amounts withheld are to be paid to
   a. ☐ The attorney (or party without an attorney) named at the top of this page.
   b. ☐ Other *(name, address, and telephone)*:

3. a. Judgment was entered on *(date)*:
   b. Collect the amount directed by the Writ of Execution unless a lesser amount is specified here:
   $

4. ☐ The Writ of Execution was issued to collect delinquent amounts payable for the **support** of a child, former spouse, or spouse of the employee.

5. ☐ Special instructions *(specify)*:

6. *(Check a or b)*
   a. ☐ I have not previously obtained an order directing this employer to withhold the earnings of this employee.
      —OR—
   b. ☐ I have previously obtained such an order, but that order *(check one)*:
      ☐ was terminated by a court order, but I am entitled to apply for another Earnings Withholding Order under the provisions of Code of Civil Procedure section 706.105(h).
      ☐ was ineffective.

....
(TYPE OR PRINT NAME)

▶

_____
(SIGNATURE OF ATTORNEY OR PARTY WITHOUT ATTORNEY)

I declare under penalty of perjury under the laws of the State of California that the foregoing is true and correct.

Date:

....
(TYPE OR PRINT NAME)

▶

_____
(SIGNATURE OF DECLARANT)

Form Adopted by the
Judicial Council of California
982.5(1) [Rev. January 1, 1993]

APPLICATION FOR EARNINGS WITHHOLDING ORDER
(Wage Garnishment)

WEST GROUP
Official Publisher

CCP 706.121

Paperwork Reduction Act Statement on Public Burden

This request for information is in accordance with the clearance requirements of 44 U.S.C. 3507. Public reporting burden for this collection of information is estimated to average 15 minutes per response, including time for reviewing instructions, gathering the necessary data, and completing the form. Send comments regarding this burden estimate or any other aspect of this information collection, including suggestions for reducing the burden, to the U. S. Office of Personnel Management, Reports and Forms Management Officer, Washington, DC 20415.

Office of Management and Budget Statement

Regulations published by the Office of Management and Budget at 5 CFR 1320.8(b)(3)(vi) require the inclusion of a statement with each collection of information that an agency may not conduct or sponsor, and a person is not required to respond to, a collection of information unless it displays a currently valid OMB control number.

<table>
<tr><td>ATTORNEY OR PARTY WITHOUT ATTORNEY (Name and Address):</td><td>TELEPHONE NO.:</td><td>FOR COURT USE ONLY</td></tr>
</table>

ATTORNEY OR PARTY WITHOUT ATTORNEY *(Name and Address)*:   TELEPHONE NO.:   ***FOR COURT USE ONLY***

ATTORNEY FOR *(Name)*:

NAME OF COURT, JUDICIAL DISTRICT OR BRANCH COURT, IF ANY:

PLAINTIFF:

DEFENDANT:

NOTICE OF OPPOSITION TO CLAIM OF EXEMPTION (Wage Garnishment)	LEVYING OFFICER FILE NO.:	COURT CASE NO.:

TO THE LEVYING OFFICER:

1. Name and address of judgment creditor   2. Name and address of employee

Social Security Number *(if known)*:

3. The Notice of Filing Claim of Exemption states it was mailed on *(date)*:

4. The earnings claimed as exempt are

   a. ☐ not exempt.

   b. ☐ partially exempt. The amount ***not*** exempt per month is
      $

5. The judgment creditor opposes the claim of exemption because

   a. ☐ the judgment was for the following common necessaries of life *(specify)*:

   b. ☐ the following expenses of the debtor are ***not*** necessary for the support of the debtor or the debtor's family *(specify)*:

   c. ☐ other *(specify)*:

6. ☐ The judgment creditor will accept $ per pay period for payment on account of this debt.

I declare under penalty of perjury under the laws of the State of California that the foregoing is true and correct.

Date:

▶

....
(TYPE OR PRINT NAME)   *(SIGNATURE OF DECLARANT)*

Form Adopted by the
Judicial Council of California
982.5(7) [Rev. July 1, 1983]

NOTICE OF OPPOSITION TO CLAIM OF EXEMPTION
(Wage Garnishment)

WEST GROUP
Official Publisher

CCP 706.128

TELEPHONE NO.:

FOR COURT USE ONLY

ATTORNEY FOR *(Name):*

NAME OF COURT, JUDICIAL DISTRICT OR BRANCH COURT, IF ANY:

PLAINTIFF:

DEFENDANT:

NOTICE OF HEARING ON CLAIM OF EXEMPTION
(Wage Garnishment—Enforcement of Judgment)

LEVYING OFFICER FILE NO.: | COURT CASE NO.:

1. TO:

Name and address of levying officer

Name and address of judgment debtor

☐ Claimant, if other than judgment debtor *(name and address):*

☐ Judgment debtor's attorney *(name and address):*

2. **A hearing to determine the claim of exemption of**
   ☐ judgment debtor
   ☐ other claimant
   will be held as follows:

   a. date: _____ time: _____ ☐ dept.: _____ ☐ div.: _____ ☐ rm.: _____

   b. address of court:

3. ☐ **The judgment creditor will not appear at the hearing and submits the issue on the papers filed with the court.**

Date:

. . . .
(TYPE OR PRINT NAME)

▶

_____
(SIGNATURE OF JUDGMENT CREDITOR OR ATTORNEY)

If you do not attend the hearing, the court may determine your claim based on the Claim of Exemption, Financial Statement (when one is required), Notice of Opposition to Claim of Exemption, and other evidence that may be presented.

(Proof of service on reverse)

Form Adopted by the
Judicial Council of California
982.5(8), EJ-175 [Rev. July 1, 1983]

NOTICE OF HEARING ON CLAIM OF EXEMPTION
(Wage Garnishment—Enforcement of Judgment)

WEST GROUP
Official Publisher

CCP 703.550,
706.105

PROOF OF SERVICE BY MAIL

I am over the age of 18 and not a party to this cause. I am a resident of or employed in the county where the mailing occurred. My residence or business address is (specify):

I served the attached Notice of Hearing on Claim of Exemption and the attached Notice of Opposition to Claim of Exemption by enclosing true copies in a sealed envelope addressed to each person whose name and address is given below and depositing the envelope in the United States mail with the postage fully prepaid.

(1) Date of deposit: (2) Place of deposit (city and state):

NAME AND ADDRESS OF EACH PERSON TO WHOM NOTICE WAS MAILED

I declare under penalty of perjury under the laws of the State of California that the foregoing is true and correct.

Date:

. . . .   ▶ _____
(TYPE OR PRINT NAME)   (SIGNATURE OF DECLARANT)

PROOF OF SERVICE—PERSONAL DELIVERY

I am over the age of 18 and not a party to this cause. My residence or business address is (specify):

I served the attached Notice of Hearing on Claim of Exemption and the attached Notice of Opposition to Claim of Exemption by personally delivering copies to the person served as shown below.

PERSONS SERVED

Name   **Delivery At**
                            Date: Time: Address:

I declare under penalty of perjury under the laws of the State of California that the foregoing is true and correct.

Date:

. . . .   ▶ _____
(TYPE OR PRINT NAME)   (SIGNATURE OF DECLARANT)

982.5(8), EJ-175 [Rev. July 1, 1983]

NOTICE OF HEARING ON CLAIM OF EXEMPTION
(Wage Garnishment—Enforcement of Judgment)

WEST GROUP
Official Publisher

Page two

ATTORNEY OR PARTY WITHOUT ATTORNEY (Name and Address):

TELEPHONE NO.:

FOR COURT USE ONLY

ATTORNEY FOR (Name):

NAME OF COURT:
STREET ADDRESS:
MAILING ADDRESS:
CITY AND ZIP CODE:
BRANCH NAME:

PLAINTIFF:

DEFENDANT:

LEVYING OFFICER FILE NO.:   COURT CASE NO.:

NOTICE OF OPPOSITION TO CLAIM OF EXEMPTION
(Enforcement of Judgment)

— *DO NOT USE THIS FORM FOR WAGE GARNISHMENTS* —

The original of this form and a Notice of Hearing on Claim of Exemption must be filed with the court.

A copy of this Notice of Opposition and the Notice of Hearing *must* be filed with the levying officer.

A copy of this Notice of Opposition and the Notice of Hearing must be served on the judgment debtor and other claimant at least 10 days *before* the hearing.

TO THE LEVYING OFFICER:

1. Name and address of judgment creditor

2. Name and address of judgment debtor

Social Security Number (if known):

3. ☐ Name and address of claimant (if other than judgment debtor)

4. The notice of filing claim of exemption states it was mailed on (date):

5. The item or items claimed as exempt are
   a. ☐ not exempt under the statutes relied upon in the Claim of Exemption.
   b. ☐ not exempt because the judgment debtor's equity is greater than the amount provided in the exemption.
   c. ☐ other (specify):

6. The facts necessary to support item 5 are
   ☐ continued on the attachment labeled Attachment 6.
   ☐ as follows:

I declare under penalty of perjury under the laws of the State of California that the foregoing is true and correct.

Date:

....
{TYPE OR PRINT NAME}

▶

_____
(SIGNATURE OF DECLARANT)

Form Approved by the
Judicial Council of California
EJ-170 [New July 1, 1983]

NOTICE OF OPPOSITION TO CLAIM OF EXEMPTION
(Enforcement of Judgment)

WEST GROUP
Official Publisher

CCP 703.550

ATTORNEY OR PARTY WITHOUT ATTORNEY *(Name, state bar number, and address):*

	FOR COURT USE ONLY

TELEPHONE NO.:   FAX NO.:

ATTORNEY FOR *(Name)*:

NAME OF COURT:

STREET ADDRESS:

MAILING ADDRESS:

CITY AND ZIP CODE:

BRANCH NAME:

PLAINTIFF:

DEFENDANT:

MEMORANDUM OF COSTS AFTER JUDGMENT, ACKNOWLEDGMENT OF CREDIT, AND DECLARATION OF ACCRUED INTEREST

CASE NUMBER:

1. I claim the following costs after judgment incurred within the last two years *(indicate if there are multiple items in any category)*:

		Dates Incurred	Amount
a	Preparing and issuing abstract of judgment		$
b	Recording and indexing abstract of judgment		$
c	Filing notice of judgment lien on personal property		$
d	Issuing writ of execution, to extent not satisfied by Code Civ. Proc., § 685.050 *(specify county):*		$
e	Levying officer's fees, to extent not satisfied by Code Civ. Proc., § 685.050 or wage garnishment		$
f	Approved fee on application for order for appearance of judgment debtor, or other approved costs under Code Civ. Proc., § 708.010 et seq.		$
g	Attorney fees, if allowed by Code Civ. Proc., § 685.040		$
h	Other: *(Statute authorizing cost):*		$
i	Total of claimed costs for current memorandum of costs *(add items a-h)*		$

2. All previously allowed postjudgment costs: . . . . $

3. **Total** of all postjudgment costs *(add items 1 and 2)*: . . . . **TOTAL** $

4. **Acknowledgment of Credit.** I acknowledge total credit to date (including returns on levy process and direct payments) in the amount of: $

5. **Declaration of Accrued Interest.** Interest on the judgment accruing at the legal rate from the date of entry on balances due after partial satisfactions and other credits in the amount of: $

6. I am the ☐ judgment creditor ☐ agent for the judgment creditor ☐ attorney for the judgment creditor. I have knowledge of the facts concerning the costs claimed above. To the best of my knowledge and belief, the costs claimed are correct, reasonable, and necessary, and have not been satisfied.

I declare under penalty of perjury under the laws of the State of California that the foregoing is true and correct.

Date:

▶

. . . .
(TYPE OR PRINT NAME)   (SIGNATURE OF DECLARANT)

NOTICE TO THE JUDGMENT DEBTOR

If this memorandum of costs is filed at the same time as an application for a writ of execution, any statutory costs, *not exceeding $100 in aggregate* and not already allowed by the court, may be included in the writ of execution. *The fees sought under this memorandum may be disallowed by the court upon a motion to tax filed by the debtor, notwithstanding the fees having been included in the writ of execution.* (Code Civ. Proc., § 685.070(e).) A motion to tax costs claimed in this memorandum must be filed within 10 days after service of the memorandum. (Code Civ. Proc., § 685.070(c).)

(Proof of service on reverse)

Form Adopted for Mandatory Use
Judicial Council of California
MC-012 [Rev January 1, 2000]

MEMORANDUM OF COSTS AFTER JUDGMENT, ACKNOWLEDGMENT OF CREDIT, AND DECLARATION OF ACCRUED INTEREST

Code of Civil Procedure, § 685.070

WEST GROUP
Official Publisher

SHORT TITLE:	CASE NUMBER:

PROOF OF SERVICE
☐ Mail ☐ Personal Service

1. At the time of service I was at least 18 years of age and **not a party to this legal action.**

2. My residence or business address is *(specify):*

3. I mailed or personally delivered a copy of the *Memorandum of Costs After Judgment, Acknowledgment of Credit, and Declaration of Accrued Interest* as follows *(complete either a or b):*

   a. ☐ **Mail.** I am a resident of or employed in the county where the mailing occurred.
      (1) I enclosed a copy in an envelope AND
         (a) ☐ **deposited** the sealed envelope with the United States Postal Service with the postage fully prepaid.
         (b) ☐ **placed** the envelope for collection and mailing on the date and at the place shown in items below following our ordinary business practices. I am readily familiar with this business's practice for collecting and processing correspondence for mailing. On the same day that correspondence is placed for collection and mailing, it is deposited in the ordinary course of business with the United States Postal Service in a sealed envelope with postage fully prepaid.
      (2) The envelope was addressed and mailed as follows:
         (a) Name of person served:
         (b) Address on envelope:

         (c) Date of mailing:
         (d) Place of mailing *(city and state):*

   b. ☐ **Personal delivery.** I personally delivered a copy as follows:
      (1) Name of person served:
      (2) Address where delivered:

      (3) Date delivered:
      (4) Time delivered:

I declare under penalty of perjury under the laws of the State of California that the foregoing is true and correct.

Date:

. . . . ▶ _____

(TYPE OR PRINT NAME)   (SIGNATURE OF DECLARANT)

Keeping Track of Costs

Date Expended	Cost Amount	Type of Cost	Expense Record	Date Costs Claimed

Keeping Track of Payments

A	B	C	D	E	F	G	H
Starting Date	Ending Date	No. of Days	Balance	Interest Due (D x ___% x C/360)	Payment	Balance Reduction (F-E)	Unpaid Interest

46

UNITED STATES BANKRUPTCY COURT _____ DISTRICT OF _____	PROOF OF CLAIM

Name of Debtor	Case Number

NOTE: This form should not be used to make a claim for an administrative expense arising after the commencement of the case. A "request" for payment of an administrative expense may be filed pursuant to 11 U.S.C. § 503.

Name of Creditor (The person or other entity to whom the debtor owes money or property):

☐ Check box if you are aware that anyone else has filed a proof of claim relating to your claim. Attach copy of statement giving particulars.

Name and address where notices should be sent:

☐ Check box if you have never received any notices from the bankruptcy court in this case.

☐ Check box if the address differs from the address on the envelope sent to you by the court.

Telephone number:

THIS SPACE IS FOR COURT USE ONLY

Account or other number by which creditor identifies debtor:

Check here if this claim ☐ replaces ☐ amends a previously filed claim, dated:_____

1. Basis for Claim
- ☐ Goods sold
- ☐ Services performed
- ☐ Money loaned
- ☐ Personal injury/wrongful death
- ☐ Taxes
- ☐ Other _____

☐ Retiree benefits as defined in 11 U.S.C. § 1114(a)

☐ Wages, salaries, and compensation (fill out below)

Your SS #: _____ _____ _____

Unpaid compensation for services performed

from _____ to_____
    (date)   (date)

2. Date debt was incurred:

3. If court judgment, date obtained:

4. Total Amount of Claim at Time Case Filed: $ _____

If all or part of your claim is secured or entitled to priority, also complete Item 5 or 6 below.

☐ Check this box if claim includes interest or other charges in addition to the principal amount of the claim. Attach itemized statement of all interest or additional charges.

5. Secured Claim.

☐ Check this box if your claim is secured by collateral (including a right of setoff).

Brief Description of Collateral:
☐ Real Estate   ☐ Motor Vehicle
☐ Other_____

Value of Collateral: $_____

Amount of arrearage and other charges at time case filed included in secured claim, if any: $_____

6. Unsecured Priority Claim.

☐ Check this box if you have an unsecured priority claim

Amount entitled to priority $_____

Specify the priority of the claim:

☐ Wages, salaries, or commissions (up to $4,650),* earned within 90 days before filing of the bankruptcy petition or cessation of the debtor's business, whichever is earlier - 11 U.S.C. § 507(a)(3).

☐ Contributions to an employee benefit plan - 11 U.S.C. § 507(a)(4).

☐ Up to $2,100* of deposits toward purchase, lease, or rental of property or services for personal, family, or household use - 11 U.S.C. § 507(a)(6).

☐ Alimony, maintenance, or support owed to a spouse, former spouse, or child - 11 U.S.C. § 507(a)(7).

☐ Taxes or penalties owed to governmental units - 11 U.S.C. § 507(a)(8).

☐ Other - Specify applicable paragraph of 11 U.S.C. § 507(a)(____).

*Amounts are subject to adjustment on 4/1/04 and every 3 years thereafter with respect to cases commenced on or after the date of adjustment.

7. Credits: The amount of all payments on this claim has been credited and deducted for the purpose of making this proof of claim.

8. Supporting Documents: *Attach copies of supporting documents,* such as promissory notes, purchase orders, invoices, itemized statements of running accounts, contracts, court judgments, mortgages, security agreements, and evidence of perfection of lien. DO NOT SEND ORIGINAL DOCUMENTS. If the documents are not available, explain. If the documents are voluminous, attach a summary.

9. Date-Stamped Copy: To receive an acknowledgment of the filing of your claim, enclose a stamped, self-addressed envelope and copy of this proof of claim.

THIS SPACE IS FOR COURT USE ONLY

Date	Sign and print the name and title, if any, of the creditor or other person authorized to file this claim (attach copy of power of attorney, if any):

Penalty for presenting fraudulent claim: Fine of up to $500,000 or imprisonment for up to 5 years, or both. 18 U.S.C. §§ 152 and 3571.

INSTRUCTIONS FOR PROOF OF CLAIM FORM

The instructions and definitions below are general explanations of the law. In particular types of cases or circumstances, such as bankruptcy cases that are not filed voluntarily by a debtor, there may be exceptions to these general rules.

— DEFINITIONS —

Debtor

The person, corporation, or other entity that has filed a bankruptcy case is called the debtor.

Creditor

A creditor is any person, corporation, or other entity to whom the debtor owed a debt on the date that the bankruptcy case was filed.

Proof of Claim

A form telling the bankruptcy court how much the debtor owed a creditor at the time the bankruptcy case was filed (the amount of the creditor's claim). This form must be filed with the clerk of the bankruptcy court where the bankruptcy case was filed.

Secured Claim

A claim is a secured claim to the extent that the creditor has a lien on property of the debtor (collateral) that gives the creditor the right to be paid from that property before creditors who do not have liens on the property.

Examples of liens are a mortgage on real estate and a security interest in a car, truck, boat, television set, or other item of property. A lien may have been obtained through a court proceeding before the bankruptcy case began; in some states a court judgment is a lien. In addition, to the extent a creditor also owes money to the debtor (has a right of setoff), the creditor's claim may be a secured claim. (See also Unsecured Claim.)

Unsecured Claim

If a claim is not a secured claim it is an unsecured claim. A claim may be partly secured and partly unsecured if the property on which a creditor has a lien is not worth enough to pay the creditor in full.

Unsecured Priority Claim

Certain types of unsecured claims are given priority, so they are to be paid in bankruptcy cases before most other unsecured claims (if there is sufficient money or property available to pay these claims). The most common types of priority claims are listed on the proof of claim form. Unsecured claims that are not specifically given priority status by the bankruptcy laws are classified as *Unsecured Nonpriority Claims.*

Items to be completed in Proof of Claim form (if not already filled in)

Court, Name of Debtor, and Case Number:

Fill in the name of the federal judicial district where the bankruptcy case was filed (for example, Central District of California), the name of the debtor in the bankruptcy case, and the bankruptcy case number. If you received a notice of the case from the court, all of this information is near the top of the notice.

Information about Creditor:

Complete the section giving the name, address, and telephone number of the creditor to whom the debtor owes money or property, and the debtor's account number, if any. If anyone else has already filed a proof of claim relating to this debt, if you never received notices from the bankruptcy court about this case, if your address differs from that to which the court sent notice, or if this proof of claim replaces or changes a proof of claim that was already filed, check the appropriate box on the form.

1. Basis for Claim:

Check the type of debt for which the proof of claim is being filed. If the type of debt is not listed, check "Other" and briefly describe the type of debt. If you were an employee of the debtor, fill in your social security number and the dates of work for which you were not paid.

2. Date Debt Incurred:

Fill in the date when the debt first was owed by the debtor.

3. Court Judgments:

If you have a court judgment for this debt, state the date the court entered the judgment.

4. Total Amount of Claim at Time Case Filed:

Fill in the total amount of the entire claim. If interest or other charges in addition to the principal amount of the claim are included, check the appropriate place on the form and attach an itemization of the interest and charges.

5. Secured Claim:

Check the appropriate place if the claim is a secured claim. You must state the type and value of property that is collateral for the claim, attach copies of the documentation of your lien, and state the amount past due on the claim as of the date the bankruptcy case was filed. A claim may be partly secured and partly unsecured. (See DEFINITIONS, above).

6. Unsecured Priority Claim:

Check the appropriate place if you have an unsecured priority claim, and state the amount entitled to priority. (See DEFINITIONS, above). A claim may be partly priority and partly nonpriority if, for example, the claim is for more than the amount given priority by the law. Check the appropriate place to specify the type of priority claim.

7. Credits:

By signing this proof of claim, you are stating under oath that in calculating the amount of your claim you have given the debtor credit for all payments received from the debtor.

8. Supporting Documents:

You must attach to this proof of claim form copies of documents that show the debtor owes the debt claimed or, if the documents are too lengthy, a summary of those documents. If documents are not available, you must attach an explanation of why they are not available.

ATTORNEY OR PARTY WITHOUT ATTORNEY (Name, state bar number, and address):	TELEPHONE AND FAX NOS.:	FOR COURT USE ONLY

ATTORNEY FOR (Name):

SUPERIOR COURT OF CALIFORNIA, COUNTY OF

STREET ADDRESS:

MAILING ADDRESS:

CITY AND ZIP CODE:

BRANCH NAME:

ESTATE OF (Name):

DECEDENT

CASE NUMBER:

CREDITOR'S CLAIM

You must file this claim with the court clerk at the court address above before the LATER of (a) four months after the date letters (authority to act for the estate) were first issued to the personal representative, or (b) sixty days after the date the *Notice of Administration* was given to the creditor, if notice was given as provided in Probate Code section 9051. You must also mail or deliver a copy of this claim to the personal representative and his or her attorney. A proof of service is on the reverse.

WARNING: Your claim will in most instances be invalid if you do not properly complete this form, file it on time with the court, and mail or deliver a copy to the personal representative and his or her attorney.

1. Total amount of the claim: $

2. Claimant (name):
   a. ☐ an individual
   b. ☐ an individual or entity doing business under the fictitious name of (specify):

   c. ☐ a partnership. The person signing has authority to sign on behalf of the partnership.
   d. ☐ a corporation. The person signing has authority to sign on behalf of the corporation.
   e. ☐ other (specify):

3. Address of claimant (specify):

4. Claimant is ☐ the creditor ☐ a person acting on behalf of creditor (state reason):

5. ☐ Claimant is ☐ the personal representative ☐ the attorney for the personal representative.

6. I am authorized to make this claim which is just and due or may become due. All payments on or offsets to the claim have been credited. Facts supporting the claim are ☐ on reverse ☐ attached.

I declare under penalty of perjury under the laws of the State of California that the foregoing is true and correct.

Date:

▶

. . . .

(TYPE OR PRINT NAME AND TITLE)   (SIGNATURE OF CLAIMANT)

INSTRUCTIONS TO CLAIMANT

A. On the reverse, itemize the claim and show the date the service was rendered or the debt incurred. Describe the item or service in detail, and indicate the amount claimed for each item. Do not include debts incurred after the date of death, except funeral claims.

B. If the claim is not due or contingent, or the amount is not yet ascertainable, state the facts supporting the claim.

C. If the claim is secured by a note or other written instrument, the original or a copy must be attached (state why original is unavailable.) If secured by mortgage, deed of trust, or other lien on property that is of record, it is sufficient to describe the security and refer to the date or volume and page, and county where recorded. (See Prob. Code, § 9152.)

D. Mail or take this original claim to the court clerk's office for filing. If mailed, use certified mail, with return receipt requested.

E. Mail or deliver a copy to the personal representative and his or her attorney. Complete the *Proof of Mailing or Personal Delivery* on the reverse.

F. The personal representative or his or her attorney will notify you when your claim is allowed or rejected.

G. Claims against the estate by the personal representative and the attorney for the personal representative must be filed within the claim period allowed in Probate Code section 9100. See the notice box above.

(Continued on reverse)

Form Approved by the
Judicial Council of California
DE-172 [Rev. January 1, 1998]
Optional Form

CREDITOR'S CLAIM
(Probate)

Probate Code, §§ 9000 et seq., 9153

ESTATE OF (Name):		CASE NUMBER:
	DECEDENT	

FACTS SUPPORTING THE CREDITOR'S CLAIM
☐ See attachment (if space is insufficient)

Date of item	Item and supporting facts	Amount claimed
	TOTAL:	$

PROOF OF ☐ MAILING ☐ PERSONAL DELIVERY TO PERSONAL REPRESENTATIVE
(Be sure to mail or take the original to the court clerk's office for filing)

1. I am the creditor or a person acting on behalf of the creditor. At the time of mailing or delivery I was at least 18 years of age.
2. My residence or business address is (specify):

3. I mailed or personally delivered a copy of this *Creditor's Claim* to the personal representative as follows (check either a or b below):
   a. ☐ **Mail**. I am a resident of or employed in the county where the mailing occurred.
      (1) I enclosed a copy in an envelope AND
         (a) ☐ **deposited** the sealed envelope with the United States Postal Service with the postage fully prepaid.
         (b) ☐ **placed** the envelope for collection and mailing on the date and at the place shown in items below following our ordinary business practices. I am readily familiar with this business' practice for collecting and processing correspondence for mailing. On the same day that correspondence is placed for collection and mailing, it is deposited in the ordinary course of business with the United States Postal Service in a sealed envelope with postage fully prepaid.
      (2) The envelope was addressed and mailed first-class as follows:
         (a) Name of personal representative served:
         (b) Address on envelope:

         (c) Date of mailing:
         (d) Place of mailing (city and state):
   b. ☐ **Personal delivery**. I personally delivered a copy of the claim to the personal representative as follows:
      (1) Name of personal representative served:
      (2) Address where delivered:

      (3) Date delivered:
      (4) Time delivered:

I declare under penalty of perjury under the laws of the State of California that the foregoing is true and correct.
Date:

▶

(TYPE OR PRINT NAME OF CLAIMANT)	(SIGNATURE OF CLAIMANT)

ATTORNEY OR PARTY WITHOUT ATTORNEY (Name and Address):	TEL NO.:
☐ Recording requested by and return to:	

☐ ATTORNEY FOR ☐ JUDGMENT CREDITOR ☐ ASSIGNEE OF RECORD

NAME OF COURT:
STREET ADDRESS:
MAILING ADDRESS:
CITY AND ZIP CODE:
BRANCH NAME:

PLAINTIFF:

DEFENDANT:

FOR RECORDER'S USE ONLY
CASE NUMBER:

FOR COURT USE ONLY

APPLICATION FOR AND RENEWAL OF JUDGMENT

☐ Judgment creditor
☐ Assignee of record
applies for renewal of the judgment as follows:

1. Applicant (name and address):

2. Judgment debtor (name and last known address):

3. Original judgment
   a. Case number (specify):
   b. Entered on (date):
   c. Recorded:
      (1) Date:
      (2) County:
      (3) Instrument No.:

4. ☐ Judgment previously renewed (specify each case number and date):

5. ☐ Renewal of money judgment
   a. Total judgment . . . . $
   b. Costs after judgment . . . . $
   c. Subtotal (add a and b) . . . . $ _____
   d. Credits after judgment . . . . $
   e. Subtotal (subtract d from c) . . . . $ _____
   f. Interest after judgment . . . . $
   g. Fee for filing renewal application . . . . $
   h. **Total renewed judgment** (add e, f, and g) . $ _____

   i. ☐ The amounts called for in items a – h are different for each debtor.
      These amounts are stated for each debtor on Attachment 5.

Page 1 of 2

6. ☐ Renewal of judgment for ☐ possession.
☐ sale.

a. ☐ If judgment was not previously renewed, terms of judgment as entered:

b. ☐ If judgment was previously renewed, terms of judgment as last renewed:

c. ☐ Terms of judgment remaining unsatisfied:

I declare under penalty of perjury under the laws of the State of California that the foregoing is true and correct.

Date:

_____   ▶   _____
(TYPE OR PRINT NAME)   (SIGNATURE OF DECLARANT)

ATTORNEY OR PARTY WITHOUT ATTORNEY *(Name and Address)*:	TELEPHONE NO.:	FOR COURT USE ONLY

ATTORNEY FOR *(Name)*:

NAME OF COURT:
STREET ADDRESS:
MAILING ADDRESS:
CITY AND ZIP CODE:
BRANCH NAME:

PLAINTIFF:

DEFENDANT:

NOTICE OF RENEWAL OF JUDGMENT	CASE NUMBER:

TO JUDGMENT DEBTOR *(name)*:

1. **This renewal extends** the period of enforceability of the judgment until 10 years from the date the application for renewal was filed.

2. **If you object** to this renewal, you may make a motion to vacate or modify the renewal with this court.

3. You must make this motion within **30 days** after service of this notice on you.

4. A copy of the *Application for and Renewal of Judgment* is attached *(Cal. Rules of Court, rule 986)*.

Date: _____

Clerk, by _____ , Deputy

[SEAL]

See CCP 683.160 for information on method of service

Form Approved by the
Judicial Council of California
EJ-195 [Rev. July 1, 1989]

NOTICE OF RENEWAL OF JUDGMENT

WEST GROUP
Official Publisher

CCP 683.160

<table>
<tr>
<td colspan="2">ATTORNEY OR PARTY WITHOUT ATTORNEY (Name and Address):

TELEPHONE NO.:</td>
<td>FOR COURT USE ONLY</td>
</tr>
<tr>
<td colspan="2">ATTORNEY FOR (Name):</td>
<td></td>
</tr>
</table>

NAME OF COURT:
STREET ADDRESS:
MAILING ADDRESS:
CITY AND ZIP CODE:
BRANCH NAME:

PLAINTIFF/JUDGMENT CREDITOR:

DEFENDANT/JUDGMENT DEBTOR:

CASE NUMBER:

PROOF OF SERVICE

1. At the time of service I was at least 18 years of age and not a party to this action, and **I served copies** of the (specify documents):

2. a. Party served (specify name of party as shown on the documents served):

   b. Person served: ☐ party in item 2a   ☐ other (specify name and title or relationship to the party named in item 2a):

   c. Address:

3. I served the party named in item 2
   a. ☐ **by personally delivering** the copies   (1) on (date):   (2) at (time):
   b. ☐ **by leaving** the copies with or in the presence of (name and title or relationship to person indicated in item 2b):

      (1) ☐ **(business)** a person at least 18 years of age apparently in charge at the office or usual place of business of the person served. I informed him or her of the general nature of the papers.
      (2) ☐ **(home)** a competent member of the household (at least 18 years of age) at the dwelling house or usual place of abode of the person served. I informed him or her of the general nature of the papers.
      (3) on (date):   (4) at (time):
      (5) ☐ A **declaration of diligence** is attached. (Substituted service on natural person, minor, conservatee, or candidate.)
   c. ☐ **by mailing** the copies to the person served, addressed as shown in item 2c, by first-class mail, postage prepaid,
      (1) on (date):   (2) from (city):
      (3) ☐ with two copies of the Notice and Acknowledgment of Receipt and a postage-paid return envelope addressed to m
      (4) ☐ to an address outside California with return receipt requested.   (Attach completed form.) ↖
   d. ☐ **by** causing copies to be mailed. A declaration of mailing is attached.
   e. ☐ **other** (specify other manner of service and authorizing code section):

4. **Person serving** (name, address, and telephone No.):
   a. **Fee** for service: $
   b. ☐ Not a registered California process server.
   c. ☐ Exempt from registration under B&P § 22350(b).
   d. ☐ Registered California process server.
      (1) ☐ Employee or independent contractor.
      (2) Registration No.:
      (3) County:

5. ☐ **I declare** under penalty of perjury under the laws of the State of California that the foregoing is true and correct.
6. ☐ **I am a California sheriff, marshal, or constable and** I certify that the foregoing is true and correct.

▶

(SIGNATURE)

ATTORNEY OR PARTY WITHOUT ATTORNEY *(Name and Address)*:

TELEPHONE NO.:

FOR RECORDER'S OR SECRETARY OF STATE'S USE ONLY

ATTORNEY FOR *(Name)*:

NAME OF COURT:

STREET ADDRESS:

MAILING ADDRESS:

CITY AND ZIP CODE:

BRANCH NAME:

PLAINTIFF:

DEFENDANT:

CASE NUMBER:

ACKNOWLEDGMENT OF SATISFACTION OF JUDGMENT

☐ **FULL**   ☐ **PARTIAL**   ☐ **MATURED INSTALLMENT**

FOR COURT USE ONLY

1. Satisfaction of the judgment is acknowledged as follows *(see footnote* before completing)*:

   a. ☐ Full satisfaction

      (1) ☐ Judgment is satisfied in full.

      (2) ☐ The judgment creditor has accepted payment or performance other than that specified in the judgment in full satisfaction of the judgment.

   b. ☐ Partial satisfaction

      The amount received in partial satisfaction of the judgment is

      $

   c. ☐ Matured installment

      All matured installments under the installment judgment have been satisfied as of *(date)*:

2. Full name and address of judgment creditor:

3. Full name and address of assignee of record, if any:

4. Full name and address of judgment debtor being fully or partially released:

5. a. Judgment entered on *(date)*:

      ☐ (1) in judgment book volume no.:   (2) page no.:

   b. ☐ Renewal entered on *(date)*:

      ☐ (1) in judgment book volume no.:   (2) page no.:

6. ☐ An ☐ abstract of judgment ☐ certified copy of the judgment has been recorded as follows *(complete all information for each county where recorded)*:

COUNTY	DATE OF RECORDING	BOOK NUMBER	PAGE NUMBER

7. ☐ A notice of judgment lien has been filed in the office of the Secretary of State as file number *(specify)*:

NOTICE TO JUDGMENT DEBTOR: If this is an acknowledgment of full satisfaction of judgment, it will have to be recorded in each county shown in item 6 above, if any, in order to release the judgment lien, and will have to be filed in the office of the Secretary of State to terminate any judgment lien on personal property.

▶

Date:

_____

(SIGNATURE OF JUDGMENT CREDITOR OR ASSIGNEE OF CREDITOR OR ATTORNEY)

*The names of the judgment creditor and judgment debtor must be stated as shown in any Abstract of Judgment which was recorded and is being released by this satisfaction. **A separate notary acknowledgment must be attached for each signature.**

Form Approved by the
Judicial Council of California
EJ-100 [Rev. July 1, 1983] (Cor. 7/84)

ACKNOWLEDGMENT OF SATISFACTION OF JUDGMENT

WEST GROUP
Official Publisher

CCP 724.060, 724.120, 724.250

JL RELEASE OR SUBORDINATON FILING INSTRUCTIONS

Please type or laser-print information on this form. Be sure information provided is legible. Read all instructions and follow them completely. Complete the form very carefully as mistakes may have important legal consequences. Do not insert anything in the open space in the upper right portion of this form as it is reserved for filing office use. Do not staple or otherwise mutilate the barcode in the upper left corner of the document, this will render the barcode ineffective.

To provide the requester with an acknowledgment of filing, the original and a duplicate copy of the statement must be presented for filing.

Section A:	To assist filing office communication with the filer, information in this section should be provided.
Section B:	Enter name and mailing address of requester in this section. This is required information.
Section C:	Enter the Secretary of State file number assigned to the original Notice of Judgment Lien.
Section D:	Enter the date the Secretary of State file date on the Notice of Judgment Lien.
ITEM 1a or 1b:	Enter the exact legal name of the organization or name of the individual that is the debtor appearing on the Notice of Judgment Lien (either 1a or 1b).
ITEM 1c:	Enter the current address of the judgment debtor.
ITEM 2a or 2b:	Enter the exact legal name of any additional judgment debtor also appearing on the Notice of Judgment Lien.
ITEM 2c:	Enter the address of any additional judgment debtor.
ITEM 3:	Enter the exact legal name and current address of the judgment creditor as it appears in the Notice of Judgment Lien.
ITEM 4:	If the lien on personal property covered by the judgment is being released, check the box and describe the personal property being released in Item 6.
ITEM 5:	If this statement is being filed to subordinate to another security interest, then check the box and describe in Item 6 the personal property to which the security interest is being subordinated.
ITEM 6:	Describe personal property being released or subordinated in this box.
ITEM 7:	This notice of judgment lien on personal property must be signed by the judgment creditor's attorney, if the judgment creditor has an attorney of record. If the judgment creditor does not have an attorney of record, then the judgment creditor must sign it. (Section 697.550, Code of Civil Procedure)
	If the individual signing the notice signs on behalf of a law firm, which is the attorney of record, the name of the law firm should be entered BENEATH, not above, the signature. If the signature is for a judgment creditor, which is an entity, the name of the entity should be entered BENEATH, not above, the signature of the person signing for the judgment creditor.

FEE:
A Statement of Release or a Statement of Subordination must be submitted with a filing fee of ten dollars ($10.00) for An original document containing two pages or less, and twenty ($20.00) for an original document containing three pages or more. Please send a check made payable to the **Secretary of State**. Contact the filing office for information concerning the establishment of prepay accounts, use of special handling services, or other payment options.

DOCUMENTS NOT ACCOMPANIED BY THE FILING FEE WILL NOT BE PROCESSED.

MAILING ADDRESS:
When properly completed, send **payment**, the **original form**, and **duplicate copy** of this statement to:

> Secretary of State
> P.O. Box 942835
> Sacramento, CA 94235-0001

NOTICE OFJUDGMENT LIEN RELEASE OR SUBORDINATION
FOLLOW INSTRUCTIONS CAREFULLY (front and back of form)

A. NAME & PHONE OF FILER CONTACT (optional)

B. SEND ACKNOWLEDGMENT TO: (NAME AND ADDRESS)

[   ]

[   ]

THIS SPACE FOR FILING OFFICE USE ONLY

C. SECRETARY OF STATE FILE NO. (ON NOTICE OF JUDGMENT LIEN)	D. DATE OF FILING (ON NOTICE OF JUDGMENT LIEN)

1. JUDGMENT DEBTOR'S EXACT LEGAL NAME – Insert only one name, either 1a or 1b. Do not abbreviate or combine names.
1a. ORGANIZATION'S NAME

1b. INDIVIDUAL'S LAST NAME	FIRST NAME	MIDDLE NAME	SUFFIX
1c. MAILING ADDRESS	CITY	STATE	POSTAL CODE	COUNTRY

2. ADDITIONAL JUDGMENT DEBTOR'S EXACT LEGAL NAME – Enter one name, either 2a or 2b. Do not abbreviate or combine names.
2 a. ORGANIZATION'S NAME

2b. INDIVIDUAL'S LAST NAME	FIRST NAME	MIDDLE NAME	SUFFIX
2\c. MAILING ADDRESS	CITY	STATE	POSTAL CODE	COUNTRY

3. JUDGMENT CREDITOR'S EXACT NAME– Do not abbreviate or combine names.
3a. ORGANIZATION'S NAME

3b. INDIVIDUAL'S LAST NAME	FIRST NAME	MIDDLE	SUFFIX
3c. MAILING ADDRESS	CITY	STATE	POSTAL CODE	COUNTRY

4.   RELEASE OF JUDGMENT LIEN ON PERSONAL PROPERTY

☐ THE JUDGMENT LIEN ON THE PERSONAL PROPERTY DESCRIBED IN ITEM 6 BELOW IS HEREBY RELEASED.

5. SUBORDINATION OF JUDGMENT LIEN ON PERSONAL PROPERTY

☐ THE NOTICE OF JUDGMENT LIEN ON THE PERSONAL PROPERTY SUBJECT TO LIEN IS HEREBY SUBORDINATED AS DESCRIBED IN ITEM 6 BELOW (SEE CODE OF CIVIL PROCEDURE, SECTION 697.650(B)).

6. DESCRIPTION OF PERSONAL PROPERTY

7.

_____
SIGNATURE OF JUDGMENT CREDITOR (SEE INSTRUCTION NO. 7

_____
DATE

FOR _____

JUDGMENT LIEN (FORM JL3) Rev 6/01
Approved CA Secretary of State

Index

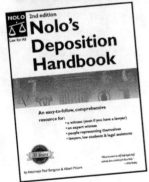